THE FLORENTINE PORTRAIT

THE
FLORENTINE
PORTRAIT

JEAN ALAZARD

SCHOCKEN BOOKS · NEW YORK

First published in Great Britain 1948

First SCHOCKEN edition 1968

Library of Congress Catalog Card No. 68–26731

Translated from the French by Barbara Whelpton

Manufactured in the United States of America

CONTENTS

CHAPTER I

FLORENTINE PORTRAITS BEFORE LEONARDO

From Giotto to Masaccio. – Andrea del Castagno. – Portraits of famous men. – Portraits of artists. – The influence of Uccello, of Piero della Francesca and of Pisanello. – Profiles. – The influence of the medal. – Wealth of portraits in frescoes from Baldovinetti to Filippino Lippi

CHAPTER II

EASEL PORTRAITS AT THE TIME OF BOTTICELLI

The Flemish influence. – Portraits by Antonello da Messina. – Antonio del Pollaiuolo. – *The Man with the Wedding Ring*. The Corsini Collection. – Domenico Ghirlandaio's easel portraits. – Those of Bastiano Mainardi. – *The Man with the Medal* by Botticelli. Botticelli's theories and influence. – *Portrait of a Man* in the former Layard Collection

CHAPTER III

LEONARDO DA VINCI'S THEORIES AND THEIR INFLUENCE ON THE YOUNG RAPHAEL

Portraits in frescoes and the theories of Leonardo da Vinci and Michelangelo. – Leonardo's conception of the portrait. – The so-called *Ginevra dei Benci* of the Lichtenstein Gallery. – *Mona Lisa*. – Leonardo's influence on Raphael. – *Maddalena Doni*. – Raphael's Florentine portraits—*La Donna Gravida.—The Woman with the Golden Chain* in the Uffizi.
– *The Donna Velata*

CHAPTER IV

PORTRAIT PAINTERS OF THE TRANSITION

The portrait of Verrocchio by Lorenzo di Credi. – Portraits with inclined heads. – Leonardo's influence on Lorenzo. – The originality of Piero di Cosimo's portraits. – The *Francesco Giamberti* and the *Giuliano da san Gallo* in The Hague.– The National Gallery *Warrior*. – Raphael's imitators. – The portrait called the *Monaca*. – Is it of Mariotto Albertinelli? – Portraits of Giuliano Bugiardini. – The influence of the fifteenth century

CHAPTER V

LEONARDO'S INFLUENCE ON ANDREA DEL SARTO

CHAPTER VI

THE DISCIPLES OF ANDREA DEL SARTO

CHAPTER VII

ANDREA DEL SARTO'S INFLUENCE ON MICHELANGELO PONTORMO

CHAPTER VIII

FRANCESCO SALVIATI AND THE VENETIAN INFLUENCE

CHAPTER IX

TASTE IN PORTRAITURE AT THE TIME OF COSIMO I DE MEDICI

CONTENTS

CHAPTER X

STATE PORTRAITS, BRONZINO

CONCLUSION

THE PLACE OF FLORENTINE PORTRAITURE IN THE
EVOLUTION OF ITALIAN PAINTING
ITS ORIGINALITY AND ITS INFLUENCE

ILLUSTRATIONS

9

ILLUSTRATIONS

INTRODUCTION

Who has not been struck on going for the first time into the Florentine churches of Santa Maria Novella, Santa Trinità or Sant'Ambrogio, by the vitality of the faces in the religious processions decorating the walls of the choir and chapel? It is almost a commonplace to say that most of the great Florentine fresco painters were at the same time great portrait painters. Their contemporaries exprienced joy and pride in seeing their features thus recorded for eternity. In the fifteenth century, which was very individualistic, it was a means of exalting the individual.

These mural painters offer us a picture of the Florentine world of the fifteenth century with its habits and customs; they are in actual fact interesting documents on the life of the period. Many of the spectators who figure in these religious scenes were patricians, influential members of great corporations, and their portraits are sometimes intermingled with those of learned men, philosophers and artists.

It might seem interesting to try to constitute an iconographical gallery, by asking the same question about each of these beautiful effigies: Whom does this represent? We must nevertheless confess that this is a pastime which is almost always deceptive and which is rarely very fruitful. In truth it is not the historical aspect which has preoccupied me. I have only considered the portraiture in the Florentine frescoes insofar as it can help us to understand the development of the easel portrait raised to the dignity of an accepted form of artistic interpretation; a development which must of necessity be thwarted by the habit of choosing the partakers in sacred subjects from the Florentine aristocracy. We see, nevertheless, this form of art becoming the fashion and submitting to the influence of medals, carved busts and portraits in frescoes.

13

In the presence of pictures which were meant to flatter the vanity of the models, the same question comes to mind as in the presence of the spectators in the religious scenes: whom do they represent? Let me state right away that my attention is not very much attracted to this problem, which is of more historical than artistic importance. It is certainly useful to know the individual whom the painter wanted to represent and to know what his conditions of life were; it is especially important to understand his moral life; this can only be of help in a better appreciation of the psychological penetration of the painter. Also, every time that it is possible to find a place for these informative elements I have not neglected them. Certainly this documentation has its value when we find ourselves in front of the portrait of a man whose personality imposes itself on the picture. But a case of this type happens but rarely. It often happens that the persons represented are of ordinary character, sometimes even second-rate; to know their names does not get us anywhere important. It is of more value to try to define the intentions of the artist, his methods and his technique.

Those who have studied the portraits of the fifteenth and sixteenth centuries, like Gruyer in his Raphael the Portrait Painter *and de la Sizeranne in his* Masks and Faces, *have only seen the historical side of the question; they have tried to solve the riddle of all the faces and, having solved it, have recounted the life story of the people thus identified. In this manner critics have restricted themselves up to the present to purely historical considerations, to the neglect of the aesthetic element.*

"There are two ways," says Baudelaire [1], "of understanding the portrait: the historical and the romantic. The first is to render faithfully, severely and in detail, the outlines and the modelling of the sitter. This method does not exclude idealisation, which intelligent painters of naturalism achieve by choosing the most characteristic pose in order to express as well as possible the temperament of the sitter. As well as this, he ought to know how to give

---

[1] Baudelaire, *Curiosités ésthetiques*, Lemerre ed., p. 141-4.

to every important detail a reasonable exaggeration, to light up everything which is naturally pronounced, emphasised and essential and to neglect or to lose in the whole effect everything insignificant or which is the effect of accidental unimportance.

"The second method, especially applicable to colourists, is to make the portrait into a picture, a poem with its accessories, full of space and thought. Here the art is more difficult because it is more ambitious. It is necessary to understand how to envelope a head in the soft mists of a warm atmosphere or to make it stand out from the depth of the half light. Here imagination plays a larger part; and nevertheless, as romance is often truer than history, it also happens that a model is more clearly expressed by the easy and full brush of a colourist than by the pencil of a draughtsman."

If we examine the development of Italian painting in the light of these strong definitions of Baudelaire's, it seems that Florence is more particularly the home of the historical portrait and Venice the home of the Romantic portrait. But this is only a superficial view, for there are romantic and historical portraits to be found in both the Florentine and Venetian schools. Much better, this definition of Baudelaire's represents almost in its general rhythm the two kinds of Florentine portraiture: before and after Leonardo da Vinci. It is in short the great division which imposes itself at first sight and which remains fundamental after a deep examination of the problems to be solved.

A great many portraits were painted in Florence between about 1470 and 1570; and there was during these years a pronounced taste for the easel portrait. In the presence of such an accumulation of works of art there can be no question of making an inventory or even a summary of them all. The innumerable works to be found in private galleries is the first obstacle in a research of this nature. Besides, the catalogues to public collections are still, for the most part, so crude that it is often difficult to trust them entirely. Finally, each time it is necessary to have recourse to photographs, one realises how rudimentary the means of working still are in this respect.

As it is impossible to know all the Florentine portraits produced at the end of the fifteenth and almost the whole of the sixteenth century, the best method is to concentrate on the most characteristic, on those which give the best feeling of the rhythm of the development. That is why I have restricted myself especially to studying the essential and typical works, only examining the secondary ones when they introduce a new note, original in some respects.

Unfortunately many of these pictures give rise to the worrying question of authorship. It is one of the great difficulties of the history of modern art to determine in an accurate way what was the creative talent of painters about whom there is little documentation. Certain catalogues are largely imaginative. It happens that only one or two authentic works by the artist are known and that all the others are added as the result of ingenious comparisons. Giovanni Morelli has been criticised for his method, which consists in studying the essential elements of a painting in order to find the personality of the painter, and to attribute to the latter all the paintings which offer similar technical characteristics. Now it seems that Morelli has been too much despised after having been too much exalted. In re-reading today the two volumes which he devoted to the study of Italian works in the Dresden and Berlin galleries and in the Roman Galleries, one is astonished at the number of successful identifications he has made.

We must take as a starting point an intrinsic analysis of a work of art, if we want to understand its tendencies and to know to what school its creator belongs. This analysis is in itself already a work of great usefulness. But this purely physical examination of the individuality of a picture can only be a starting point. A wider and deeper study must follow. Whatever may be the importance of technical details, the drawing of the hands or of the ears, when it is a question of determining the character of a picture, the study of these details is vain if we never succeed in penetrating the spirit in which the work was carried out. It is for having neglected this side of the problem that the method of Morelli has often missed its goal and given the impression of empty words. It is no less true that when controlled it is still a powerful help.

I have shown its drawbacks, in particular that it gives too much importance

1. Salviati. *The Lute Player*. (Musée Jacquemart-André, Paris)

·:TADDEVS·GHADDI·:· ·:GADDVS·ZENOBII·:· ·:AUGEVS·TADDEI·:·

2. Florentine School of End of Fourteenth Century. *Portraits of the Gaddi.* (Uffizi)
3. Paolo Uccello. *Portraits of Giotto, Uccello, Donatello, Manetti and Brunelleschi.* (Louvre)

to intuition. Now intuition is not to be condemned when used prudently. It is not unusual for an art historian to give his personal impression as the principal reason for an identification. Just as today it is quite easy to recognise in an exhibition the treatment of many of the artists without having to consult the catalogue, so in a museum one can put names to many of the pictures, trusting in a kind of instinct to which constant frequenting of the galleries gives birth. But there are imitations and replicas, there is the whole output of the painter's "Bottega", and the further we get away from genius or real talent the more difficult it is to discriminate between original works and those of pupils.

By trusting only to the personal factor many blunders can be made. It would be easy to compile, in the case of certain pictures, a list of the various attributions they have been given which could only make us very sceptical. Mr. Berenson himself, who has created with full documentation that curious and, on the whole, real personality Amico di Sandro (which is a sufficient proof of the sureness of his intuition) has admitted, however, that in many cases he has made mistakes. When he attributed to Brescianino de Siena the Raphaelesque portrait of Montpellier (which makes one wonder who could possibly have seen a Raphael there), he had already a very deep knowledge of the Sienese and Florentine schools. He nevertheless confesses today that his diagnosis is not infallible and that he has now changed his mind. Thus on occasions he has to deny what he affirmed earlier.

His example should make us extremely cautious especially in the domain of portraiture, where the causes of mistakes are more numerous than in any other type of painting. In an imaginative work or in a genre painting, the personality of the painter shows up more; the anatomical drawing, the landscape, the general composition show clearly the essentials of his tendencies. A portrait is not so much of a revelation; even in the romantic portrait (if we adopt Baudelaire's classification) there is a struggle between the artist and the model; when the model is a characteristic type with powerful or charming features, the artist is easily subjugated, but he is very much less so if the face

---

[1] *Gazette des Beaux-Arts*, 1907, p. 208 and following.

is commonplace and does not impose itself on his mind. In any case the personality of the painter is limited to a certain extent by the very existence of the model whose essential features at least must be rendered; it even, on occasions, forces him to modify his technical principles; it can lend vigour to him who, up till that time, has employed a subtle and soft technique; it can also on the other hand give elegance and charm to a painter who is above everything powerful.

It often happens (as we shall see throughout this book) that a mediocre painter raises himself for a moment to the ranks of the great, if he is strongly impressed by a face which is very full of character; his work takes on a brilliance of which we doubted him capable. And it creates yet another difficulty in the attribution of painted portraits. It is not always easy to recognise the painter's style in an imaginative scene. It is even less easy to say who has drawn a portrait, since what strikes us to begin with is the intensity of the life of the model. When it is a question of the fifteenth century the problem is even more complicated in that painters considered accuracy of features before everything else; hence their pre-occupation with precision in drawing and modelling. The artists of the fifteenth century were ambitious to make real likenesses, and that is why their style is less obvious and attributions are more difficult.

After Leonardo it seems that they had been less preoccupied with this necessity and they had been drawn more by the psychological truth of a portrait. The mere fact of placing a model in its milieu is already a great advance along this path; it was inevitably accompanied by an interpretation of its character. It is then that the personality of the painter expresses itself still more. If he has any sensibility he does not bind himself solely to making a faithful likeness. He will be caught up into expressing some of his own feelings; there is an instinctive tendency to interpret the moral life of others according to one's own; it is difficult to imagine ways of thinking and being which are entirely different from our own. Also the so-called psychological portrait brings out the greatest self-expression of the artist and reveals his manner to the utmost; that is why it is easier to recognise a portrait by Botti-

*celli or his school than to distinguish, by means of a portrait, the technique
of an artist who painted without emotion, like Domenico Ghirlandaio or
Cosimo Rosselli.*

*It is natural therefore that it is easier, or at any rate less difficult, to make
attributions of the work of the painters of the first half of the sixteenth
century. Andrea del Sarto, Franciabigio and Puligo have a conception of the
face and of attitudes which is not the same as that of their predecessors. Their
eye is more easily inclined to note what gives softness to a face and renders
it less coarse. Let us think of Piero della Francesca's relentless profiles, which
do not spare any detail of the features, however unpleasant. What is indefinable and deep in the gaze escapes him; but on the other hand, no-one has
rendered with the same hardness the fixed, haughty and chill expression of
the condottiere. On the other hand Andrea del Sarto is seduced by the charm
of a feminine face; and does not look for characteristic and pronounced
profiles; the likenesses which he leaves us of some of his contemporaries are
beautiful and subtle, simply because we find there a little of his sensibility,
we see them living this curious inner life in a way which is reminiscent of the
models of Leonardo.*

*The style of Andrea del Sarto, of Pontormo and other painters as well,
is thus more easily recognisable. But we must not on their account fall into
the sin of over-confidence. What is true of the fifteenth century is also true
of the sixteenth, that the "Botteghe" were full of artists who easily caught
the methods of the master; and although it is not a question of works of the
first rank, there is inevitably more uncertainty in the attributions.*

*Fortunately, as well as the pictures, we have some documentation for our
guidance, although it is not as ample as could be desired. Researches into
archives are seldom fruitful: it is often chance that leads to an important
discovery. Moreover a document which would seem to have a great deal of
significance for the identification of a canvas often turns out to have only
slight value. The contracts discovered by Mr. Biscaro in the Record Office
of Milan are a striking example of this. They have enabled us to clear up*

certain obscure points concerning the problem of the two Virgins of the Rocks *by Leonardo da Vinci; but they have not solved them in a conclusive way; again it is the considerations of style which are more convincing. We must rely on them to establish between the two pictures in the Louvre and the National Gallery, the essential differences which distinguish the first, the work of Leonardo, from the second, painted by a pupil. In this way the considerable research work into the records does not always end in a useful result.*

It is again Vasari who remains the best source of information for the period which concerns us. When he speaks of the school of Giotto or the painters of the fifteenth century, he refers to traditions which he is often unable to substantiate; fiction and truth are often intermingled. But from the end of the fifteenth century his documentation is much more precise; he was closer to the artists he was speaking of; those whom he did not know personally were known by others from whom he got reminiscences. Born in 1511, he came to Florence in 1524 in Cardinal Silvio Passerini's suite; he stayed for some time in Andrea del Sarto's studio; then it was through the work of Bandinelli that he became familiar with the grandeur of Michelangelo's school. From his youth, then, he was put in contact with several of the greatest artists of the period; he must have known well the studio stories remembered by his masters. From the beginning of the sixteenth century we can consider him as a major historical source; if we take into consideration his usual verbiage, a redundance of style at times disagreeable, a monotony of expression which sometimes bores us, he gives, concerning many painters and sculptors, the appreciation of a man of taste. His scale of values is not very far removed from the one we can establish today.

For these historical and artistic reasons we frequently come back to Vasari's Lives; *Raffaello Borghini and Baldinucci, who often do nothing but paraphrase or reproduce his text, are less important; they are neither of them, besides, very explicit when they speak of portraits. Therefore it is obvious we are far from having in many cases the precise elements without which there is no historical certainty.*

Profile Portraits of the Fifteenth Century.

4. *Paolo Uccello.* (National Gallery, London)
5. *Alessio Baldovinetti.* (Kaiser Friedrich Museum, Berlin)
6. *Antonio del Pollaiuolo.* (Poldi-Pezzoli Museum, Milan)

7. Domenico Ghirlandaio. *Pope Honorius III Approving the Rule of Saint Francis*. (Santa Trinità, Florence)

8. Botticelli. *Adoration of the Magi*. (Uffizi)

It is from a study of the pictures themselves that enlightenment so often comes and we can apply to the painters of the fifteenth and sixteenth century the remark—so true—by Renan: "We know very little of the artists who created the masterpieces of Greek art. But these creations tell us more of the personality of the artists and the public who appreciated them than the most reliable narrations or the most authentic documentations" [1].

What I have tried to study above everything else is the evolution of a particular aspect of painting. A portrait by Bronzino is essentially different from one by Andrea del Castagno or even by Domenico Ghirlandaio; it is interesting to note through what influences Florentine art finally came to the style of Bronzino and Pontormo. These influences are not only artistic; the atmosphere also played its part. It is quite helpful to know how the court of Cosimo I de Medici lived and that Florentine Dukes liked luxury and display, to understand the talent of their official painters or the artists who lived under their protection.

It is one of the most important facts in the history of Florentine painting that portraiture finally became the principal element. There are sixteenth-century painters who were, above all, painters of studio portraits, which would have been impossible in the fifteenth century when a taste for individual portraits was very rare. Now at the time when the art of Florence tended to become more and more academic, it still kept a certain vitality, thanks to the painters who understood how to draw the features of a face. It is interesting to study these impulses of energy. After having known hesitant beginnings in Tuscany, portrait painting ended by becoming the greatest glory of Florentine art. Its slow but sure evolution conferred on it an originality which it did not possess in other countries, which reached definite formuli far more quickly. In Florence it was the reflection of an active civilisation and of an often troubled history; it tells us at one and the same time the aspirations of the artists and those of an élite society.

Studying its history principally from an aesthetic point of view we should

---

[1] Ernest Renan, *Les Apôtres*, Introduction, p. VIII.

be led to establish preferences. Besides, the history of art cannot be entirely dissociated from criticism of art. The mere study of a picture is already a form of appreciation. And who can say that there are not works which are worthy of consideration and others which are not? It is useful to take interest in all the artistic manifestations of a period, whatever their value, but it is doubtless better still to show how an Andrea del Sarto or a Pontormo left his stamp on his epoch.

CHAPTER I

FLORENTINE PORTRAITS BEFORE LEONARDO

From Giotto to Masaccio. Andrea del Castagno. Portraits of famous men. Portraits of artists. The influence of Uccello, of Piero della Francesca and of Pisanello. Profiles. The influence of the medal. Wealth of portraits in frescoes from Baldovinetti to Filippino Lippi.

We know that Flemish art from its beginnings was an art of the portrait painter; some of the most beautiful Nordic portraits were in fact those by Van Eyck. There is nothing comparable in Florentine art, which subsisted to begin with on general ideas and deep feelings and did not arrive until rather late at a precise and detailed analysis of the outside world.

The first great Tuscan painters seem to have ignored—or almost ignored— the art of portraiture; in their modest craft there was a kind of hierarchy of styles; the most worth while work seemed to them to be church frescoes and there they expressed, in general, their conception of life and of the world, for they had their thoughtful side.

Let us first consider Giotto and his followers. They were above everything astonishing interpreters of religious emotion: the admirable movement of Franciscan piety was still too close to them for its impression to have weakened. Furthermore, with Giotto, the breadth of composition destroyed, as it were, secondary detail; everything is subordinated to a certain state of feeling which shows us the work as a whole. It is a characteristic of decorative painters to sacrifice detail to the line which surrounds the mass of forms. The moment the strength of this principle weakens, fresco loses its grandeur and unity.

Nevertheless Giotto himself cast a quick look over the world around him and included a few portraits in his frescoes. In the Palazzo Vecchio in Florence he painted Charles, son of the Duke of Calabria, on his knees in front of Notre Dame. The portraits of Dante and of Boniface VIII [1] are broadly brushed in with the firm hand of a fresco painter; but they already show a timid attempt at individualization and one can regard them as first examples of studies in physiognomy.

It was the great masters of the first half of the fifteenth century, Masaccio, Paolo Uccello and Andrea del Castagno, who created something quite new in painting. Neither Gentile da Fabriano nor Fra Angelico were from this point of view of decisive importance. Neither of them had the extraordinary decorative power of Giotto. They come under the influence of the miniaturists; it is therefore natural that detail should be more important to them; also one sees that Fra Angelico already brings out certain individual types. Cristofero Landino, the famous annotator of Dante, wrote in 1481 that Masaccio was 'an excellent imitator of nature' [2]. But this definition of the painter's talent applies above all to the remarkable way in which he caught the tragic side of human destiny. His work shows a wonderful unity. He only took from everyday life those things which helped to accentuate the dramatic side; in this he was a great innovator.

It was this powerful and synthesising genius who left the most impressive example of a portrait at the beginning of the fifteenth century. In fact great significance is given to the *Trinità* of Santa Maria Novella by the two figures of the donors kneeling at the foot of beautiful columns on which rests a solidly constructed arch. The lines of the drapery are of an extraordinary breadth and the individual portraits show precise characterisation: these two portraits are still treated as frescoes, but for the first time it seems we have

---

[1] To these celebrated portraits, which are to be found in the Bargello and Saint Jean de Latran respectively, one must add that of Bishop Pantano, in the Basilica at Assisi; it has been much repainted and it is thus seems difficult to affirm that it is "the first example of the portrait" as does Venturi, *La basilica di Assisi*, 1908, p. 127: Cf. Supino, *Giotto*, 1920, p. 311.

[2] "Optimo imitator di natura, nuono compositor et puro, sensa ornato: perche solo si dette all imitazione del vero" (*La Commedia*, ed. 1481).

9. Antonio Pollaiuolo. *The Man with the Ring.* (Corsini Gallery, Florence)
10. Piero Pollaiuolo. *Portrait of Galeazzo Maria Sforza.* (Uffizi)

11. Botticelli. *Portrait of a Young Man.* (National Gallery, London)

a full-length portrait with all its importance; perhaps it is not necessary to search here for a Flemish influence; a personality such as Masaccio's lives outside tradition.

On the contrary we must consider his work as a point of departure. Although true portraiture appeared but rarely in the Brancacci Chapel frescoes, it is none the less true that they give a great lesson in the importance of the observation of human nature to those who study them. With Giotto, dramatic force is given by the moving beauty of the postures; Masaccio adds to this a stressing of the character of the figures. After him this research into expression was carried even further by emphasising still more the individual features of each face.

The posing of Masaccio's donors has a wonderful statuesque effect. Other works have a similar aspect: since the middle of the 14th century had been seen in profile on the walls of the Communal Palace at Siena the *Guidoriccio dei Fogliani*, by Simone Martini [1]. It was customary to produce equestrian portraits in praise of the virtues of captains who defended Italian States. Tuscan artists excelled in this kind of monument. In 1444 Padua commissioned Donatello to make a statute of Gattamelata. Later on it was Verrocchio's turn, who was called in by the Venetian Republic. In Florence itself the glory of the "Condottiere" is magnificently displayed on the inner wall of the façade of Santa Maria del Fiore. It was Giovanni Acuto, painted in 1436 by Paolo Uccello, to whom Andrea Castagno gave, a few years later (in 1455), a worthy companion, Nicolada Tolentino [2].

In these equestrian portraits the "terre verte" has left a patina which recalls the old "pietra serena" of Florence and gives the illusion of a statue. They are characteristic of the first conception of the portrait, considered as such, in Florence—the only heroes regarded above all as symbols of the art in which they excelled—in other words the art of fighting.

When Andrea del Castagno had to portray the *"famous men"* commissioned by Pandolfo Pandolfini, he also gave them a statuesque pose, set them

---

[1] Van Marle, *Simone Martini et les peintres de son école*, 1920, p. 58.
[2] *Il libro di Antonio Billi* (ed. Frey), p. 22 and 24. *Il Codice Magliabechiano* (ed. Frey), p. 98–99.

on a base and in a niche [1]: Dante, Petrarch and Boccaccio on one side, and on the other Filippo degli Scolari called Pippo Spano, Farinata degli Uberti and Niccolo Acciaiuoli.

In truth, the idea of giving an important place in painting to famous men goes back to Giotto and the paintings he did for King Robert of Naples in a room of the Castel Nuovo [2]. They are to be found again in the processions representing the *Triumph of Virtue, the Liberal Arts, Fame*.

A "Cassone" in the Gardner Collection at Boston [3] attributed to Pesellino, shows to the left of the "Fame", heroes of the sword, and on the right those of the spirit. They liked to evoke in this manner the great figures of the past; at the end of the fifteenth century Ghirlandaio was to paint antique characters on the walls of the Belfry Hall in the Signoria of Florence [4]. In the Italian Courts, these illustrious Romans were to be considered something like the ancestors of the reigning sovereigns. In Florence, where there were no Princes to flatter, they more often extolled the valour of those who had brought honour upon the city. The cult of Great Men was there expressed in a less symbolic, more direct and more naturalistic way.

In the portraits which he produced for Pandolfini, Andrea del Castagno could only, of course, show the generic features handed down by tradition. Thus his portrait of Dante has much in common with the one by Domenicino di Michelino for the cathedral in Florence, after a drawing by Baldovinetti (this last being only a copy of the Dante of Taddeo Gaddi at Santa Croce).

"Famous Men" only come into the history of art indirectly. It is rather the imaginative pictures which were destined to give, for example, the pattern of the Condottiere. We are still very far from the documentary portrait. When a personality is isolated it is because it belongs to the glorious past,

---

[1] *Il memoriale di Francesco Albertini* (ed. Horne), p. 19. Consult also *Codice Magliabechiano*, p. 99.

[2] *Il Codice Magliabechiano*, p. 53.

[3] Schubrig, *Cassoni*, 1915, p. 279 (IX). – Cf. Weisbach, *Francesco Pesellino und die Romantik der Renaissance*, 1901, p. 80–90.

[4] Vasari, *Le vite dei pittori scultri e architetti*, ed. Gaetano Milanesi, III, p. 2269; Gaye, *Carteggio inedito degli artisti*, 1839, I, p. 577–81; Gaye, *Carteggio...*, II, p. v. Vasari, I, 574.

that past which is symbolised for Florence by a Niccolo Acciaiuoli, Lieutenant of the Realm of Naples, a Pippo Spano, Fortunate Conqueror of the Turks, proud as Donatello's Saint George, and a Farinata degli Uberti who has not the ardour of the young Condottiere, but the calm assurance of a statesman certain of his experience and of his power [1].

These painters also sometimes took the trouble to leave us portraits of each other. These groups of artists are one of the most interesting manifestations of Florentine art, of which the oldest seems to be the one in the Uffizi where the three Gaddi are represented. They appear against a blue background; one, Taddeo Gaddi, turned three-quarters to the left, the other, Gaddo Gaddi, facing us, and the third, Agnolo Gaddi, in profile looking towards the right. Each of these faces has deep wrinkles and hollow cheeks; the flesh tones go from pink to yellow, allowing the underpainting of "terre verte" to show in certain places (Plate II, fig. 2) [2]. The whole picture is not lacking in life, in spite of the difficulties encountered by the artist in trying to bring out the individuality of these three people of the same family.

The paintings of Giotto, Uccello, Donatello, Manetti and Brunellesci in the Louvre are more distinctive. They are handled in a more precise manner, the observation is carried further than in those of the Gaddi (Plate II, fig. 3). It was evidently to these that Vasari referred in a well-known passage, "Paolo Uccello admired the qualities of artists [3], and so that posterity might keep some remembrance of them he painted with his own hand in one long picture portraits of five remarkable men and he kept it in his own home in their

---

[1] Also attributed to Andrea del Castagno is a *Portrait of a Man* three-quarter view where the features seem to be drawn with a certain strength. It is now in the P. Morgan Collection in New York, after having belonged to the R. Kann Collection (Cf. *The R. Kann Collection Pictures*, vol. II, 1907, p. 27). In his catalogue to the Widener Collection Mr. Berenson does not doubt its authenticity.

[2] Uffizi Gallery (*autoritratti dei pittori*). These portraits belong in all probability to the end of the fourteenth century: the three inscriptions are: Taddeus Gaddi, Gaddus Zenobii, Angelus Taddei.

[3] Vasari, II, 215. The tradition of these group portraits was not lost in the sixteenth century. A curious example to be found in the Mond Collection shows Giotto, Donatello, Michelangelo, Raphael and Brunellesci. J. P. Richter attributes them rather dubiously to Francesco Salviati (*The Mond Collection*, 1910, II, p. 476).

memory. One was the painter Giotto, personifying the beginning of art, Filippo di ser Brunellesci representing architecture, Donatello sculpture, himself perspective and the painting of animals, and lastly Giovanni Manetti representing mathematics." [1]

This evidence of Vasari's is a little suspect since the 1550 edition of *The Lives* attributes the group to Masaccio. Nevertheless it is only reasonable to suppose that such a personality as Uccello would show a keener sense of observation in studying the faces of his contemporaries than his predecessors would have done. In the *Battle Piece* in the National Gallery some of the profiles seem to have been taken from living models [2], such as that of the young page in the middle of the picture, which, by its delicacy of features and tone, reminds one of another work in the same gallery: a portrait of a young woman with a very prominent nose and a rather receding forehead. Her hair is arranged with complicated artistry; a rich jewel made of several pearls adorns the top of her head. A bandeau hides her ears and holds back her hair, letting fall a few locks of pale gold. The beautiful light yellow sleeves of her dress are embroidered with strange black palm leaves; through the colouring of the face one can make out the underpainting of "terre verte", a device which Uccello always uses *(Plate III, fig. 4)*.

This is not the place to discuss the conjectures made regarding this portrait. The most probable is that which attributes it to Uccello, who would thus have a place apart in the evolution of Florentine portrait painting for having produced one of the first known profile portraits in which one can see an obvious preoccupation with making a likeness.

Piero della Francesca developed this theme in the middle of the fifteenth century by painting two powerful portraits: the Duke of Urbino and his wife, Battista Sforza. In 1439 he worked in Florence under the direction of Domenico Veneziano. In actual fact it was not from Veneziano that he found

---

[1] The first edition of *The Lives* (1550) gives this mathematician the name of Antonio Manetti which is the exact name and person to figure in the Louvre picture.

[2] Vasari (II, 208 and X, 213) said definitely that Uccello painted battle pictures "con assai ritraitti di naturale".

the deepest inspiration, but from the Brancacci Chapel and from Paolo Uccello. Piero was profoundly influenced by this art so full of force and grandeur. It would be tempting, from the logical point of view, to count him as Uccello's pupil, both from his portrait painting and his large frescoes. Here is a pupil, moreover, with a strong personality. Although he only spent his youth in Florence and his art developed after that in Rimini, Ferrara, Urbino, Perugia and Rome, there is no doubt that its radiance spread over the whole of central Italy. It is a happy innovation in the *Storia dell' Arte Italiano* that Arnolfo Venturi puts the art of Piero della Francesca back in its place—a place of honour [1].

This artist, who is remarkable for his solid grouping of forms, looked on a portrait as forming a part of a whole. He is preoccupied with geometry in his portraits, allowing the lines to unfold with exactitude and precision. He is nevertheless an implacable and accurate observer. In 1451, at Rimini, he painted a fresco in the "Tempio Malatesta" representing Sigismondo Pandolfo Malatesta kneeling in front of Saint Sigismond. The profile stands out from an almost plain background and the features are strikingly similar to those on the medal made by Pisanello.

On the other hand connoisseurs and critics are so impressed by the beauty of the portraits of Federigo and Battista that they often conclude that Piero della Francesca was the author of certain other similar paintings. But we must realise that the use of the profile spread very rapidly. It is delightful to recapture the calm repose which a powerfully drawn relief gives to a medal. In fact great medallists of the mid-fifteenth century come quite naturally to mind when one looks at similar works. It is to Pisanello at least as much as to Piero della Francesca that we must attribute the vogue for this kind of portrait. He lived in Florence much longer. We know that he spent his youth there, and he was probably there in 1439 for the Council, and it was during

---

[1] National Gallery, London, No. 758. Cf. Loeser, *Repertorium für Kunstwissenschaft,* 1898, p. 88. This portrait is attributed by Crowe and Cavalcasselle to Piero della Francesca. It is in too strong relief to be by Baldovinetti as Mr. Roger Fry believes (*Burlington Magazine,* XVIII, p. 311). Cf. as well J. P. Richter, *Italian Art in the National Gallery,* 1883, p. 17.

this stay that his medal of Jean Paleologue was struck. He undoubtedly went back again because he was commissioned to cast one of Paolo Toscanelli [1].

Pisanello's portraits are simply coloured translations of his medals. They were so famous that they were often copied by second-rate painters, who were far from having his talent. The practice was not lost for some time after his death; and mistakes in research for his authentic works are due to this. It is further proof that he also played a dominant part in the evolution of portrait painting.

From the earliest beginnings painters liked to show their skill in portraiture in frescoes. In Saint Francis d'Grezzo, Piero della Francesca shows us in his *Miracle of the True Cross* the inhabitants of a little town, full length portraits, three-quarters and full face, giving a powerful effect of life. When he was called to Rome to take part in decorating the Vatican he peopled with famous contemporaries what was to become later on, in the time of Raphael, the Hall of Heliodorus [2].

In this artist's work the contrast is very striking between the monotonous posing of his studio portrait and the variety of attitude and modelling which lends vigour and individuality to the persons in his frescoes.

In Florence Baldovinetti was one of the first to give the portrait an important place in mural painting. Although this cannot be taken as a fixed rule, it is clear that this idea was conceived to please painters gifted with little imagination. If Masaccio painted Saint Paul with the features of a certain Bartolo Angiolini it was because those features seemed to him to have exceptional character. He has expressed them with such force that they are almost frightening. But he was too much concerned with the unity of effect to draw systematic inspiration from the living model.

On the other hand, Baldovinetti, feebly sustained by his own imagination, searched around him for interesting heads. He spent less effort in reproducing

---

[1] G. Uzieli,"Sui ritratti di Paolo del Pozzo Toscanelli fatti da Alessio Baldovinetti e da Vittore Pisano"(*Bollettino della Societe geografica italiana*, 1890, p. 586).

[2] Vasari, II, p. 492.

an exact likeness of them. His frescoes in Santa Trinità—which have since disappeared—were full of people easily identified by Vasari. In the *Story of the Queen of Sheba* who goes towards Solomon attracted by his famed wisdom, we find a "portrait of Lorenzo the Magnificent", the father of Pope Leo X; and one of Lorenzo of Volpaia, an "excellent astrologer". In the scene opposite we find "Luigi Guicciardini the Elder, Luca Pitti, Diotisalvi Neroni, Julius de Medici". And all these people are easily recognisable, because of their similarity to the portraits or busts in the house of their descendants [1].

One knows that this tendency to fill frescoes with portraits had a wide influence and imposed itself even on the most gifted of painters. Throughout the second half of the fifteenth century it became a fixed tradition from which no one dared depart; the greatest, like Botticelli, and the mediocre, like Cosimo Rosselli, conformed to it.

The speed with which this idea developed is in part explained by the number of scenes from the Old and New Testament which were enacted in the fourteenth and fifteenth centuries for the benefit of the Florentine public [2]; artists were thus tempted to call to mind certain details. They loved to paint in the backgrounds of their frescoes or pictures the clean lines of the Tuscan landscape; in this they liked to evoke the memory of the brilliant ceremonies which had caught their imagination.

The year 1459, when Benozzo Gozzoli was working on the frescoes in the Medici Chapel, was a time of gaiety and festival in Florence. Pope Pius II was received there with great solemnity and also the young Count Galeazzo Maria, son of Francesca Sforza [3]. It is very likely that there is some connection between the portraits one finds in the Gozzoli frescoes and the famous personages who were fêted in that year. These festivals, organised in honour of the Pope, who wanted to exterminate the Turks, reminded the spectators and painters of the celebrations twenty years earlier to the glory of Byzantium

---

[1] Vasari, II, p. 593–594.

[2] Cf. on this subject of the "Sacre Rappresentazioni" of this nature the book by Ancore, *Origini del teatro italiano*, 1891, I, p. 246, 272-277.

[3] J. Mesnil, *Rassegna d'arte*, May, 1909.

and its Emperor John Paleologue. It had been a memorable date for the
Medicis, when they had received the ruler from the Orient with great pomp.
Also it is for this reason that the artist had to evoke on the walls of their
Palace these two glorious moments, 1439 and 1459.

At the same time as Benozzo Gozzoli, Filippo Lippi went to the living
model for inspiration. It was he who so often included in his religious scenes
portraits of the donors. "At Arezzo", said Vasari [1], "he carried out for Carlo
Masupini a *Coronation of the Virgin* where many saints were present." One
of the most striking of the faces in this picture [2] is that of the donor, on his
knees with hands folded, being presented to the Madonna by a friar of the
Order of St. Benedict. In *The Death of St. Jerome* in the Cathedral at Prato
is another portrait of the donor, the provost Inghirami. Besides these, Alessandro degli Allesandri figures with his two sons in the *St. Lawrence* which
he had painted for his villa in Vincigliata [3].

Filippo Lippi, then, followed the example of the Flemings by his habit
of including in his works portraits of those who had commissioned them.
He also occasionally included his own features as in the *Coronation of the
Virgin* in the Uffizi [4]. He also made one of the greatest contributions towards
individualising the heads of the saints. This artist monk "with the light and
worldly heart" conceived his religious scenes in the form of human scenes
in which real living beings took part. In actual fact, contrary to what Vasari
says [5], the spirit of Masaccio never entered into him. The frescoes in the
cathedral at Prato are the best proof of this; in the *Funeral of St. Stephen*

---

[1] Vasari, II, p. 618.

[2] Vatican Gallery.   Given the advanced years of Carlo Marsupini, secretary of the Florentine Republic born in 1399 and died in 1453, this work must be dated between 1445 and 1450
(Cf. Supino, *Fra Filippo Lippi*, 1902, p. 60—61).

[3] Vasari, II, 626. This picture is today in the Alessandri Collection in Florence.

[4] In an article in the *Burlington Magazine*   (XXI, p. 194), Mr. Carmichael says that the
portrait of the person kneeling and with folded hands is of the donor, Francesco di Antonio
Maringhi, Canon of San Lorenzo, and not that of Filippo Lippi; but there seems no reason to
doubt the traditional identification. The portrait is very similar to the one Vasari puts at the
beginning of his life of Filippo Lippi and, besides, "is perfecit opus" means very definitely: this
latter finished the work.

[5] Vasari, II, p. 613.

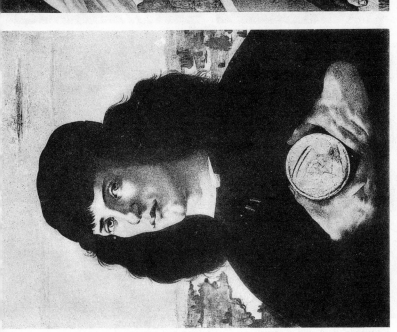

12. Botticelli. *The Man with the Medal.* (Uffizi)
13. School of Botticelli. *Portrait in the former Layard Collection.* (National Gallery, London)

14. Leonardo da Vinci. *Portrait of Mona Lisa, Gioconda.* (Louvre)
15. Raphael. *Portrait of Maddalena Doni.* (Pitti Palace)
16. Raphael. *La Donna Gravida.* (Pitti Palace)
17. Ridolfo Ghirlandaio. *Portrait of a Woman.* (Pitti Palace)

the spectators are very numerous; the painter has chosen them from among the élite of Prato as a means of rendering homage to them. At Prato, as in the Medici Palace Chapel, Filippo Lippi and Benozzo Gozzoli portrayed important contemporaries who are placed in the first row at religious ceremonies as in the city fêtes.

This tradition soon imposed itself on all artists, and evidently reached Botticelli through Pollaiuolo's contacts. Nevertheless it was he who least felt the necessity for inspiration from the living model, for he was sustained by the flame of real genius. It is quite possible that the strange *Allegory of Spring* consists only of idealised figures. On the other hand, in the *Adoration of the Magi* in the Uffizi (*Plate IV, fig. 8*) there are some of the most beautiful portraits of the fifteenth century. Efforts have been made to identify them all [1]. It is not difficult to recognise many members of the Medici family. Although the family likeness in their faces might induce mistakes, it seems that it is Cosimo the Elder, clothed in robes bordered with ermine and embroidered in gold, who kisses the feet of the Infant Christ. The other people of whom Vasari speaks [2] are certainly there, but they are not always in the places indicated. Julius de Medici could not be the back view of the King, already aged, in the centre of the picture, who has a strong resemblance to Peter the Gouty; he is more likely to be the young man with head bowed sadly to the ground. As for John, the favourite son of Cosimo, he is very likely the one suggested by Vasari: kneeling, he looks towards the left and offers a present to the Virgin. Tradition by then had become a convention [3] and so when, in his series of the twenty-four Medicis, Bronzino had

---

[1] Ullman also claims to have found portraits of Politicus and Lorenzo Tornabuoni (*Sandro Botticelli*, 1893, p. 59–60). Cf. Horne, *Sandro Botticelli, Florentine Painters*, 1908, p. 38 and following. Cf. also the article by Henri Hauvette (*Etudes Italiennes*, 1919, p. 193). According to Horne the probable date of this work is 1477.

[2] Vasari, III, 315. Cf. also *Il Libro di Antonio Billi*, p. 58.

[3] What seems also likely is the presence of Botticelli in this picture; the person on the right draped in a full coat of saffron colour. He has in fact a strong resemblance to Botticelli's features, which Filippino Lippi painted in the *Crucifixion of Saint Peter*, painted in the Carmine about 1484 after Botticelli's return from Rome (Vasari, II, 325).

John to paint, he gave him the same features and the same bowed head as the young man in the Adoration of the Magi.

These portraits are nearly all presented in the form of admirable profiles. The faces of the Medicis and their household, so full of character, gain by being viewed thus. Besides, it is easier to seize the fundamental contours of a face from this angle. These kinds of portrait were for Botticelli an excuse for an astonishing study in lines. He has shown this admirably in the incomparable frescoes which went in 1882 from the Villa Lemmi, between Florence and Fiesole, to the Louvre. This villa belonged for almost a century (from 1469-1541) to the Tornabuoni, and it was from this illustrious family that Botticelli received the commission for mural paintings in which he was to commemorate with honour the marriage of Lorenzo Tornabuoni and Giovanna degli Albizzi (1486). On one side the Three Graces come to visit the young fiancée and one of them makes an offering of flowers; on the other side it is the Liberal Arts, Dialectics, Grammar, Arithmetic, Music, Astrology, Philosophy, who receive the homage of Lorenzo Tornabuoni.

The portraits of the two betrothed [1] are astonishingly lifelike: Lorenzo Tornabuoni with his handsome curly hair is the same as on the medal by Niccolo Fiorentino, whose other side bears the impression of Mercury. This delicate scholarly youth, whose portrait fascinated Politien, and whose death was so tragic, stands out from a neutral background with the same clarity as does the head of Giovanna degli Albizzi. These features recall those of another medal by Niccolo Fiorentino where one finds, falling over the breast of the beautiful Florentine, the same necklace as in Botticelli's picture, whereas framed on the other side are the same Three Graces with the inscription: Caritas, Pulchritudo, Amor.

The contrast between these Three Graces and Giovanna degli Albizzi is striking. Two have something indescribably exquisite and languorous, which is a peculiar gift of this painter's genius. The other's pose is full of dignity:

---

[1] It is equally possible that in the procession of the Graces and the Liberal Arts the painter has made use of the features of some pretty contemporaries.

one sees in her the proudness of the patrician who wishes to show, even to the carriage of her head, that she has distinction.

One finds almost exactly the same profile of Giovanna in the *Visitation* scene in the church of Santa Maria Novella in Florence. There is a little more youthfulness in the Louvre portrait than in that of the Tornabuoni chapel: But each has the same nose, the same mouth and the same pearl necklace with a pendant.

Ghirlandaio's work began in 1486; it is not, therefore, impossible that Botticelli's painting was known to him and that he was inspired by it, so similar is the pose of the head seen three-quarter view in both works [1]. This was one of the few occasions on which Ghirlandaio submitted to the influence of Botticelli. The temperament of these two artists are so different that such a reconciliation is quite exceptional. One has the sensibility of a great emotion and the other is an exceptionally gifted chronicler.

I think that is the best definition one can make of Ghirlandaio's art—the art of the chronicler. He has also an important place in the history of fifteenth-century portraiture as a whole. Already in the *Last Supper* in the Church of Ognissanti one notes the care taken over characterisation and over bringing out the individuality of the people in a fresco. This developed into an even more dominant preoccupation when he became the almost regular painter to the great Florentine families. In the *Calling of St. Peter and St. Andrew* in the Sistine Chapel he placed behind the two kneeling apostles a wonderful array of spectators with marked individuality. Commissioned to decorate the Sassetti Chapel at Santa Trinità, he dedicated it to the greater glory of this family. At the time when he received commissions from other rich Florentines, no-one was better qualified to carry them out; he knew how to flatter their patrician pride.

In the Santa Trinità frescoes he is already a master of the portrait. He brings

---

[1] The date of the frescoes in the Villa Lemmi is 1486. Now the contract between Ghirlandaio and Giovanni states that the artist must begin the frescoes in the choir of Santa Maria Novella in May 1486. This contract has been published by Milanesi in his *Nuovi documenti per la storia dell'arte toscana dal XII al XVI secolo*, 1893, p. 134.

to mind the pictures of donors as conceived by Masaccio at Santa Maria Novella, and at the base of the central wall of the chapel he instals superbly Filippo Sassetti and his wife; making use of extreme simplicity of technique, he is careful at the same time to get a likeness and to give a unified and beautiful decorative effect. This is one of the principal works of Ghirlandaio, one where he shows himself to be at the same time a great fresco painter and a great portrait painter. The outlines of the bodies are so firmly drawn as to acquire almost the power of a bas-relief.

Now this chapel is really dedicated to the glory of the Sassetti family. It seems that even the religious scenes are only an excuse to bring well-known faces before the spectator's eyes. Many patricians watch the miracle in which St. Francis's intervention saves the life of a child of the Spini family, and Vasari complacently gives us their names. Ghirlandaio's desire for accuracy went to the length of making him paint the whole extent of the Santa Trinità square with the Spini Palace [1]. His artistic aim here is very different from that of Giotto or Masaccio, who thought of nothing but the unity of composition or the intensity of a dramatic event. It is quite clear that the new conception of chapel decoration was no longer religious and that the faithful considered it with feelings of curiosity. They would not experience any emotion in front of the suffering of the Spini family, as expressed by Ghirlandaio, posing as they do like models in front of the painter, unmoved by a scene in which they should have been the principal actors. When Pope Honorius III is approving the rule of St. Francis (Plate IV, fig. 7), it is not this important event which holds our attention, because the painter transports us right into the Piazza Signoria and makes us look on at the Triumph of Filippo Sassetti appearing to the left of Lorenzo the Magnificent.

In the Santa Maria Novella frescoes one can see the qualities and the weaknesses of those at Santa Trinità developing. The great number of portraits ends by becoming an obsession. "When he was a goldsmith", says Vasari, "Ghirlandaio used to amuse himself by drawing the people who came into

---

[1] Vasari, III, 255–256.

the workshop and he was extremely good at catching a likeness". One of his first works was in fact a group of portraits drawn together under the ample cloak of a *Virgin of Mercies* in the church of Ognissanti in Florence. It was fatal that he was tempted to abuse his great talent as a portrait painter. Besides he was obliged to do so. A Giovanni Tornabuoni meant to be well served, if he took the trouble to indicate very precisely all the episodes which the painter ought to depict; and if he commissioned him to submit all his plans it was because he was a master of staging. The text of the contract is very clear. "Execution", he says, "shall be in all and for everything preceded by my desires".

Ghirlandaio responded admirably to these desires. *Joachim Driven out from the Temple, The Visitation* and *The Angel Appearing to Zacharias!* are a kind of apotheosis of the great Florentine family. In the first fresco one sees Lorenzo Tornabuoni with three friends; in the second it is a beautiful patrician, gorgeously clothed, who watches the scene of the *Visitation*. Vasari gives the name of Ginevra dei Benci, which is rather difficult to believe [1]. According to Enrico Ridolfi, it would be the wife of Lorenzo, Giovanna degli Albizzi; now she, as we have already seen, is in the second rank in the suite of the beautiful aristocrat. The owner of this excellent profile remains a mystery; actually it is perhaps best to consider it as insoluble.

Like Filippo Sassetti at Santa Trinità, Giovanni Tornabuoni wanted to figure as a kind of donor at Santa Maria Novella; this practice shows the patrician Florentine's great taste for glory and fame. In the *Angel appearing to Zacharias* he is surrounded by a complete court of relations, of scholars and artists. These portraits are today very well known and it is no use dwelling on them [2]. They are full of life; but the requirements of the

---

[1] The reason why it is difficult to take this for a portrait of Ginevra dei Benci is not that of chronological order given by Enrico Ridolfi (*Archivio storico italiano*, 1890, p. 226 and following). Ridolfi believed Ginevra died in 1473. Now Carnesecchi has shown that she was still living in 1490 (*Rivista d'arte*, Sep.-Dec. 1909). The real reason is that it is unbelievable that the Tornabuoni would have placed in the first row of the fresco of Santa Maria Novella a Florentine with no tie of relationship to unite her with their family.

[2] Cf. Vasari, III, 263 and following. *Il libro di Antonio Billi*, p. 58.

Tornabuoni family and the facility with which the artist submitted to these desires has taken away from the beauty as a whole. The setting absorbs all our attention, and by setting I mean not only the architecture, which crushes the spectators, but the spectators themselves, who, enveloped in huge cloaks, form independent groups, discussing the affairs of the city or philosophical questions.

At the end of the fifteenth century this tradition still persists with Filippino Lippi. Following the example of his father, he mixes with those taking part in religious scenes, kneeling and isolated donors. In the Brancacci chapel on the other hand, he has imitated Filippo Lippi and Ghirlandaio rather than the Master whose decorative work he ought to have completed [1]. Filippino's frescoes are conceived in a completely different spirit from those of Masaccio and one can measure on the same wall the great distance which separated these two artists, the one at the beginning, the other at the end of the fifteenth century. With Masaccio it is the intensity of religious and human drama, with Filippino the charm of an anecdote delightfully told, whose interest is enhanced for contemporaries by the inclusion of familiar faces [2].

There is no doubt that this abuse of portraiture was a source of weakness for Florentine art. Nowadays we are carried away by the lively portraits of bourgeois, rich merchants or bankers, which are enlivened by fine and astute intelligence, but we must make no mistake; after the art of Giotto and Masaccio that of Ghirlandaio and Filippino Lippi is almost an art of decadence.

When Vasari wrote, in speaking of Filippino Lippi, that in the Brancacci chapel he carried on the work begun by Masaccio "to its final perfection" it seems that he did not appreciate the two artists at their full value. Masaccio

---

[1] In the Fresco in the Carmine representing the *Curing of the Child*, Vasari mentions the names of the spectators: the father of the historian Francesco Guicciardini the poet Luigi Pulci, Antonio Pollaiuolo; the nude child is also a portrait of Francesco Granacci whilst young; the artist painted himself in this composition, young as he was at the time, a thing which he never did again in the course of his career. "In the following scene", adds Vasari, "there is Botticelli and a number of friends and important people".

[2] Vasari, III, 462-463.

gave his frescoes an architectural unity, whereas with Filippino Lippi and Ghirlandaio the interest ends in concentrating on portraits which people their mural decorations. Leon Battista Alberti, a contemporary of theirs, understood them well when he wrote, "One can form an idea of what a painter ought to seek after principally on seeing what passes for a picture in which one finds the face of some well-known man; it is well that there are other faces of finer artistry than this, for it is this familiar face which attracts the eyes of those who look at the picture" [1]. Thus the unity of the whole is in part destroyed and its power to evoke our sensitivities is less intense and less moving.

---

[1] Leon Battista Alberti, *della Pittura*, (ed. Janitschk, 1887), III, p. 153.

CHAPTER II

EASEL PORTRAITS AT THE TIME OF BOTTICELLI

The Flemish Influence. Portraits by Antonello da Messina. Antonio del Pollaiuolo.
The Man with the Wedding Ring. The Corsini Collection. Domenico Ghirlandaio's
easel portraits. Those of Bastiano Mainardi. *The Man with the Medal* by Botticelli.
Botticelli's Theories and influence. *Portrait of a Man* in the former Layard Collection.

At the same time as a taste for the collective portrait was developing, a
favourable atmosphere for the easel portrait was created. Perhaps the Florentine bourgeois were more sensitive to the honour of figuring in the magnificent assemblies in frescoes. Their pagan feeling for glory was satisfied
by this distortion of religious painting. But they came, in spite of everything,
to appreciate isolated portraits, which in the second half of the fourteenth
century were beginning to appear more frequently than previously.

As a matter of fact, if one thinks of the great number of busts and medals
which have come down to us from the fifteenth century, the number of
painted portraits is by comparison very small. One may suppose that many
were lost [1]. Nevertheless, it seems evident that this kind of effigy was not
fashionable and there are none mentioned in the inventory of Lorenzo the
Magnificent's collection.

Among those which have come down to us there are some of excellent
workmanship, but they generally conform to certain traditions. This explains
why they are not animated by the same life and freedom as those of Flanders.

From early times portraiture in Flanders was developed without hindrance,

---

[1] Perhaps a fairly large number were lost in the "destruction by fire" brought about by
Savonarola's preaching.

whether it was the donor or a rich merchant who posed before the artist. Now the painters of the Low Countries were not unknown in Italy, especially in Venice. Without mentioning the possible journey of one of the Van Eycks, we might note that in 1449-50 Roger de la Pasture went there and received a flattering welcome; he worked for the Duke of Ferrara [1] and even, it seems, for the Medicis[2].

A self portrait by Roger de la Pasture dated 1463 is in a Venetian collection[3]. In Lorenzo the Magnificent's collection (who seemed nevertheless little disposed to buy Flemish paintings), we find works by John of Bruges (who was perhaps Jan van Eyck) and of Petrus Christus [4].

Between 1450 and 1480 the Italians were to some extent infatuated with Flemish painting. Zanetto Bugatto, the official portrait painter to Francesco Sforza, was sent from Milan by his master to the Low Countries, there to learn from Roger de la Pasture. Duke Federigo of Montefeltro ordered Juste de Gand to come to his palace; and it was under his influence that the talent of Giovanni Santi, the father of Raphael, was formed. We must also take this fact into account in the development of Florentine painting even before the days of the famous Van der Goes Triptych, commissioned by Tommasso Partarini, arrived at the hospital of Santa Maria Nuova.

After the death of Zanetto Bugatto "quale retraseva dal naturale in singolare perfectione", the duke Francesco Maria Sforza called in a Sicilian painter [5]; it was very likely Antonello da Messina, because several portraits by him are still to be found in Milan. This Antonello da Messina was evidently the most powerful and lively portrait painter of all the fifteenth-century

---

[1] Campori, *I pittori degli Estenti* (reg. deputazione di storia per le provincie della Emilia, series II, vol. III). Cf. Roger Fry, *A Portrait of Leonello d'Este by Roger Van der Weyden* (*Burlington Magazine*, XVIII, p. 200).

[2] A picture by Roger de la Pasture in the Städel-Institut represents the *Virgin and Four Saints* of whom two are the patron saints of the Medici, the saints Como and Damien. Cf. J. Mesnil, *L'art au Nord et au sud des Alpes a l'époque de la Renaissance*, 1911, p. 15. Eug. Muntz, *Roger van der Weyden à Milan et à Florence. Les portraits des Sforzas et des Medicis* (*Revue de l'art chrétien*, 1895, p. 190).

[3] *Notizia d'opere di disegno* (de Marc Antonio Michiel), ed. Frizzoni, 1884, p. 206.

[4] Cf. Eug. Muntz, *Les collections des Medicis au XV siècle*, 1888, p. 206.

[5] Di Marzo, *Di Antonello da Messina e dei suoi congiunti*, 1903, p. 64.

Italians. Whether or not he went to the Low Countries, his art remains very much, in technique as well as spirit, under the influence of Flanders. The tradition of Roger de la Pasture and his contemporaries was that of precise realism, which carefully included every characteristic in a face and expressed it with accurately drawn contours. For a long time portraits by Antonello and Memlinc were difficult to distinguish from each other; this fact alone is significant, and proves the part played by Flemish realism in the formation of the style of Antonello.

Antonello's influence was very great in Venice and was felt even as far away as Florence. In the middle of the fifteenth century people were accustomed to the clean and powerful lines of the profile. Baldovinetti had tried to temper this vigorous conception with a certain softness. His *Head of a Young Woman*, which is today in the Kaiser Friedrich Museum, is painted with much grace *(Plate III, fig. 5)*; and this grace delightfully humanises the style of Uccello, which must have been somewhat after that of Domenico Veneziano, if we can judge by the latter's religious paintings [1].

Antonio del Pollaiuolo followed only the method of his master Baldovinetti; and when he took up the theme of the profile again, it was in order to recapture the cold and severe expression against which the charming master of the Madonnas of the Louvre, of the Edouard André Museum and the Berenson Collection reacted. This is why the profile in the Poldi Museum [2] is so different from that in Berlin where the body is arched as in Uccello's painting in the National Gallery.

Pollaiuolo has depicted a young woman, erect and stressing the fine curves of her hips. He has modelled her face vigorously and given her a severe and proud bearing *(Plate III, fig. 6)*. He has in this way, to a certain extent,

---

[1] This explains why the attribution of this profile to Domenico Veneziano is in no way acceptable. It is Mr. Bode who claims it *(Jahrbuch der königlichen preussischen Kunstsammlungen,* 1897, XVIII, p. 187).

[2] Formerly on the back of the picture the following words could be read: *Uxor Joannis de Bardis;* they were effaced after a restoration: the dei Bardis were a very well-known Florentine family.

recaptured the tradition of Pisanello, whose temperament is not unlike his own.

In early times there was an idea that easel portraits were simply pieces taken out of large mural compositions. Thus the portrait of a woman by Ghirlandaio in the old R. Kann Collection [1] keeps the handling of a fresco. It has the appearance of a sketch for the tall and beautiful figure of the *Visitation* in Santa Maria Novella. The fair hair is full of life, and that, in the fifteenth century, was an essential element of beauty; her dress is that of a woman of quality at the end of the fifteenth century, that is to say of a more simple and refined elegance than of Uccello's, Francesca's or Baldovinetti's models. The elegance of the clothes and coiffures is in better taste; the folds of the dress, which do not depart far from the lines of the body, are more supple. Little by little the adornments become less complicated and this development helps the artist to concentrate on the ethical worth of the portrait. But with Ghirlandaio this tendency scarcely showed itself. What is most striking in a picture of this kind is the persistent influence of the fresco. This noble Florentine is destined to take part in the parade of a brilliant fête.

Compared with that of Ghirlandaio, Antonio Pollaiuolo's art is therefore more original. He brought to Florence a spirit similar to that of Antonello da Messina. This artist, who, according to Albertini and the author of the *Codice Magliabechiano*, painted as a pastime, was an innovator. His *Man with the Wedding Ring* [2], three-quarter view, has the same pose as a portrait by Roger de la Pasture or Memlinc; but the character is in every way different *(Plate V, fig. 9)*. Between the brown of the coat and the white of the shirt, the trimming is an ingenious repetition of the red colour of the cap, and the paler colouring of the face is contrasted well against this brilliant colour, where the handsome brown eyes have a penetrating soft gaze. The

---

[1] *The R. Kann Collection Pictures*, 1907, II, p. 28. Cf. the article by Paleologue, *Gazette des Beaux-Arts*, Dec. 1897. This portrait any more than the young woman to be seen in profile in the *Visitation* at Santa Maria Novella does not represent Giovanna Tornabuoni. Cf. also the article by Thieme (*Zeitschrift für bildende Kunst*, 1898, p. 192).

[2] Previous to its attribution by Crowe and Cavalcaselle the portrait was attributed to Masaccio (*Storia della pittura in Italia*, 1883, II, 327). It is in the Corsini Gallery in Florence.

paintings of Antonello are thus stripped of their roughness by this sensitive and taking artist who was the genial master of Botticelli. The features of the *Man with the Wedding Ring* are the same as those in Antonio Pollaiuolo's *Bacchus* in the Berlin Museum; he searches out with happy effect the living model; according to Vasari his *Saint Sebastian* in the National Gallery is the portrait of one of his contemporaries, Gino Capponi [1].

Piero, Antonio's brother, contributed just as much in his way to giving life to the studio portrait; the Galeazzo Maria Sforza in the Uffizi, which by its technique comes very near to certain "virtues" of the Marcanzia, is in a freer style than the profile portraits; the gesture of the gloved hand brings life to an expressive face *(Plate V, fig. 10)*.

It was thus through the two Pollaiuolos that the art of Antonello and of Flanders became familiar to the Florentines. The pose of the model followed an almost unalterable rule. The medal type of profile was abandoned in favour of a detailed facial study, a three-quarter view was preferred, even sometimes an almost full-face rendering of the model. If a head and shoulders study was made it was in unconscious imitation of the practice in sculpture. The beautiful series of effigies in the Bargello in Florence shows just how much the Florentine patricians loved to see their features immortalised in marble or bronze. One work by Desiderio da Settignano and Antonio Rossellino was so realistic that it fascinated even the old masters; it is an additional example to that of Antonello and the Flemings.

It is probable that the Florentines also must have been a little influenced by what was going on in other artistic capitals. If they liked to have their portraits painted in frescoes and thus force themselves on the attention of those who came to pray, the Venetian pride and the pontifical pride had other requirements.

In Venice the Doges were too conscious of their power and dignity not to commission the artist to perpetuate their memory by pompous separate portraits. In Rome the Sistine Chapel had to be adorned with portraits of numer-

---

[1] Vasari, III, 292.

ous Popes considered as illustrious ancestors. The painters who had developed there a beautiful series of frescoes were ordered thus to complete the decoration: Ghirlandaio, Fra Diamente—the pupil of Filippo Lippi—Botticelli and Cosimo Rosselli. In these simple portrait busts, which can have no iconographic value, they tried to bring out the individuality of the faces[1]. It is easy nevertheless to recognise there the style of Ghirlandaio and that of Botticelli. Vasari himself cites these pictures of the Popes[2] among the known works of Botticelli. They have the same refined features and thoughtful gaze, just as in the *Evariste* with the head slightly inclined, which is a beautiful personification of melancholy and Christian gentleness. With Ghirlandaio, on the contrary, the heads have a majestic gentleness. The two painters' temperaments are contrasted there as in the church of Ognissanti in Florence, where the *Saint Jerome* and the *Saint Augustine* are so different in spirit and in appeal.

In Rome they considered the Florentines to be the best of all portrait painters; it was Florentines who were commissioned to create this pontifical gallery. And similar works must have helped besides to give them the taste for a deeper study of individual heads. In Florence, commissions also came in little by little. But it is curious to note that in contrast to the masters of other states, the Medicis hardly ever asked to be painted separately. It seems that they were quite content with medal profiles, sculptured busts or a place of honour in a fresco.

We must not forget the impression produced by the realism of Hugo van der Goes' triptych, a work very much admired by the Florentines. An artist like Ghirlandaio must have been struck above all by the beauty and powerful life of the donors[3]. Now it was his ambition to get a likeness, to fix accurately all the details of a face. *The Old Man* in the Louvre shows the pleasure the

---

[1] Cf. Ernst Steinmann, *Die Sixtinische Kapelle*, 1901, I, p. 201 and following.

[2] Vasari, III, p. 317.

[3] Hugo van der Goes' triptych executed in 1475 was placed in Santa Maria Novella probably about 1482. Cf. Joseph Destree, *Hugo van der Goes*, 1914, p. 108.

artist took in bringing out every detail which would make the face more ugly—despite its kindly appearance—and to contrast with it the charm of the child's face; through a window looking on to the mountainous countryside, a golden light illuminates the group and helps to accentuate the contrast in the two faces.

The Francesco Sassetti in the Benson Collection [1] is presented in a similar way. This man who gave Ghirlandaio the important commission for the Santa Trinità Chapel is here seen standing with his son. In spite of numerous repaints the whole is not lacking in appeal. Portraits of this kind show a new tendency: the painter groups two heads together in order to study them to better advantage and to try to rid them of all traces of artificiality. But he did not show their inner feelings; incapable of interpreting the depth behind a face, he veiled it, so to speak, not daring to catch its real intensity. He pre-occupied himself a great deal about posing his model naturally. When working on his frescoes he learnt how to arrange figures so as to make a good composition; and this feeling for construction is found again in certain of his studio portraits, which also reveal the Flemish influence in precise rendering and the seeking out of picturesque detail. The technique of painting in oils allows the artist to give a more careful analytical study of the faces, whereas that of mural painting necessitates a rapid synthesis, a drawing of the general silhouette with its essential features.

In spite of Ghirlandaio's example there were some artists who still had a preference for profiles; they often painted them to commemorate a marriage, the husband and wife seeming to look towards each other, as in the picture of the Duke and Duchess of Urbino. When Bastiano Mainardi shows them facing each other against a landscape background, as in the two pictures in Berlin, he was simply imitating Piero della Francesca. This practice of placing a profile against a charming landscape, so as to render it softer and less arid, spread even outside Florence.

---

[1] *Catalogue of Italian Pictures collected by Robert and Evelyn Benson*, 1914, no. 272, p. 51. This Francesco Sassetti must be a little later than the frescoes in the Santa Trinità Chapel. The son of Sassetti, Theodore, born in 1479, is in this picture about twelve years old: which makes the probable date of the work 1489.

This type of double portrait seems to have appeared fairly frequently. In the National Gallery and in the Arconati-Visconti Collection we see some in a similar style. One is tempted to attribute them to the same artist. This Mainardi, who was a pupil and collaborator of Ghirlandaio's, did not succeed in drawing the contours of a face with that power which made a portrait by his master a finished and, so to speak, permanent work. Whereas Ghirlandaio was able to achieve charming effects in his treatment of hair, Mainardi painted it without any sense of delicacy. In the Berlin Gallery the accessories have little justification: they show the same taste for insignificant and superfluous detail as does Ghirlandaio's *St. Jerome*. The portrait is separated from the background by a parapet from which rises two columns, the harmony of the verdant landscape is brought out and also the vigour of the face, which is characterised by a certain lack of balance.

In commemorative portraits the tradition of the profile is not forgotten, nor for that matter in the others. Second-rate artists remained faithful to the canons of Piero della Francesca and by this process were able to seize a likeness more easily. Among the examples (which are numerous enough) we can cite at least one which is quite striking—the head in the Pitti Palace which is not, as was thought, Simonetta Vespucci, nor a work by Botticelli or his school (as the catalogue states) [1]: in this rather dry profile that care for cold precision which is predominant in the group of Ghirlandaio is manifested.

The conceptions of the School of Botticelli were in fact quite different; and it is quite easy to see that there is nothing in common between this soulless kind of painting and the *Young Man* in the National Gallery or the *Man with the Medal* [2] by Botticelli, which are among the most remarkable Florentine portraits of the second half of the fifteenth century.

There is an obvious kinship between the *Man with the Medal* and the *Man*

---

[1] Mr. Berenson (*The Study and Criticism of Italian Art*, 1903, I, page 622) attributes it to Amico di Sandro, but he himself realises that the expression is "foolish", which takes us far away from the circle of Botticelli's followers.

[2] The same technical methods are employed as in the *Death of Holofernes* in the Uffizi; that is why there can be no doubt about its attribution to Botticelli.

with the Ring by Antonio Pollaiuolo; it is certain that the master has here influenced the pupil, as in one of the *Virtues* in the Mercanzia. The expression of the face is entirely in Botticelli's manner; the painter's personality is already forcefully expressed here. The vigorous construction of the head, the strongly contrasted modelling of the cheeks is reminiscent of Pollaiuolo; besides, Botticelli remains one of the most moving draughtsmen that painting has ever known. The contrast of light and shade delicately indicated helps to give this face a troubled feeling quite different from any conception up to now. Note also the simplicity of the dress, the extraordinary head-dress and the dark colour of the hair; all this contributes to the full value of the pale face and the troubled look of the eyes. The hands are shaded in the same way as the face: they are the hands of a highly strung person. Even the landscape has here its significance; in the case of Ghirlandaio it appears through a window, whereas with Mainardi it fills almost the entire background. Here it is only an accessory which might be dispensed with. It plays apparently a more useful part in the *Man with the Medal*; are not the sinuous lines troubled like the face of the sitter *(Plate VII, fig. 12)*?

It is difficult to say who the model is; anyway it is only of anecdotal interest; before such a strong work the identity of the sitter is entirely secondary; only notice that, since he holds between his hands the medal of Cosimo de Medici, "Pater Patrie" (and this gesture gives a strange life to the picture), it is almost certain that it is a member of that family, perhaps a close relation of Cosimo's [1].

The pose of the model, looking straight ahead, is one that pleased Botticelli particularly. *The Young Man* in the National Gallery has a face to which all the character is given by the eyes, eyes of dark brown into which a little of that bitter melancholy which scornfully folds the corners of the mouth seems to pass. There is nothing to take the attention away from the pupils, which fascinate us; the costume is extremely sober—a brown jacket edged

---

[1] M. Friedländer claims, without any good reason, that Botticelli has here represented the medal-maker Niccolo Fiorentino, maker of Cosimo the Elder's medal (*Die italienischen Schaumünzen des fünfzehnten Jahrhunderts*, 1882, p. 146).

18. Raphael. *The Woman with the Golden Chain.* (Uffizi)
19. Mariotto Albertinelli (?). *Portrait called "The Monaca."* (Uffizi)

Lorenzo di Credi.
20. *Head of an Old Man.* (Uffizi Drawing Office)
21. *Portrait of Andrea Verrocchio.* (Uffizi)
22. *Portrait of a Young Man.* (Uffizi)

with a narrow strip of fur. The background is plain; Botticelli has banished landscape in order to make the emotion stronger *(Plate VI, fig. II)*.

Some of his other portraits, the *Lorenzo Lorenzano* in the Johnson Collection [1] and the *Young Woman* in the Städel-Institut [2], although less impressive, show similar handling. In the solid face of the learned doctor, framed in a grey background, it is the brilliance of the eyes which gives the expressive note; as for the lovely portrait at Frankfurt, it is very sensitive in design and has a taking charm [3].

These portraits certainly impressed contemporaries very much. There is in fact a series of portraits which seem to belong to the same period, from 1475 to 1490, inspired by identical principles [4]. During a period of several years there was no doubt of the preponderance of Botticelli's influence. The faces have that nostalgic expression which it is surprising to find in a period of easy living. They seem to foretell the evil days to come. The authority of the Medicis no longer had the solid foundation of Cosimo's time, and the plotting of the Pazzi were soon to terrify the hearts of the Florentines. The portraits of him who was to become an unfortunate hero, Julius de Medici, seem to be agonised by a presentiment of his sad end. We see him with his head bowed in a melancholy fashion to the ground in the *Adoration of the Magi* in the Uffizi, as in the portrait at Bergamo, and in the one in the Kaiser Friedrich Museum in Berlin. It is said to have been painted after the tragic ambush of the 26th April 1478. The medal by Antonio Pollaiuolo which commemorates this event also represents Julius, with tired features, bowing

---

[1] B. Berenson, *A Catalogue of a Collection of paintings and some objets d'art in the possession of John G. Johnson, Philadelphia*, 1913, I, *Italian Paintings*, p. 29 and 30. Cf. the article by Leon Dorez in the *Bulletin de la Société française d'histoire de la médecine*, 1907.

[2] *Katalog der Gemäldegalerie des Städelschen Kunstinstituts*, 1909, pp. 43, 44.

[3] Cf. the drawing in Oxford University reproduced by S. Colvin (*Drawings of the Old Masters in the University Galleries Oxford*, I, pl. 4) was carried out from the Frankfurt portrait by a second-rate pupil.

[4] In his volume *Die Einzelporträte des Sandro Botticelli*, 1911, Kroeber attributes to Botticelli almost all the portraits which are in his style. He thus includes thirteen, also the so-called Simonetta in the Pitti. It is unnecessary to say that this catalogue is highly imaginative.

his head with a like sadness; it is this that gives some weight to the conjecture of Frizzoni that this portrait is a reproduction of the death mask [1].

The dominating effect in the pictures in Berlin and Bergamo is an impression of exhaustion. Neither of these works is obviously by Botticelli himself; the one in Berlin is second-rate; the features are less lifelike than those in the example in Bergamo, where the modelling is more delicate. In neither of them do we find the beautiful emphasis of the faces by Botticelli in the Uffizi and the National Gallery.

The *Young Man* in the Louvre [2] is of a superior quality; the lips are accurately drawn like those in the *Young Man* in the National Gallery. There is in this face with its surprized gaze a touch of Botticelli. The planes of the face recall those of the *Man with the Medal;* the hair is treated broadly; the dress and the hair-style are conceived in the same spirit of simplicity. But it is not difficult to tell that this is the work of a pupil. Mr. Berenson states that the pupil is Amico di Sandro [3]. One is today tempted to attribute to him some portraits with a Botticellian physical structure where there is nevertheless no deep inspiration of the master. These faces are very lifelike and look out with an ardent curiosity. The Smeralda Bandinelli (which has gone from the Ionides Collection into the Victoria and Albert Museum) has this animation of the face which is even more attractive than the rather irregular features.

The *Young Man* in the Lichtenstein Collection [4] and the one in the former Layard Collection [5] are even more characteristic. The latter, especially, has a strain of sincerity which makes it superior to the others *(Plate VII, fig. 13)*. A picturesque landscape with rocks and slender trees hovering airily in the foreground; a certain warmth of colour, especially felt in the yellowish-pink above the head of the model; the general attitude, full of life; a hand resting on the balustrade, the other slipped into the opening of a large coat; the dishevelled hair floating in the wind; a certain astonished

---

[1] G. Frizzoni,*La Galleria Morelli in Bergamo*, 1892, p. 10.

[2] G. Frizzoni,*La Galleria Morelli in Bergamo*, 1892, p. 10.

[3] B. Berenson, *The Study and Criticism of Italian Art*, I, p. 46.

[4] W. Bode, *Die fürstliche Liechtenstein'sche Galerie in Wien*, 1896, p. 72.

[5] In the National Gallery Catalogue it is attributed to Botticelli himself.

anxiety in the features; all this indicates a vigorous temperament in whoever painted this powerful portrait. It is not altogether Botticelli and neither is it Amico di Sandro. The artist is gifted with a dramatic sense which to a certain extent exceeds that of Botticelli, for by him the life of a face is expressed with more ease.

The evolution of Florentine portraiture leads us then to a technique which differs essentially from that which artists employed at the beginning of the century. Florentine painting was, to begin with, a linear painting: portraiture could only have a small part to play in it. As long as painters were invincibly attracted by scenic unity we find very few exceptions to this fundamental rule. Nevertheless, the new ideas came to those among them whose chief preoccupation was the impression of unity: Paolo Uccello, Andrea del Castagno, Piero della Francesca. A portrait executed from the likeness on a medal was their work; and during a great many years it was not considered possible to give life to a portrait. The monotony in the middle of the fifteenth century (about 1440-1460) of all the heads left to us is due to this, as is their rarity: medals and sculptured busts were more in fashion.

But with the help of the cult of personality, Florentine pride found means of expressing itself elsewhere than in medals and busts: and from the day when portraiture invaded the realm of frescoes, these lost in grandeur and beauty. No one doubts that the *Funeral of Saint Francis* has a much greater breadth than the frescoes by Ghirlandaio. From frescoes portraits developed into easel portraits; and at times were inbued with a new life. Although profiles kept a certain popularity, the main interest eventually was concentrated on the whole face. But these were only slight indications, because they were still carried out as busts, as if sculpture exercised an influence over painters from which they were unable to free themselves.

Features set against a neutral background can be very precisely drawn, but the work of a careful draughtsman gives but slight presentation of character; it lacks life, the life of the gaze. Now Botticelli and his followers brought something new, and it was precisely this. In this sense they sowed the seeds of a revolution. This great painter has been much criticised for not being a colourist, and it is true that his colours are in general quite weak; they were not meant to excite those for whom painting is only a passionate game of unusual colours. But line, outline, has never had a more subtle analyst. And this subtlety, of such great charm, is an essential element of his portraits.

To assess the development let us compare the profile in the Kaiser Friedrich Museum, where the influence of Piero della Francesca is tempered with Tuscan grace in portraits of the Botticelli school, including even those which are the work of his pupils; the art of portraiture has gained in life and depth, and in this Botticelli's example had been fertile. There was also a tendency to make the pose more natural. Ghirlandaio grouped two people together and by the ingenuity of the presentation produced a lively effect. But these two masters were not the only ones to contribute to the formation of the style of painters working in Florence at the end of the fifteenth and beginning of the sixteenth century; other influences were going to be superimposed on theirs, and they were going to be deeper and more decisive.

CHAPTER III

LEONARDO DA VINCI'S THEORIES AND THEIR INFLUENCE ON THE YOUNG RAPHAEL

Portraits in frescoes and the theories of Leonardo da Vinci and Michelangelo. Leonardo's conception of the portrait. The so-called *Ginevra dei Benci* of the Lichtenstein Gallery. *Mona Lisa*. Leonardo's influence on Raphael. *Maddalena Doni*. Raphael's Florentine portraits. *La Donna Gravida*. *The Woman with the Golden Chain* in the Uffizi. *The Donna Velata*.

The originality of Botticelli's portraits rather lessens in our eyes the importance of the part played by Leonardo. The portrait of *The Man with the Medal*, contemporary with the *Saint Sebastian* at Berlin and the *Judith* of the Uffizi, dates from about 1475; it is certainly earlier in date than any important work by Leonardo. Nevertheless Leonardo had the merit of creating a set of doctrines, of establishing laws to which his followers submitted. At the beginning of the 16th century he became the great Florentine master, Botticelli being an old man besides being so profoundly influenced by the Savonarola drama that his painting was almost unrecognisable. Thus as Benvenuto Cellini says in a well-known passage, the board on which Leonardo sketched the *Battle d'Anghiari* for the great hall of the Palazzo Vecchio became, at the same time as the one by Michelangelo "the school of the world". Leonardism and Michelangelism suddenly became the fashion: few influences since that of Giotto have been so deeply felt in the history of Florentine painting.

---

1 Benvenuto Cellini, *Vita* (edition Guasti, p. 30).

It was inevitable that the evolution of portrait painting should be affected by these influences. The strongest of these was Leonardo's. Even in his very first works he departed from the ideal set by Ghirlandaio. He considered that a religious scene should inspire feelings quite different from those of curiosity. Already in Botticelli there was a definite subordination of detail to the central theme: but famous Florentines were not lacking in the backgrounds of his pictures.

With Leonardo the revolution was complete and radical. Although Vasari says that there are portraits in the *Last Supper*, it is rather doubtful whether he interpreted the painter's intention correctly. In a work of painting, says Leonardo, it is the effect produced by a composition that should be sought after by the painter; the action should be in harmony with this effect. In a general way, a painter should represent two things: man and the contents of his soul [1]. "You shall paint the faces in such a way that it will be easy to understand what is going on in the mind, otherwise your art is unworthy of praise", he adds.

Leonardo insists on the importance of the idea the painter wishes to express; everything in a work of art should lead towards the same goal, which is to give it profound unity. "Whether a scene represents terror", says he, "or fear, or suffering or pleasure, the spectators must act in such a way as to seem to take part in it and be animated by the feelings which it ought to inspire; if this is not the case, the artist's work has no interest whatsoever" [2]. Is not that exactly what Leonardo wanted to do in his *Santa Maria della Grazia*? In his *Treatise on Painting*, he often comes back to the necessity of "composing" a picture with great care. "Dei componimenti delle storie", "Precetti del Comporre le storie" are titles which we are always finding, more or less modified. The artist should group his figures in such a way that their gestures and expressions are in harmony with the fundamental idea of the picture. Everything foreign to the scene should be removed. "When one wishes, for

[1] Leonardo da Vinci, *Trattato di pittura* (ed. Ludwig), 1882, p. 134.
[2] *Trattato di pittura* (ed. Ludwig), I, p. 222.

example, to depict a work of great moral seriousness few young men should figure in it since youth is apt to avoid the councils of the wise" [1].

Leonardo thus criticises indirectly the tendency which used to give portraits a leading part in frescoes. He always contended that "among painters who make a profession of portrait painting, those who give the closest likeness are the most mediocre of historical painters", historical (*historie*) indicating all those important and impressive subjects which the painters of the 15th century used to illustrate. Well, here the portrait painter has really no part to play; he spoils a work which could be beautiful. When an artist excels at one thing, it proves that nature has blessed him in that direction and not in another; and thus he applies himself to it with love and this love makes him diligent. But as "he has only one bent his preoccupation with only a part of his work means that he abandons the universal for the particular. The influence of such a mind is only felt over a narrow field." It makes one think of "those concave mirrors which only give off a slight warmth when they reflect the sun's rays in their greatest diameter, but on the other hand give off a great deal if they reflect them from a small portion. It is thus with those painters who in their art concentrate on the human face and ignore the other parts" [2].

Since, according to Leonardo, painting should deal with the universal, it is obvious that those who get involved in the study of detail are mediocrities—they are attracted by accessories and lose sight of the essential function of a work of art, which is to fill with emotion the heart of him who contemplates it. Leonardo has thus the highest ideas of the mission of a painter; nothing is beautiful unless it approaches complete perfection. If a painter neglects a single aspect of his art he is not worthy of the name of master.

One must "like equally all things in the realm of painting" and this is why Leonardo gives so much importance to landscape [3]. To consider it as only

---

[1] *Trattato di pittura* I, p. 376.
[2] *Trattato di pittura*, I, p. 112.
[3] *Trattato di pittura*, I, p. 116.

worthy of superficial study, like Botticelli, is to have a very narrow conception of things. The mission of an artist is a very vast one. It is almost encyclopaedic. "People who hail as a master the man who is only capable of doing a head or a face well deceive themselves. It is not a very great accomplishment to attain a certain degree of perfection by giving up a lifetime to the study of a single aspect of art. To us who know that all that nature can produce is united in a painting, and that all that the human hand can make and finally all that the eye can take in, he seems a poor master who can only succeed in representing a face. Cannot we see how very varied are the actions of man, how many different kinds of animals, trees, plants and flowers there are, what variety there is to be found in mountains, plains, fountains, rivers, towns, in public and domestic buildings, in a word in all that serves man? Here are the things which ought to be understood, studied and analysed by anyone who wishes to earn the title of a good painter" [1].

The teaching and example of Leonardo were of such a kind as to make inevitable the renunciation by his disciples of the formuli laid down by Ghirlandaio and the Lippis. So striking were Leonardo's theories that young artists could not resist being seduced by them. Consequently one can understand the resultant progressive disappearance of portraits in frescoes and sacred paintings; the great masters of the end of the fifteenth and beginning of the sixteenth century were not always liberated from fifteenth-century tradition. They nevertheless searched honestly, without always succeeding, to fix the attention on a central theme.

Did not Savonarola himself condemn Ghirlandaio's tradition in vehement terms? From the religious and moral standpoint he considered that this tradition revealed great contempt for divine things. "You would do well," said he to painters, "to eliminate those heads which call to mind the features of so many contemporary men and women because that is a very dishonest way of painting." At the same time as deploring these "vanities" he laid down a theory of beauty according to which not only the harmony of bodily

---

[1] J. P. Richter, *The Literary Works of Leonardo da Vinci*, 1883, vol. I, p. 250–251.

proportions should be emphasised, but to an even greater extent the charm of mind and heart [1].

Michelangelo also considered it absurd and unworthy for a great artist to turn a fresco into a collection of portraits. According to Vasari, he had a horror of recording in detail the exact features of a living model [2]. It sufficed for his figures to have a clearly defined human character; he recreated their faces, expressing in them his own feelings. Power of imagination dominated all his work. Though it may be impossible to compare the artistic forms of Leonardo and Michelangelo, it is by no means impossible to establish a similarity between some of their ways of thinking. Certain general principles of Leonardo's could not have met with Michelangelo's disapproval, particularly insofar as art in general should aim at expressing the universal. Michelangelo thought that one should only represent those human features which were really beautiful and that as the artist's craft was often incapable of rendering this beauty, it was better not to attempt it. When the poet Gandolfo Porrino asked him to paint a portrait of his mistress Mancina, the artist replied that only God, who had formed the flesh, could reproduce its brilliance [3]. This is why representations of individual heads is almost entirely absent from his works; he idealised the features he took from life; they became elements in a harmonious whole and served, as did the *Lorenzo* and the *Julius*, in the Medici Chapel at St. Lorenzo, to express a profound sentiment.

The influence of Michelangelo added to that of Leonardo encouraged painters gradually to suppress everything in their work which took away from the theme. The tendency which was already making itself felt with Botticelli took shape in their theories and their works. It was an innovation similar to the one which Giorgione introduced among the Venetians. As soon

---

[1] *Prediche quadragesimale del R. frate Jeronimo Savonarola da Ferrara sopra Amos propheta,* Venice, 1539, p. 169 and 229 ("tanto piu bello il corpo, quanto e piu bella l'anima"). Cf. P. Villari, *La storia di Girolamo Savonarola,* 1887, I, p. 518 and following. – G. Gruyer, *Les illustrations des écrits de Savonarole publiés en Italie au XV et au XVI siècles et les paroles de Savonarole sur l'Art,* 1879, p. 190–1.

[2] Vasari, VII, p. 271–272.

[3] *Die Dichtungen des Michelangelo Buonarotti* (ed.Frey, 1897,   CIX, p. 172).

as Giorgione appeared on the scene, painters quickly gave up the Bellini tradition. But in Venice there were men of genius able to take the theories of Giorgione to their logical conclusion. It was not all the same with Florence, and that which ought to have brought new life into Florentine art ended by weakening it.

A first point is obvious: talent was less freely expressed in what Leonardo da Vinci calls "componimenti". In a painting, for instance, of *The Adoration of the Magi,* an artist's first consideration should be grouping and composition; if portraits are found there it is exceptional and because artists of the second rank found it difficult to give up such a strong tradition.

From then onwards, when a Florentine patrician wanted to hand his features down to posterity, he was satisfied with an isolated portrait. And it was thus that, at the end of the fifteenth century, the taste for easel portraits spread even at the expense of sculptured busts which in the sixteenth century were fewer in number than paintings. This is one of the important results of Leonardo's theory.

Since it was necessary to make expression of first importance, it followed that the character of the portrait should be transformed. It is an idea which often recurs in the *Trattato di Pittura;* if it be true that the painter must aim at expressing the universal, then it is equally true that the point of departure for all his works must be nature [1].

"No-one should imitate the style of another for he would thus only be the grandchild (nipote) and not the child of nature. Works of nature offer us such abundance of material that it is better to have direct recourse to them than to the masters who owe all their knowledge to nature." In a very rapid survey of the evolution of painting, Leonardo sees in Giotto an artist who was inspired by nature and submitted his genius to her dictates, and since Giotto's time art loses some of her vigour because everyone imitated existing works; thus "art was in a decline until the time of Tommaso of Florence,

---

[1] *Trattato di pittura,* I, 140.

called Masaccio, who shows by his works that he who takes any guide but nature, the supreme mistress, works in vain" [1].

At the same time it is not necessary to copy slavishly what one sees. According to Leonardo a "work in its entirely should express a collective idea; and the figure most deserving of praise is one which reveals the passion of its soul" [2]. Is it not obvious that the same formula should hold good with portraiture? A portrait should reveal the mind or soul of the model. If the model in question has only mediocre soul or spirit, it is certain that a genius like Leonardo will endow him with profounder feelings more in keeping with his own. With him, more than with any other painter, portraits bear a certain family likeness.

Landscape is of the utmost importance. We have already seen how much Leonardo disapproved of the fifteenth-century painters who treated it as an accessory. He loved nature for herself; he understood her deep beauty as an artist and a scholar. "Everything born of her is sensitive, growing and rational . . . .We can say that the earth has a growing soul and that her flesh is the soil and her bones the framework of rocks which go to make up the ranges of mountains, her sinews the foundation of the earth and her blood the rivulets of water" [3]. Landscape is in no way a drop curtain as in the works of the primitives; it is part of the life of the painting. Leonardo loved the more tortuous formations of nature; he describes with admiration the beauty of the mountains; his *Treatise on Painting* contains curious passages on this subject, notably his famous description of Taurus that might lead one to believe that he had travelled in the East. Already in his Uffizi drawing of 1473 we see a preference for majestic horizons. This carries us far away from the tradition to which Florentine painters remained so faithful—depicting in a simple way the hills around them bathed in limpid atmosphere. But Perugino's Umbrian landscape already shows more variety than that of the

---

[1] Richter, *The Literary Works of Leonardo da Vinci*,   I, p. 331–332.
[2] Richter, *The Literary Works of Leonardo da Vinci*,   I, p. 292.
[3] Richter, *The Literary Works of Leonardo da Vinci*,   II, p. 220–221.

Tuscan painters. It is in certain ways more original and more personal, and in Verrocchio's studio must have had an influence on Leonardo.

The Apennines, and his stay in Milan near the Alpine Lakes, made him still more familiar with turbulent landscape. From that time the backgrounds of his pictures are extremely vivid; we must not look for an exact representation of an aspect of nature which he had caught sight of and admired; his mind recreated what was before his eyes and he liked to give free play to fancy. The landscape being part of the matter depicted in the foreground, it is obvious that nothing should interfere with the harmony of the painter's conception. In the portrait in the Lichtenstein Gallery he has achieved this magnificent unity in a more strikingly intimate and poetic rendering than in *The Man with the Medal* (Botticelli).

Several tendencies which were to develop with Leonardo's maturity are already evident. Waagen and Wilhelm Bode were the first to lay claim to recognising the portrait of *Ginevra dei Benci* which Antonio Magliabechiano [1] considered, like Vasari, worthy of admiration: "Leonardo painted Ginevra, wife of d'Amerigo Benci, in so perfect a manner that it was in truth a really faithful likeness."

Mr. Bode's arguments can be summed up as follows: the background itself is composed of a magnificent foliage of junipers, some of which are reflected in the still waters; the painter must have intended them as a symbol alluding to the model's christian name. Also the young woman's coiffure belongs to a definite period (1470-1490); so we must presume that the picture was painted between these two dates. In gathering together these data from history, Mr. Bode comes to the conclusion that this must be the portrait of Ginevra dei Benci, painted by Leonardo. He backs up his proof by claiming to have found the copy of this portrait at the Marchese Pucci's in Florence, a work of no great artistic value (which nevertheless Mr. Berenson attributes to Lorenzo di Credi) on the back of which are two indications that Mr. Bode finds very important: an inscription dating from the sixteenth century:

[1] *Antonio Magliabechiano*, ed. Fry, p. 111; Vasari, IV, 39.

"Ginevra d'Amerigo Benci" and a design representing a sprig of juniper surrounded by two branches of laurel and palm bound by a scroll with the words "Virtutem forma decorat".

The argument which might seem to have the most foundation at first sight is that which makes us identify the model with Ginevra dei Benci; however, we must admit that there is no similarity between the portrait of the Pucci collection and the one in the Lichtenstein Collection. Mr. Bode insists on the likeness between the two faces, but this resemblance is an illusion. The Pucci portrait shows a much longer and entirely insignificant face; if one is a portrait of Ginevra Benci, then it is difficult to imagine that the other can have the same attribution. On the other hand it is not without interest to note that one of these portraits is painted down to the middle of the body, the other just to the beginning of the breast. The problem of the model's identity is thus difficult to solve; besides, there is nothing to prove that the inscription on the Pucci portrait has any importance whatsoever. One can quite easily take no account of it and maintain that the picture in the Lichtenstein Gallery is of Ginevra Benci. Nevertheless the whole question is a matter of some doubt. On the other hand, it is the name of the artist that compels recognition. This work calls to mind Verrocchio's *Woman with Flowers* [1], but the interpretation is so personal that this fleeting likeness is forgotten. One feels here the presence of his famous pupil, Leonardo. The clearness with which the cheek bones are given their right value, the play of light and shade which accentuates the modelling of the lower half of the face are the work of a very personal painter; the whole rendering of the face is of a depth not to be found in the Pucci portrait. This strange head with its delicate neck interested the painter, who took a great deal of care in drawing the features and in rendering the curious attraction of the almond shaped eyes [2] which are so far removed from the quiet inexpressive eyes of the portrait in the Florentine collection. Let us consider as well the delicacy

---

[1] Bargello Museum, Florence.

[2] It has been noted that the eyes give a curious exotic character to the whole head (A. Chiaparelli, *Leonardo ritrattista*, 1921, p. 15).

with which the light plays across the hair whose waves are accentuated by those metallic glints which later Lorenzo di Credi was to love so much. The landscape sketched in the background has a certain melancholy, with its blue hills and maroon-coloured bushes softly mirrored in the sleeping waters; it admirably furnishes the background of the picture, filling the whole of it, as did later the background to the *Mona Lisa*. The rendering of the ivory and pink skin shows an extraordinary scientific knowledge of the blending of colours, anticipating the art with which Leonardo was to paint the flesh tones of the *Mona Lisa*. Consider, above all, the brown eyes with their gentle expression which remain perhaps the most remarkable part of the picture.

All this belongs to a very fastidious type of art and takes us far away from Verrocchio's conception. In the few pictures of his which remain to us there is dryness and sharpness, and they never achieve a like softness of colouring. Leonardo's name comes forcibly to mind [1]. He already applies the principles which were to develop later on in the picture of the *Mona Lisa* (*Pl. VIII, fig. 14*). Leonardo began work on this last portrait almost certainly on his return to Florence right at the beginning of the sixteenth century. The model was a Neapolitan, third wife of Francesco del Giocondo. Her likeness, undoubtedly transfigured by the painter, exercised a veritable fascination over his contemporaries and its influence was just as great as that of the cartoon for the *Battle of Anghiari*. Vasari, who did not know this work, because in his time it already formed part of the collection of the King of France at the Palace of Fontainebleau, describes it at length. Many copies were made of it, and it left a lasting impression on those who saw the original. Also the terms employed by Vasari in his description had as much force as though he had seen the actual painting. A contemporary critic [2] infers that the Mona Lisa in the Louvre is a replica of Jean Charpentier's painting, which thus assumes

[1] In the *Burlington Magazine* (XX,   p. 345), Mr. Herbert Cook attributes this portrait to Leonardo, W. Bode to Morelli and Mr. Berenson to Verrocchio, Venturi to Lorenzo di Credi, and so does Frizzoni (*Nuova Antologia*, July 1911). An equally difficult question to solve is that of the date. It is very likely that it was painted before Leonardo's departure for Milan. From this point of view the traces of Verrocchio's influence are of great importance.

[2] Roger Miles, *Leonardo da Vinci et les Jocondes*, 1923.

the value of the original admired by Vasari. One of his principal arguments for its authenticity is this very vivacity of the description made by the historian of *The Lives of the Painters;* but Vasari often described with the same vividness pictures he had never seen. It is one of his weaknesses to drift into exaggeration or pompous admiration. A second argument is drawn from the description made by De Beatis of three works which Leonardo showed to Cardinal d'Aragon [1] during the latter's stay at Amboise; there was, among others, "portrait of a certain Florentine woman" which had been commissioned by Julius de Medici. Well, Vasari says that Mona Lisa's portrait was commissioned by her husband. But there is nothing which makes us believe that this portrait represents the wife of Francesco del Giocondo; when Cardinal Louis d'Aragon went to see Leonardo da Vinci, it is possible that the picture of the Mona Lisa already formed part of Francis I collection and also that we may have lost all trace of the one which he saw. We may equally suppose that De Beatis' memory on this point is inaccurate and these conjectures have as much value as those of Mr. Roger Miles[2].

Anyway there seems to be practically no doubt that the work which, in 1550, Vasari knew to be at Fontainebleau is the same as the one P. Dan mentions [3]. Besides, it is psychologically impossible to suppose that the impulsive Leonardo should have painted the Mona Lisa twice. As he very seldom finished a work there is all the more reason to believe him incapable of beginning one again after he had tried to express the best that he was capable of.

To contemporaries Mona Lisa came as a great innovation in portrait painting. Compared with earlier portraits it seemed as though the model was enveloped in atmosphere. "When the contrast between light and shade is too violent," says Leonardo da Vinci, "a picture lacks beauty, also when the human body is painted in the open air, it is better that the faces should not be directly illuminated by the sun, but that there should be a few clouds partly

---

[1] Cf. Ludwig Pastor, *Beschreibung der Reise des Kardinals Luigi d'Aragona,* 1905.

[2] This complex question has been studied in detail by M. Rene Schneider, *L'insoluble problème de la Joconde (Etudes Italiennes,* October-December 1923).

[3] P. Dan, *Le trésor des merveilles du Château de Fontainebleau,* 1642, p. 136.

obscuring it, thus the change from light to shade will be more subtle" [1]. "Shadows must be softly graduated to give grace to a face."

To this must be added the charm of landscape. In the portrait of the Mona Lisa, it is even more expressive than in the Lichtenstein picture. "It is obvious that the higher up one goes the more subtle the atmosphere becomes. Things at a distance are much less distinct when they are high up than when they are low down." "Also when you paint mountains, O painter, do them in such a way that in the hills which succeed each other, the lower portion is much more distinct than the heights" [2]. Mountains in the background of a picture are thus a study in the play of air and in its differing transparency according to their distance from the painter.

Leonardo da Vinci might have been thinking of the Mona Lisa when he wrote that for a painter to be successful he must give his faces beautiful features [3].

"Nelle eletioni delle figure sia piutosto gentile che secco o legnioso" [4]. "Limbs which are destined for work should be muscular and those which are not thus destined should be softly drawn. They must be elegantly depicted when the face bears distinction, avoiding straight lines by outlining them with gracious curves".

As for costume, Leonardo likes it to be as simple as possible, without many folds, the material falling naturally [5]. According to Mr. Salomon Reinach, Mona Lisa is dressed in mourning. Her sadness would thus have a natural explanation. Nevertheless this conjecture, attractive at first sight, lacks conviction [6]. We must recognise above everything in this portrait the expression of Leonardo's art and a summary of an entire series of new tend-

---

[1] *Trattato di pittura*, I, p. 144.
[2] *The Literary Works*...... I, p. 161.
[3] *Trattato di pittura*, I, p. 182.
[4] *The Literary Works*, ... I, p. 294. Cf. also p. 295 and 300.
[5] *Trattato di pittura*, I, p. 520–522.
[6] S. Reinach, *La Tristesse de Mona Lisa* (*Bulletin des Musées de France*, 1909, no. 2). Mona Lisa's mourning, going back to 1499, when she lost her little daughter, was hardly likely to be still worn in 1501, when Leonardo began the portrait. And we must not forget that according to Vasari the painting took four years to carry out.

Piero di Cosimo.
23. *Portrait of Francesco Giamberti.* (The Hague)
24. *Portrait of Guiliano da San Gallo.* (The Hague)

25. Piero di Cosimo. *Portrait of a Warrior*. (National Gallery, London)

encies which can be seen in embryo in Botticelli's *Man with the Medal* and the *Young Woman* of the Lichtenstein Collection.

Vasari tells us that Leonardo surrounded his model with singers and musicians; this great artist loved everything that might add an atmosphere of charm to his pictures; he had a strong leaning towards music, and if in his *Trattato di Pittura* he gives the first place to painting, it is not for lack of a deep emotional feeling for the art of sound. In the portrait of the *Mona Lisa* he would have liked thus to dispel "this feeling of melancholy which painting so often gives to a head" [1]. A strange enough intention if one thinks of the usual expressions of Leonardo's portrait heads.

He wished to give to his faces a deeply personal accent, he did not think it necessary to animate them with the model's own sentiments; a familiar precept of his was "fare di fantasie appresso gli effetti di nature". Neither did he adhere to a physical likeness. When Cecilia Gallerani, Ludovico il Moro's mistress, sent the portrait Leonardo had painted of her to Isabella d'Este in 1498, she complained of the imaginative treatment of the picture: "I am sending it to you", she said, "but I would send it more willingly if it were like me" [2].

Mona Lisa symbolised, then, without any doubt, ideal feminine beauty as conceived by Leonardo; it is one of those portraits in which the artist endows his model with feelings which satisfy his reason and his heart, without any relation to reality.

Leonardo applied himself to the task of seizing the slightest detail of a face in order to make a deeper analysis of it. In several rapid sketches in the Ambrosiana Library, Leonardo took care to indicate the name of the person represented; on the other hand, Vasari says that he took great delight in drawing curious heads [3]. These are the portraits where Leonardo exaggerated the essential character of the face to the extent of making it ridiculous; they have the value of "studies in expression" as Gabriel Séailles justly says [4].

---

[1] Vasari, IV, p. 40.

[2] Uzielli, *Leonardo da Vinci e tre gentildonne del secolo* XV, 1890, p. 22 and following.

[3] Vasari, IV, p. 26.

[4] Cf. R. Schneider, *Le Réalisme de Léonardo da Vinci* (*Gazette des Beaux-Arts*, Nov. 1923).

Leonardo studied passionately the way the features of a face became modified when ruled by strong emotion. He was also a lover of unusual sensations; we know that at Milan he often watched capital executions [1]. He must have noted with perfect composure the terror of the last moments of the condemned. A drawing in the Museum at Bayonne is a study of this kind. It is of Bernado Bandini, one of the conspirators who on April 26, 1478, assassinated Julian de Medici in the Cathedral in Florence—a relentless portrait in which he analyses the terrible effects of death on the face and body of a hanged man.

A Ghirlandaio or a Cosimo Rosselli would have been only interested in the physical form of the face, by the outline without its content, so to speak: and that is why the profiles or three-quarter portraits made towards the middle of the fifteenth century impress us by their clarity and precision of line. On the other hand Leonardo was not interested in perfect verisimilitude to nature or in the painted portrait being so lifelike as to be taken for the model itself. He preferred that the soul of the model should be expressed in her eyes or in the smile which lighted up the face.

Such are the new precepts; they are of very great importance, for as soon as contemporary painters began to understand them, the current conceptions of sacred paintings and portraits were modified by them; unity of interest and unity of feeling became essential in both; costume and background landscape became subsidiary to the central theme and had no other function.

It remains to be known whether the influence of the Mona Lisa's portrait was immediate and profound, and whether during the first ten or twenty years of the sixteenth century many works where inspired by it. The answer would seem at first sight to be "yes" for there are few pictures of which we possess more copies or replicas [2].

There are some copies where the model is represented with naked breasts, which makes some people believe that Leonardo had the idea of painting

---

[1] Lomazzo, *Trattato dell'arte della pittura.* ... V, chap. I.

[2] Cf. an article on this subject by M. Seymour de Ricci reproduced in the *Revue Archéologique,* July-December 1911, p. 193.

the Mona Lisa in this way. A strange assumption when one thinks of what
he wanted to express in the Louvre picture. This was not at all Leonardo's
conception of a portrait. Besides, the Gioconda with naked breasts is solely
the Leonardesque type of woman that the great masters' disciples reproduce
to excess. These numerous imitations prove at least the admiration in which
this painting of rare perfection was held by contemporaries. Every first class
work is copied or distorted by pupils willing to sacrifice themselves to public
taste. The same thing happened in Giorgione's time when the cultivated
public demanded "Concerts" and in Watteau's time when the fashion was
for *Fêtes Galantes*.

The most interesting thing to find out is the influence these new ideas
were able to exercise over painters of marked personality [1] and to begin with,
on Raphael, who arrived in Florence with his mind filled with traditional
formulas and not yet liberated from the influence of Perugino.

In spite of the efforts which have been made for several years to present
Raphael as an artist full of originality, there is, nevertheless, no doubt that he
was often dominated by geniuses who were superior to him in strength. From
his youth he had shown an extraordinary facility for assimilating the style
of his masters, whether it was Timoteo della Vite or Perugino. We know at
exactly what date he arrived in Florence; Giovanna, wife of Giovanni della
Rovere, wrote to P. Soderini, the Gonfaloniere of the Florentine Republic
on the 1st of October, 1504, to recommend the young painter to him. And
according to Vasari, what struck him most on arrival were the famous
cartoons of Leonardo and Michelangelo: "The city delighted him as much
as its works, which seemed to him divine; and that is why he decided to stay
in Florence for some time" [2].

On leaving Perugino's studio, Raphael was thus put in contact with the

---

[1] In the University of Oxford there are some drawings by Michelangelo which show that he
himself was not insensitive to the charm of a Leonardesque face. Cf. Sidney Colvin, *Drawings
of the Old Masters in the University Galleries and in the Library of Christ Church, Oxford*,
1907, V I, p. 27.
[2] Vasari, IV, p. 320.

principal works of Florentine art, in such a way that they imposed themselves on him in all their brilliance and novelty. Raphael's temperament had
more in common with Leonardo's than with Michelangelo's; it was not only
the *Battle of Anghiari* which filled him with astonishment, but also the portrait of the Mona Lisa. He was inspired by it when he painted both the
portrait of Angiolo and of Maddalena Doni [1].

In studying these two pictures it is very easy to grasp the dominant tendencies of Raphael's work at this period and to assess how far he had super-
ficially assimilated the spirit of Leonardo.

In about 1506 Raphael probably painted the portrait of Maddalena Doni.
She was the daughter of Giovanni Strozzi and she had married Angiolo Doni
in 1503. M. Davidsohn published her birth certificate: 19th February 1488 [2],
and he concluded that it was not she whom Raphael had painted; Maddalena
Doni would have only been eighteen or nineteen years old when Raphael was
in Florence; this picture seemed to him to be of a mature woman. Nevertheless
it is difficult to doubt what Vasari says: "During Raphael's stay in Florence,
Angiolo Doni, who liked to spend money on works of art, commissioned
him to paint his own and his wife's portraits" [3]. At the time when Vasari
was writing, these two pictures were to be found in the collection of
Angiolo's son, Giovanbattista, in the palace which Angiolo himself had had
built in the Corso dei Tintori. It was not until the nineteenth century, in
1826, that the descendants of this family sold them to the Grand Duke of
Tuscany, Leopold II [4]. Their record is therefore extremely precise.

Is it so certain on the other hand that the features of Maddalena Doni
are those of a mature woman, as M. Davidsohn claims? The portrait is
rather of a young woman prematurely heavy whose beauty is in no way
comparable to the Mona Lisa's. The painter posed his model in the same
way as did Leonardo. She is seen almost full face: her body framed in a

---

[1] Gallery Pitti.

[2] R. Davidsohn, *Das dem Raffael zugeschriebene Portrait der Maddalena Doni* (Repertorium
für Kunstwissenschaft, 1900, p. 451).

[3] Vasari, IV, p. 325.

[4] G. Gruyer, *Raphael peintre de portraits*, 1881, I, p. 103.

slightly sketched landscape bathed in very clear atmosphere. The hands are placed one on top of the other. An entirely formal resemblance, because the spirit of the pictures is completely different; while admiring Leonardo's work profoundly, Raphael was not able to absorb enough of his genius to express the same strange beauty. Again the landscape is treated as an accessory; and in the details of her dress, as in the representation of features, it seemed that Raphael followed more the tradition of Ghirlandaio or of his master, Perugino. The fair hair, carefully parted in the centre and bound by a fine net, falls thinly over her neck. The features are regular but thick; there is in this face, saddened by a slight smile, a youthfulness which seems to have escaped M. Davidsohn *(Plate VII, fig. 15)*.

The rich Florentine was bent on posing in her most beautiful jewellery. Her neck is encircled by a fine golden chain with a lovely pendant made from a ruby, a sapphire, an emerald and a pearl, and there are also emeralds and rubies in the three rings. The materials of the costume are just as rare as the stones are precious; the pink moire bodice harmonises well with the pink flesh tones from which it is separated by the scarcely visible white shift, set off by a blue velvet edging; the puffed sleeves are of magnificent blue silk and they are embellished with white slashes at the top of the arms.

How different from the idealised features of the Mona Lisa! This Florentine with plump hands and opulent contours (in spite of the impeccable curve of the shoulders) expresses only the pride of being magnificently attired. Her gaze lacks depth. Raphael kept conscientiously to the model. That is why, in spite of the slight Leonardesque feeling given by the picture, it remains nevertheless faithful to the conception of Perugino which was also the Florentine conception at the end of the fifteenth century.

One is even more struck by it on looking at the husband's portrait Angiolo Doni. This three-quarter view picture of a face framed in a mass of hair is not lacking in character; his eyes are piercing; the hands with their short fingers are covered with rings; the Umbrian horizons figure in the luminous background. In spite of the awkwardness of the pose, which is rather stiff, a searching realism, a stress and a soberness relate it to the style of Ghirlandaio.

The two portraits were certainly commissioned at the same time and they were meant to hang together. In making comparisons we must bear in mind that the one of Angiolo Doni was earlier than that of Maddalena Doni; there is less skill in presentation than when Raphael, who by then had complete control over his medium, painted the rich wife. Leonardo's influence is scarcely seen in the portrait of Angiolo, although it is already beginning to appear in that of Maddalena. Raphael's drawings show, better than his paintings, the hold Leonardo's genius had over him. They show the faithfulness with which Raphael imitated the style of the master of the moment; they are Mona Lisas, not dreaming, but cold and unfeeling. They are always posed in the same way. One of them might even be the first sketch for the portrait of Maddalena Doni [1]. She has the same hands and the drawing of the face is of the same nature, full of freshness and youth.

With Raphael the Perugino tradition and the new spirit united harmoniously. Perugino, having lived a great deal in Florence, brought the preoccupations of the colourist to a country whose artists were great admirers of the flexibility of line. He had depicted the Florentine Francesco dell'Opere, brother of Giovanni delle Corniole, full face, his hands resting on the edge of a balustrade [2] in a pose which reminds one of the Venetian style [3]. The hair is untidy, the gaze is calm and the composure of the face is only slightly troubled by a few lines on the forehead. The warm tones with which he paints the hands and the face recall the Venetian style, but the harmonious landscape, with its few trees lightly sketched in, is illuminated by the Umbrian light.

The colouring of *The Woman with the Golden Chain* [4] in the Uffizi makes one think of the tones of the portrait of Francesco dell'Opere. This "gentil-

---

[1] Cf. drawing No. 3882 in the Louvre. Cf. also the two drawings in the British Museum reproduced in Oskar Fischel, *Raffaels Zeichnungen*, E923, I, 333-34.

[2] Uffizi.

[3] Perugino went to Venice in 1494 and the portrait of Francesco dell'Opere dates from exactly that year (Cf. Vasari, III, p. 604; Knapp, *Perugino*, 1907, p. 49).

[4] Uffizi. Cf. Gruyer, *Raphael peintre de portraits*, I, p. 118.

donna" who was formerly in the place of honour in the hall of the Tribuna, was a model of rare distinction; she is represented half-length, seated and looking towards the right, her head slightly turned to three-quarter view. The face, framed in fair hair, is unforgettable; she attracts us by the aristo-cratic turn of her features; we see there the elements of Florentine beauty, formed not by regularity, but by a lively expression of subtlety: it is interest-ing to compare the pasty face of Maddalena Doni with the elongated oval of her face and the hair falling delicately over the shoulders *(Plate IX, fig. 18)*.

In this face everything is brought out: the forehead is impeccably drawn; the slim neck helps to give further lightness to the head as a whole; as to the modelling of the cheeks, it is expressed with a deep feeling for gradation. There is not a single detail which is not rendered with perfect care and precision, or which does not reveal the character of this noble Florentine of high culture and dignified standing; the nose is short and delicate; the lips are only slightly full and the eyes have a certain haughty coldness. The hands are one of the most beautiful parts of the portrait; the forefinger of the left hand wears a ring; that on the right is curiously separated from the other fingers, it points with an authoritative gesture and is also adorned with a beautiful ring. The costume is of the greatest simplicity, the simplicity which is the sign of taste and elegance. Thanks no doubt to Leonardo, the craze for excessive adornment, which was one of the fashionable characteristics of the fifteenth century, was tending to fade out. The head and body of this portrait show rather more sensitivity and distinction than that of the Mona Lisa, but it is impossible not to find traces of the influence of that great work; the pose of the model and the placing of the hands are proof of this. To tell the truth, the painter has preferred a uniform background to a landscape background; and if the portrait of the Mona Lisa is the expression of a state of mind, then in this one there is the wish to stress the nobility and dignity of a beautiful patrician. The artist in depicting her has paid more attention to her physical charm than to her sensibility; he has not, however, neglected this attribute. The eyes and the movement of the lips suggest a disillusioned sadness, but leaving only fleeting traces on the features of this elegant woman who is conscious of her great distinction.

The technical qualities of this picture, where there is none of the "sfumato" of Leonardo, are on the other hand very great. The drawing of the face is clear and precise. The colours harmonise and evoke the warmth of Perugino's portraits [1]: nothing jars; everything is as the model (who would never countenance a lapse of taste) wished it to be. We are in the presence of one of the masterpieces of Florentine art, one in which the artist has remembered the Mona Lisa, without it making anything but the slightest impression on his mind because his model had so much originality and created such a great impression on him.

It is obvious that from certain aspects this is a work of transition. The young patrician is here represented full of dignity, like a Tornabuoni in Ghirlandaio's frescos, although the creator of this portrait drew it with more subtlety than the fresco painter of Santa Maria Novella. It recalls the impassive character of numerous portraits of the fifteenth century, and that is perhaps why he gave this Florentine woman a slightly frigid look.

This picture evidently dates from the beginning of the sixteenth century. The costume is very much like that of Maddalena Strozzi. In the inventory of the Pitti Palace of 1710 it was attributed to Raphael (for a long time it was believed to represent the wife of Angiolo Doni); M. Gruyer considers it to be one of this artist's works painted in 1506. Passavant, Crowe and Cavalcaselle, and Adolf Venturi make the same conjecture, which seems the most probable [2]. Between Maddalena Strozzi and this elegant Florentine there are many differences. The technique of Maddalena Strozzi is less refined; the colouring is colder. It is a proof that Perugino's influence is less felt.

The Woman with the Golden Chain was most probably painted by

---

[1] Mr. Berenson goes as far as to attribute it to Perugino (*The Central Italian Painters of the Renaissance*, 1909, p. 219).

[2] G. Gruyer, *op. cit.*, I, p. 40-41. Cf. also A. Venturi, *Raffaello*, 1920, p. 125. Enrico Ridolfi, *Archivio storico dell'arte*, 1891, makes an impossible attribution to Leonardo.

Raphael at the time when he had just left Perugino and begun to know Leonardo. He still respected the fifteenth-century tradition, but he understood how the new conception could give life and stress to a portrait. This distinction of feature and the lovely golden tones of Perugino appear to an equal extent in Raphael's self-portrait [1] which is drawn just as minutely, just as subtly, just as elegantly, and where one finds, in the form of the lips particularly, certain characteristics of the sketches in the Louvre and the British Museum.

During his stay in Florence, Raphael was gradually caught by the charm of Mona Lisa's portrait. It was during the period when Madonnas like *The Virgin with the Goldfinch*, painted for the marriage of Lorenzo Nasi, and the *Madonna of the Meadows* in the Vienna Museum have that sweetness of expression not to be found in any earlier pictures by Raphael, which could only have come from Leonardo. But in the painter's portraits of *Julius II* and *Leo X* it is only a fleeting impression. The influences Raphael absorbed from the great painters he was in contact with finished by giving his pictures the dominating aspect of unity and balance. These influences while not creating anything really new, delight us because there is nothing out of place. The portraits carried out by Raphael later on in Rome remain superb examples of painting where the models are posed in rather the same way as Maddalena or Angiolo Doni; they seldom betray their thoughts. The artist regards them with a cold eye; he is a remarkable but insensitive interpreter of the human face.

Raphael (and this is something not sufficiently realised) is one of those painters in whom the fifteenth-century tradition is very much alive. He could not resign himself to abandoning entirely those which had formerly been so successfully applied. Thus it is that he, like Gozzoli or Ghirlandaio, could not conceive of a fresco which did not include portraits. Vasari, speaking of *The School of Athens*, recognises there several illustrious figures;

---

[1] Uffizi, *Autoritratti dei pittori* (collection).

the young man, exceedingly handsome, who flings out his arms and bows his head, so great is his astonishment, is Frederick II, Duke of Mantua, who was then in Rome; the man who is bending down with a pair of compasses in his hand, which he twists on the table, is the architect Bramante, who appears full of life; and to one side is Raphael, the author of this work, who painted himself by looking in a mirror: it is a head full of youth and of a very modest aspect, wearing a black cap [1]. Raphael has given himself a companion in this fresco, not (as has been believed for some time) Perugino, but possibly Sodoma, who was his collaborator in the decoration of this Stanza in the Segnatura.

The *School of Athens* is one of the first large frescos that Raphael had carried out since his arrival in Rome. He was still under the Florentine influence, and there is in the Sistine Chapel an example of what the painters called in by Sixtus IV would have liked to have done. Clearly he remembered Santa Trinità and Santa Maria Novella, and he produced for the Popes what other painters had done for the Medici family; in his religious frescoes he perpetuated the glory of his patrons.

Two other portraits in the Uffizi, where we find the tradition of the fifteenth century and the influence of Leonardo at the same time, seem also to be works of Raphael: I mean those known under the titles of *The Donna Gravida* and the *Donna Velata*.

The Donna Gravida [2] very much resembles Maddalena Doni in its method of handling. The pose is almost the same; the physical type is more pronounced, the hair, which is very fair, is bound in a net which follows the shape of the waves and frames a high receding forehead; the eyebrows are carefully plucked, as fashion dictated; the whole face, which has a certain youthfulness, is delicately drawn. As in the portrait of Maddalena Doni, the painter has neglected nothing which would help to enhance the beauty of the dress, which is of an almost identical style *(Plate VIII, fig. 16)*.

---

[1] Vasari, VI, p. 331.
[2] Pitti Palace. Cf. Gruyer, *Raphael peintre de portraits*, I, p. 124.

The hands are very similar to those of Angiolo's wife, and the short fingers are covered with rings. There is an obvious similarity between the two works, but the *Donna Gravida* shows better technique. The face has more life in it, the flesh tones are more delicate, and against the neutral background the youth and the freshness of colouring are of a charm stressed by a happy use of the science of chiaroscuro specially marked in the folds of the garments.

There is no doubt that once again the painter had the picture of *Mona Lisa* in mind. But all the characteristics of Raphael's technique are to be found here—the contour is of an impeccable precision, and there is nothing of the "sfumato" of a Leonardo. The expression of the face reflects a great internal calm, the eyes, a little almond-shaped, are more animated than those of the *Maddalena Doni;* they are those of a Florentine bourgeoise, who awaits with extreme calm the happy event.

The *Donna Gravida* does not differ in essentials from the preceding portraits; carried out in the same spirit, they doubtless belong to Raphael's Florentine period, during which time Perugino's pupil combined the charm of colour of his masters with fifteenth-century draughtsmanship and the application of certain of Leonardo's precepts.

The Donna Velata[1] is far removed in conception from *The Woman with the Golden Chain, Maddalena Doni* and the *Donna Gravida.* We know the exact history of this picture. Vasari tells us that the only authentic portrait of Raphael's mistress was in the hands of a Florentine merchant, Matteo Botti, some years after the death of the painter[2]. In 1591 this portrait was still in the possession of the Botti family[3], which explains why it is not possible to identify it with the famous *Fornarina* which has been under so much discussion and is to-day attributed to Sebastiano del Piombo.

The relationship between the *Donna Velata* and the famous type of the

---

[1] Pitti Palace.

[2] Vasari, IV, p. 335, Raffaello Borghini affirms that this portraits was to be found at this time with the descendants of Matteo Botti (*Il Riposo,* 1584, p. 392).

[3] Bocchi-Cinelli, *Le Belleze di Firenze,* 1677, p. 173.

Sistine Madonna of the Dresden Gallery is obvious; it is a first indication to which another can be added: M. Enrico Ridolfi has published part of the will of Marquis Botti, who in 1619 made the Grand Duke Cosimo his heir. This Botti was descended from the man who had the good fortune to own the portrait of Raphael's mistress; among other works of art he inherited a picture painted on canvas: "dipontove dentro una giovane sino a cintola, di mano di Raffaello da Urbino con adornomanto di noce scorniciato".

It seems likely that this is the portrait in the Pitti Palace. An unknown hand has written in the margin of this description these few words: "Si trova in Palazzo (obviously the Pitti Palace) e non fu stimato". If in general it is better not to put too much faith in 17th-century attributions, it is evident that this scepticism can be exaggerated in this instance, for the attribution made in the inventory of Marquis of Botti's estate goes back to the sixteenth century, and Vasari supports it. There is no reason for doubt; the picture thus described is certainly by Raphael.

The *Donna Velata* has a very young face, the pink of the cheeks recalling the brilliance of Venetian colouring. This lovely rose colour has lost nothing of its freshness and it is astonishing to see how the tones have kept their value.

Look carefully at the hands. Although for a long time in the fifteen century they had not been included in portraits, they have now become an important element. In all the pictures which we have just studied they are characteristic and full of life; the painter draws them with careful precision, neglecting nothing which will make them expressive; some are covered with jewels and show us the model's wealth; others have purity of line as their only adornment. Those of the *Donna Velata* with their tapering fingers are beautifully drawn. The dress is quite simple, but is set off with gold embroidery and the sumptuous contrast of whiter areas dazzling as those in the portrait of Gardena Bibbiana. Finally the grey veil which covers the head and the top of the body stands out against a neutral background.

In its entirety the pose is rather like the Mona Lisa's, but there is nothing else to remind us of the Louvre picture. The *Donna Velata* is simply a woman content with life, happy in her youthfulness. It certainly belongs to Raphael's

Roman period, and is contemporary with the *Sistine Madonna*. It shows the hold Leonardo's conception of pose had taken of the artist. During his most successful period in Rome, Raphael nearly always used the same attitude for his portraits, the Mona Lisa, which tended to become classic. In *Baldassar Castiglione* in the Louvre and in the Gallery Barberini *Portrait of a Woman*, exactly the same principles hold good, but one only finds in them a faint echo of the reforms initiated by the master of the *Last Supper*. Raphael had not enough inner life of his own to be able to endow his models with any. Even in his Madonnas, which were sometimes, like Filippo Lippi's, actual portraits, we find nothing but the model's own expression. Has the *Madonna of the Chair* anything in common with the *Virgin of the Rocks*?

CHAPTER IV

PORTRAIT PAINTERS OF THE TRANSITION

The Portrait of Verrocchio by Lorenzo di Credi. Portraits with inclined heads. Leonardo's influence on Lorenzo. The originality of Piero di Cosimo's portraits. The *Francesco Giamberti* and the *Giuliano da San Gallo* in The Hague. The National Gallery *Warrior*. Raphael's imitators. The portrait called the *Monaco*. Is it of Mariotto Albertinelli? Portraits of Giuliano Bugiardini. The influence of the fifteenth century and of Leonardo combine in Ridolfo Ghirlandaio. He also felt Raphael's influence. *The Old Man* in the National Gallery. *The Man with the Jewel* in the Pitti Palace.

The attraction felt for the portrait of the Mona Lisa in the first half of the sixteenth century is an obvious fact. Even those painters who were most imbued with fifteenth-century tradition had to make some concession to the new taste. It is also important to find out just how far these went. Transition periods which give birth to a complexity of tendencies are always of great interest.

There were painters living in Florence at the beginning of the sixteenth century who, having been brought up in the fifteenth-century school, were a long way from being freed from its influence and to a certain extent carried on its tradition. Nevertheless, Leonardo's example suggested several new ideas to them. But as they could not really understand their value they remained unconscious to the essential meaning of his reforms. They could see what could be made of this with a painter so extraordinarily gifted as Raphael: and some of them were tempted to imitate his manner, gathering in this way certain of Leonardo's influences which had passed into Raphael's art. The beautiful Raphaelesque portrait, well conceived, with firm and sometimes brilliant tones, had its imitators.

78

In the two paintings *Maddalena Doni* and the *Woman with the Golden Chain*, the styles of the fifteenth century and of Perugino combine happily with the new ideas. Some painters were inspired by this example; others remained under the influence of Leonardo until the day when, from this contact with varying precepts, an original form of portraiture was born, characteristic of Florentine art.

Lorenzo di Credi and Piero di Cosimo were both interesting products of this period of transition, when artists borrowed sometimes from the masters of the fifteenth century, sometimes from Leonardo, sometimes from Raphael. The first of these, with a talent more subtle and less individual, seemed to adapt himself more easily to the new tendencies, whereas the second only achieved this slowly and by degrees.

"Lorenzo di Credi carried out many portraits; in his youth he painted a self-portrait which is today in the possession of Gianjacopo, his follower, a Florentine painter who also had many other things left him by Lorenzo, and among them a portrait of Pietro Perugino and one of Andrea del Verrocchio, his master. He also painted a portrait of Girolamo Benivieni, a very learned man who was his intimate friend" [1].

Such are the meagre particulars which Vasari gives us of Lorenzo's portraits: we know practically nothing about the history of his pictures. It is only by chance that they have been discovered. For a long time one of his best works in the Uffizi [2] was thought to be by a northern artist; in the inventory of 1704 it was classified as a *Portrait of Martin Luther*, painted by Holbein; in 1784 Luther's name disappeared, but Holbein's was still there. The publisher of *The Lives*, M. Milanesi, was the first to correct this obvious mistake. There is nothing Germanic about this portrait; it is easy to recognise it as a Florentine work, and the features have a close resemblance

---

[1] Vasari, IV, p. 566.
[2] Uffizi, collection *"Autoritratti dei pittori"*.

to those of the print which Vasari placed in the beginning of his *Life of Verrocchio* [1] (*Plate X, fig. 21*).

Another characteristic of Lorenzo's style is the landscape seen to the right; it is lightly sketched in; the hills, which fade into the sky, shade into tones of blue. Lorenzo often uses this device: he paints the mountains in the *Annunciation* in the Uffizi in the same way [2]. Note also the delicate way in which he details the foliage of the trees, underlining them with touches of white, with those light brush strokes so often found in his work.

The portrait is full of life; the brilliance of the eyes is accentuated by the firmly drawn arched eyebrows; the painter has taken the greatest care over this; he has made them the centre of the picture, putting in with complete assurance all the vibrations of the skin around these luminous points out of which emerges a fresh and spontaneous soul. The rest of the face is massive; the wrinkles are very obvious and the chin shows several rolls of fat. It is the portrait of a man who is past fifty [3]. If the hands seem less expressive than the face, it may be due to repainting, but we must not forget that it was a habit of Lorenzo di Credi to paint hands without paying much attention to structure and joints.

This picture vaguely recalls the portraits of the fifteenth century. Nevertheless if one compares it to the likenesses of the second half of the fifteenth century there is only a superficial resemblance to the work of Ghirlandaio and his disciples. One might even say that there is a modern touch about it. The model, who has deeply inspired the artist, is dressed in a dark suit and wears a dark-coloured skull cap with thick hair falling from beneath it. Nothing distracts our attention from this striking head; here the landscape is only an accessory. The life in the eyes and the trembling nostrils have struck Lorenzo to such an extent that he has neglected the rest of the picture. He understood his master Verrocchio so well that he seems to have caught him when his features were at their most expressive.

---

[1] Cf. the second edition of *Le Vite de Vasari*, 1568, I, p. 480.

[2] Uffizi.

[3] This makes it quite easy to date the portrait. Verrocchio was born in 1435, it was towards 1485 that this picture was painted. Lorenzo di Credi, born in 1459, was then twenty-six years old.

Ridolfo Ghirlandaio.
26. *The Funeral of Saint Zanobius* (Uffizi)
27. *Portrait of an Old Man.* (National Gallery, London)

Ridolfo Ghirlandaio.

28. *Portrait of a Young Man called "The Goldsmith."* (Pitti Palace)

29. *Portrait of a Man* (Corsini Gallery)

Thus Lorenzo di Credi's work is very far removed from those inanimate portraits in profile or three-quarter view; for a better study of a head he painted it full face. In this he fell slightly under the influence of Perugino and the portrait of Francesco dell'Opere [1]. It was in Verrocchio's studio that he got to know the Umbrian painter, whose seductive and sometimes vigorous art left such a profound influence on his mind. He also met there Leonardo da Vinci, whose style pleased him "beyond all words". From the very beginning of his artistic career Lorenzo di Credi was inspired by him [2]; Vasari draws attention, among his youthful works, to a picture which was sent to Spain and which was so like a painting by Leonardo "that one could not distinguish between them". Constant association with Leonardo gave him food for thought, which made work difficult for him; he dared not paint large pictures; his conscience as a colourist was such, in fact, that he feared he would never master this medium; he also used colours which were rather too skilfully mixed.

He kept something of Verrocchio's teaching—a taste for simple settings, for example. We must also add those essential fifteenth-century characteristics of precision of outline and flawless draughtsmanship. Although he had learnt from Leonardo the secret of skilfully compounding colours, Lorenzo nevertheless kept plenty of clarity and transparency in his own pigments. The flesh tones are delicate, almost fragile; his brushwork is of a rather monotonous immaturity which is in contrast with the deep inspiration of the master of the *Last Supper*. This apprentice could not make up his mind to renounce completely all that he had been taught. His simple palette was not equal to the refined technique of the master. He was, besides, too superficial to get lost in deep thought; his curiosity was restricted to translating the life of the face, whose charm came from liveliness and precision of rendering; he was a long way from the mysterious poetry which enveloped Leonardo's heads.

All these characteristics are seen again in his portrait drawings. One of

---

[1] Mr. A. Venturi goes as far as to attribute the portrait of Verrocchio to Perugino himself (*l'Arte*, Jan.-Feb. 1922), forgetting that if the construction of the head recalls Perugino by its solidity, on the other hand the landscape is not at all Umbrian in style.

[4] Vasari, IV, p. 564.

them [1] in the Uffizi represents the head of an *Old Man* which recalls in certain ways the type dear to Perugino. The head is seen almost full face and slightly bent; the white with which he brings out the essential features reminds one of those metallic highlights which he so skilfully includes in his paintings; as in the portrait of Verrocchio the thick hair falls from beneath a narrow cap. The dress, which is lightly sketched in, is also like that of Verrocchio. What is most striking is the similarity of the two faces—the same squat nose, the same thin and tight lips; in the Uffizi drawing the curve of the lips is more cheerful. It is obviously not of the same person, but it is certainly very much the same style *(Plate X, fig. 20)*.

A beautiful drawing in the Louvre shows a similar line and expression. According to M. Loeser, it is a study for the portrait of Perugino which has been lost. But there is little or no connection between this wrinkled and emaciated face and the healthy countenance of Cambio. It is drawn with all the precision that the painters of the middle of the fifteenth century favoured; to this extent the fifteenth-century Florentine influence is as living with Lorenzo di Credi as the influence of Leonardo or Perugino.

Among the portraits of Lorenzo's indicated by Vasari, that of Verrocchio is not the only one which has been found [2]; a self-portrait has also been found recently, which after having belonged to M. W. Beattie's collection in Glasgow has now passed into the hands of M. Widener of Philadelphia. Both Berenson and Loeser have analysed it in enough detail to give us a fair idea of it. On the back of the picture is a description which seems to date from the end of the fifteenth or beginning of the sixteenth century, says Mr. Loeser: "Lorenzo di Credi, Pittori ecc... te (eccellente) 1488 aetatis sue 32 ..." If we believe these few words, Lorenzo would thus have been represented in full youth, and we should have one of his most authentic works which would enable us to identify others.

---

[1] Uffizi, Drawing Office. Cf. Berenson, *The Drawings of the Florentine Painters*, II, p. 35. This work is considered by Mr. Berenson to be a possible work of Perugino's.

[2] No trace remains of Girolamo Benivieni. Nevertheless Milanesi, in his edition of *The Lives* of Vasari (I, p. 567), claims to have recognised it in a painting which he found during his lifetime in the collection of a certain Giuseppe Volponi.

The set of the head is typical. It is slightly bent, but the eyes look straight in front, whereas the bust is turned towards the left. The hair falls down to the shoulders as in the portrait of Verrocchio. The landscape is the same as in Lorenzo's religious pictures with a background of blueish hills.

M. Loeser, who saw this work in Glasgow, was struck with the liveliness of colouring and the delicate sensibility expressed; the modelling of the face is, according to him, full of spontaneity. This inclination of the head, which gives the face a certain languorous expression, is to be found in many of his figures in other paintings and in his drawings. It is equally characteristic of a portrait in the Uffizi, whose affinity with that of the Widener Collection (*Plate X, fig. 22*) indicates that it must be the work of the same artist.

It was considered in the eighteenth century as being by Leonardo and it was exhibited under his name in the Hall of the Tribuna. In fact there is no doubt that the influence of the great master was felt in it, indicated by the gentleness of the gaze and the slightly nostalgic expression of the face; but that is all. The drawing of the face is very exact and the landscape in no way recalls the powerful and distorted nature which pleased Leonardo; it is designed in great detail with some sepia tones in the foreground, almost the same tones which one finds in all Lorenzo's works; the same clear and transparent horizon, the same blue hills.

Thus in looking through his portraits, the art of Lorenzo di Credi presents itself to us, at times trying to express strength under the influence of Verrocchio and Perugino, at others sometimes interpreting (but to a lesser degree) themes of a Leonardesque sensibility. But his talent is always of a certain quality; his drawing is gracious. It is also unjust to add to the catalogue of his works some mediocre and ill conceived portraits; Berenson [1] attributes to him a portrait of this kind from the Pucci Collection where M. Bode would like to find the imitation of the beautiful Lichtenstein picture. Is it possible to connect the very finished, sometimes too finished paintings, the flawless drawings of Lorenzo with such an ordinary picture, where the hands are just

---

[1] *The Florentine Painters*, 1908, p. 132.

roughed in and the landscape treated in an elementary fashion? This picture is rather the work of a clumsy imitator of Lorenzo or a weak pupil of Leonardo.

One might with more reason at first consider Lorenzo as the creator of a *Portrait of a Woman* in the Museum of Forli, which was for some time falsely attributed to Marco Palmezzano [1]. In this presentation there are some passages which make one think of Lorenzo di Credi and which remotely recall the *Young Woman* of the Lichtenstein Collection—the slim tapering fingers, the landscape with the far distance blurred, where the trees have those little accents of white which give them life. These recalls certain characteristics of the *Annunciation* in the Uffizi or the *Virgin* in the Borghese Gallery. But the almost lifeless eyes and the slightly indicated modelling of the face are less worthy of Lorenzo. The quality is much inferior to that of his portraits with the inclined heads. It is quite reasonable to believe that this young woman was painted by one of Lorenzo's disciples who had assimilated to some extent the fundamental elements of his technique and was partly inspired by Leonardo. He had a good conception of the part played by landscape in a portrait; but he did not express the possible depth of emotion created by placing a model in front of nature; that is why he makes the fair hair and pale pink face stand out against a red hanging which falls between two columns. The painter had not enough courage to imitate Leonardo completely. He knew the Mona Lisa portrait but was rather clumsily inspired by it, he did not dare to leave the hands inactive, so he employed them in picking a flower from a vase on the table. It might have been an interesting and new idea; but here it is more than anything the indication of a mediocre talent which, incapable of expressing a sentiment or an idea, gets lost in anecdotal detail, thus completely distorting Leonardo's conceptions.

Some of the principal tendencies of the beginning of the sixteenth century are reflected in the vigorous temperament of Piero di Cosimo with more originality than is the case with Lorenzo di Credi. For one thing Piero was

---

[1] *The Florentine Painters*, 1908, p. 132.

the pupil of Cosimo Rosselli one of the chroniclers of the fifteenth century, and through him he clung to the traditions of Ghirlandaio's contemporaries; for another he knew Leonardo, who passed some of his principles on to him; we must not forget, as well, that he was the master of Andrea del Sarto and that his influence on Fra Bartolommeo and on Mariotto Albertinelli was far from being negligible. He is therefore one of the links which joined two very different periods of art.

Among his works there are several which are clearly fifteenth century in character; among others is the picture at Chantilly which has for some time been considered the authentic portrait of Simonetta Vespucci. It is obviously this picture to which Vasari refers: "una testa bellisima di Cleopatra con uno aspido avvolto al collo" [1]. The inscription "Simonetta Januensis. Vespuccia" which is not contemporary with the work has, it seems, no value whatsoever. If in this Cleopatra are represented the features of Simonetta, whose life story had stirred every heart, Vasari would not have failed to take the opportunity of pointing it out; besides, she died in 1476 when Piero di Cosimo was only fourteen years old. It is certainly then an idealised face of Cleopatra to which he has given a pronounced Florentine type of beauty, with a turned-up nose. Moreover, and this is important, it is the point of departure of Piero di Cosimo, who painted a profile in the manner of a fifteenth-century painter so well that it could have been mistaken for the work of Antonio del Pollaiuolo.

It also seems that Piero di Cosimo had afterwards, like Domenico Ghirlandaio, a tendency towards the Flemish conception of realism. In the same way as Lorenzo di Credi at certain moments in his career, he was interested in expressing vigour; he was carried away by contrasts of tone; he was certainly much more of a colourist, and that is why his portraits have more emphasis than those of Leonardo's friend. What we know of Piero di Cosimo's life is besides instructive. He did not despise fantasy in life, a fantasy which he sometimes carried too far, according to his contemporaries. His work is often out of harmony and his figures seem animated with feelings of unusual violence.

---

[1] Vasari, IV, p. 144.

Two pictures in The Hague are, from this point of view, remarkable; one represents Francesco Giamberti, and the other Giuliano da San Gallo. Here it is the influence of the realists which is dominant. Frizzoni is the first to notice that they correspond to the mention made by Vasari of the works of Piero di Cosimo which were to be found in the collection of Francesco da San Gallo[1]. This latter possessed, in fact, at the same time as the Cleopatra, "two portraits, one of Giuliano da San Gallo his father, and the other, of Francesco Giamberti his grandfather, both of which seemed really to live". Frizzoni was struck by the resemblance of one of the Hague portraits to the picture which Vasari had had engraved of Giuliano da San Gallo, in *The Lives*. There is no possible doubt. The Hague possesses the two portraits of Francesco da San Gallo's ancestors painted by Piero di Cosimo *(Plate XI, fig. 23, 24)*.

It is easy to date them approximately: Giuliano's hair is turning grey and his features are those of a man between fifty and sixty years old[2]. As he was born in 1445, it was then at the end of the fifteenth or beginning of the sixteenth century that he was thus represented. Piero di Cosimo tried to give Giamberti's face a very definite character. It is emaciated and the skin is ivory in tone, scarcely heightened with pink, which accentuates his aesthetic appearance. Piero also drew the fair and very distinct lashes very carefully and the lively intelligent eyes. The dress is very simple, dark in colour, with the white line of the shirt visible on the arms. Giuliano da San Gallo has a softer expression, but realistic details are no less lacking; the furrows of the wrinkles, the prominent blue veins on the temple, and the ear which is pushed out of shape under the weight of the cap.

This elaborate analysis of the features of the face brings out the fifteenth-century origins of Piero di Cosimo. But there are other elements which indicate that the artist had come under different influences since the time when he was the disciple of Cosimo Rosselli. To begin with, the very an-

---

[1] Frizzoni, *Arte italiana del Rinascimento*, paggi critici, 1891, p. 247 and following.

[2] The portrait of Francesco Giamberti, who died in 1480, was evidently painted from another earlier one. Cf. G. Clausse, *Les San Gallo*, 1900, Vol. 1.

imation of the two faces, presented to us almost full face, looking straight ahead, have a spontaneity and vigour which is lacking in any of Ghirlandaio's portraits or even in Botticelli's; the colours have a certain brilliance, especially in the landscape which is a fundamental element in both paintings. Nature is seen with an eye which does not arrange or stylize it in any way. Here the painter has studied the characters with as much precision as he has the features of those he had to portray. He did not understand them in the same way as the fifteenth-century painters, who gave them more harmony but less variety. This certainly is not Leonardo's method. Beginning with a realistic study of nature, the Leonardesque landscape becomes real, to such an extent does the artist recreate its structure and colouring in order to make it harmonise with the scene or people in the foreground, that is to say, with his own ideas and thoughts.

On the other hand, Piero di Cosimo tends to reproduce precisely everything that interested him in a certain aspect of nature without in any way modifying it. In *The Death of Procris* in the National Gallery, *Venus, Mars and Love*, in Berlin, *Hylas and the Nymphs* in the Benson Collection, he draws and paints a different landscape every time, flowers, foliage, birds, everything in it beautifully detailed and a lovely light brightening the whole. It was, according to Vasari, because he had a very different spirit from other painters and he excelled at analysing the "sottigliezze" of nature. He painted them regardless of the effort it cost him, solely for the pleasure it gave him and for the love of art [1]. Perhaps it was Piero di Cosimo who had, among the artists of this generation, the most direct feeling for the character of landscape. His example certainly contributed to the development of taste for living portraits which made the fresh colours stand out against a very blue sky, with scattered grey and white clouds, and with a green horizon which is animated in the Francesco Giamberti by a procession.

Piero di Cosimo must have made many other portraits, especially during his stay in Rome, where he accompanied Cosimo Rosselli and helped him with the decoration of the Sistine Chapel. It was then that he may have done

---

[1] Vasari, IV, p. 142.

the one of Cesare Borgia which had already disappeared in Vasari's time. According to this latter, he very much admired Leonardo's style of painting: "although he was very far from achieving it" he tried to imitate it, and we find proof of this in his series of *Perseus and Andromeda* in the Uffizi.

He had a great curiosity concerning everything, a desire for originality, and "one might say that he changed his style with every work he painted" [1]. This explains the difficulty we find in recognising them, especially when it is a case of portraits. Many have been attributed to him, among which some have a certain affinity with those in the Hague and others have nothing in common with them. This is the case with *The Young Man* in the Dulwich Gallery, which is later than the portrait of the *Mona Lisa*, as it is inspired by it, but it does not in any way bear the stamp of Piero's genius (even taking into account his curious diversity). The landscape background is barely sketched in. There is a glimpse of the sea and bluish hills, a tower, a belfry, several other buildings; the whole is softly lighted. The head is without much expression and the eyes dull. There is nothing left of that love of physical life which inspired Piero.

On the other hand, as far as one can judge from a photograph, two portraits in the Johnson Collection at Philadelphia seem more likely to be by him; one is *The Portrait of a Man*, posed almost full face, who holds in his hand a bronze "caducée" decorated with laurels. It was for some time believed to be of the humanist Francesco Filelfo. It has so much similarity with the Hague portraits that the attribution at first sight beems obvious. Mr. Berenson in his catalogue of the American collection has come back to his first conclusion. "The character of face, the composition, seem", he says, "to be by Piero di Cosimo". On the contrary the construction of the hand does not seem to be by him, but rather by a follower of Dosso Dossi.

In the attribution of another *Portrait of a Man* in the same collection there is a similar variation. The right hand of the model holds a folded letter on which is written the date 1512. "The face is long, with a vividly drawn nose and mouth, the forehead rather wide, large, calm grey eyes and a short and

---

[1] Vasari, IV, p. 134.

ragged brown beard." Here again attribution to Piero di Cosimo seems, even from a photograph, probable, and this was Mr. Berenson's first impression. Nevertheless a more detailed study made him attribute it to Palma Vecchio: "the shape of the nose, the moulding of the ear and the left hand are by this latter" [1].

It is difficult to make any assertions without seeing the originals. Notice however that we get here an actual exaggeration of Morelli's method of criticism, which Mr. Berenson has brought up to date and often used most successfully. The great family likeness which these portraits of the Johnson Collection have with those of the Hague is an argument which might be alone decisive even if certain details of drawing do not seem to be by Piero di Cosimo. Let us go back to Vasari's remark about the artist's inquisitive temperament, for we can easily conclude from this that we must expect to find in him disconcerting elements, which seem foreign to him and are quite simply manifestations of his enquiring mind.

Can one, supported by this diversity of talent, attribute to him, as has already been done, *The Warrior* in the National Gallery, so different from the portraits in the Hague?

It is a handsome portrait of a soldier, which expresses a deep feeling for volume, perspective and values *(Plate XII, fig. 25)*. A rather gentle face stands out against an architectural background; the light, coming from the right, illuminates it brilliantly and picks out the details of the armour plate. The face is almost round and encircled by a beard. Across the slim hands highlights play like those in the *Man with the Jewel* by Ridolfo Ghirlandaio. The background reveals remarkable qualities of colour; the Piazza della Signoria and the Loggia dei Lanzi are depicted; the Marzocco is gilded by the sun's rays; one can make out, further away and contrasted with the dark mass of the Palazzo Vecchio, the pink-roofed houses which occupy the actual site of the Uffizi, a street charmingly lighted, and the large white spot made

---

[1] Berenson, *Catalogue of Italian paintings from the Johnson Collection at Philadelphia*, I, p. 113. Cf. also *Rassegna d'Arte*, 1905, p. 120 (article by Mason-Perkins), and the *Connoisseur*, XXI, p. 147.

by the Michelangelo statue of David, painted with plenty of vigour with two strokes of the brush, the head being simply a stroke of white.

Was it Piero di Cosimo who left us such a brilliant painting of the Piazza della Signoria at the beginning of the sixteenth century [1]? At first sight, it must be admitted we do not think of this artist. And yet do not the lovely warm tones which emphasise this face recall those which light up the *Death of Procris*? Further, if one compares *The Warrior* of the National Gallery with *Perseus delivering Andromeda*, which is one of the last works of Piero di Cosimo, one of those in which he was influenced by Leonardo's spirit, one finds several similar technical details. The colours of the houses are the same as in the Piazza della Signoria; and in particular, the drawing of Perseus' hand, lifting his sword with a vigour identical to that of the right hand of the Warrior, bears a striking resemblance. These observations give birth to the conviction that the portrait in the National Gallery is undoubtedly one of the most characteristic works of the last period of Piero's artistic career, one where the outlines are softened and where the harshness of his realism is toned down.

Even a man of such talent was attracted by Leonardo's style. It is not surprising that less gifted men should have been attracted towards this greatest of masters. Also, there is a strong similarity between portraits of this period; the same motive is repeated, in some feebly and indifferently, in others with greater subtlety.

Besides, in imitating Leonardo, the Leonardism of Raphael is often expressed. This is most striking in the Uffizi portrait which is called, curiously enough, *The Monaca* [2] (*Plate IX, fig. 19*). Perhaps it was thus named because through the windows one can see in the foreground the Convent of St. Paul's

---

[1] This portrait was for a long time considered to be of Francesco Ferrucci, defender of Florentine liberty; and it is a rather attractive conjecture. It was attributed to Lorenzo Costa. G. Frizzoni (*Arte italiana del Rinascimento*, p. 152) corrects this mistake. Ullman mistakenly sees here a Ridolfo Ghirlandaio (*Jahrbuch der k.p. Kunstsammlungen*, 1896, p. 137). Cf. Knapp, *Piero di Cosimo*, 1898, p. 91-92.

[2] This picture was, until 1919, in the Pitti Palace.

in Florence and in front of the portico three people who look like nuns. At the same time the black and white of the dress gives an air of severity to the pose. Dressed in almost the same style as the *Maddalena Strozzi* and the *Donna Gravida*, she has a more original headdress—a transparent veil lightly flows over the net binding the hair, which is parted in the middle. The form of the breast shows clearly through the bodice; the rather hard line of the open neck is softened by a border of lace; at the top of the sleeves the white of the billowing material repeats that of the hair net. The model is holding a prayer book in her left hand, whereas the right is lightly resting on the balustrade; the forefinger is stretched out like that of the *Woman with the Golden Chain* by Raphael, but with less authority and decision. The artist has taken a great deal of care with the drawing of these hands and has made them the most gracious and expressive part of the picture. By contrast there is a certain feebleness in the outline of the face, especially in the lower part, which is heavy; as for the eyes, they have a fixed and unseeing gaze.

The painter must have been thinking of the portrait of the Mona Lisa when he posed his model, almost full face, against a landscape background which stretches into the distance; the study of light and shade proves that he profited by Leonardo's teaching without always achieving that great Florentine master's subtle representation of velvety softness and "sfumato". This portrait is the work of a fifteenth-century painter who, having seen Leonardo's paintings, was moved by their originality of treatment; his artistic outlook was modified by it but he was not able, in spite of everything, to forget the precepts which up till now he had respected. In the background is a lovely Tuscan landscape with its hills, its slender trees and the far distant summits of the Apennines. Unfortunately it has no value except as a setting, for the artist has not dared to do as Leonardo and Botticelli did before him; he has separated the portrait from the background by the arches and pillars of a kind of loggia. It shows the diffidence of a painter who has seen works full of the poetry of landscape, but who stops half way, incapable of placing his model in a lovely landscape setting, realising the difficulty of paying such honour to such an uninspired portrait.

Certain rose-coloured flesh tints recall the style of Mariotto Albertinelli in the same way as the background, lighted by the setting sun, is similar to that of the *Meeting of Christ and Mary Magdalene* in the Pitti Palace. A drawing in the Uffizi of a pretty, slightly inclined head of a woman which Mr. Gamba justifiably attributes to Fra Bartolommeo [1] perhaps inspired this portrait which also shows the collaboration of Albertinelli and Fra Bartolommeo. There was, in fact such intimacy between the two painters that according to Vasari, they were "un'anima ed un corpo" [2].

Fra Bartolommeo was sent to Leonardo's school of painting after having worked in Cosimo Rosselli's studio; having studied his works with enthusiasm he made such progress that "he very quickly acquired the reputation of being one of the best of the young painters as much for his colour as for his drawing" [3]. Thus he adopted the Leonardesque technique, making his heads stand out in such a way as to give them as much relief as possible. But he did not apply, or rather he applied but rarely, these principles to portraiture. Caught up in the Savonarola movement, like Botticelli and Lorenzo di Credi, he preferred to consecrate his life to the glorification of God. He had little time for painting portraits, and those which he did paint were religious in conception. It seemed natural to him, for example, to immortalise the features of the great preacher who had made the true nature of Christianity known to him, or to paint his companions in the monastery; the portrait of Savonarola [4] is treated in the most simple style, and in profile, like a medal. Fra Bartolommeo made no concessions to public taste and he represented the severe likeness of the Dominican against a neutral background; nevertheless he did not fail to apply Leonardo's technical methods and to employ great skill in making the light and shade play round the powerful and energetic features of his sitter.

While he was at the Dominican Monastery of San Domenico de Prato,

---

[1] Cf. Gamba, *Disegni di Baccio della porta detto Fra Bartolommeo* (I disegni della R. Galleria degli Uffizi, fasciolo II, serie II).

[2] Vasari, IV, p. 217.

[3] Vasari, IV, p. 175.

[4] Vasari, IV, p. 179.

Bartolommeo was commissioned to paint a *Last Judgment* for Santa Maria Novella; and he conceived his work rather after the manner of the fifteenth-century painters, not disdaining to surround himself with models for the figures. Vasari gives us the following precise details [1]: he painted from nature the director of the hospital and some of the brothers; he added portraits of the donor Gerozzo Dini, and his wife kneeling; he also did one of Giuliano Bugiardini one of his young pupils, wearing a "zazzero" according to the fashion of the time. He includes a self-portrait and among the elect he depicts Beato Angelico.

Those interested in the game of identification can try to recognise the people indicated by Vasari in the *Last Judgment* in Santa Maria Novella. It is interesting at least to notice the presence of all these people in a fresco which has a great deal of importance in the development of the monumental style, and which was carried out at the time when Fra Bartolommeo was very deeply impressed by the preachings of Savonarola, who was so much against this type of painting. This more than anything shows how strong this tradition was [2].

Mariotto Albertinelli was inspired by similar aesthetic principles. Vasari tells us that master and pupil collaborated in the execution of the *Last Judgment*. Crowe and Cavalcaselle try to give us the exact part played by Albertinelli and say that he only really finished off the lower portion and added the portraits of the donors, Gerozzo Dini and his wife (portraits which are today in a bad state) [3]. This is pure supposition based on no precise data. There is nothing to support the idea that we have here two portraits by Albertinelli; in a work of this kind it is difficult to pick out the part played by each artist.

In very truth, there is no doubt that there was a portrait painter called

---

[1] Vasari, IV, p. 180.

[2] As for the portraits of monks by Fra Bartolommeo which are to be found in the lower dormitory of the monastery of San Marco in Florence, they have only an indifferent interest for the history of Florentine portraiture; these medallions show no feeling of the new state of mind of the Florentine portraitists.

[3] Crowe and Cavalcaselle, *Storia* ... V, p. 272.

Albertinelli. According to Vasari he was very greatly helped in the early part of his career by Alfonsina Orsini [1], the wife of the unfortunate Piero de Medici and mother of Lorenzo, Duke of Urbino; and in gratitude he painted a portrait of her which the author of *The Lives* found excellent. M. Gamba's conjecture, which has been explained further back, can be considered as additional substantiation that the so-called *Monaca* of the Uffizi perhaps represents Alfonsina Orsini. This picture leads us to believe that Albertinelli was one of those painters trained in the tradition of the fifteenth century but beginning to be conquered by other ideas. We must not conceal the weakness of the conjecture which makes Albertinelli a portrait painter of some attraction; at any rate it does not seem to be unlikely [2]. This conjecture is in no way the same as that given by Emil Schaeffer, who attributes to Giuliano Bugiardini this so-called *Monaca*, which reveals qualities of technique and mind with which this mediocre painter was never gifted. He was, in fact, one of the least talented of Raphael's imitators. He could not understand the deep feeling of the works which he tried to imitate. If Vasari does not speak of him too badly it is because Vasari was at times full of indulgence [3]. He considered that to have worked under Michelangelo was an extenuating circumstance. Nevertheless several passages in *The Lives* show us the small esteem in which he was held by the author, since Michelangelo was obliged to send him away from the Sistine Chapel because he found his work inferior.

Bugiardini had some fifteenth-century leanings, as he worked under the direction of Domenico Ghirlandaio at the time when the latter was working on the decoration of the choir chapel of Santa Maria Novella. Later we see him under a different discipline; he finished a picture partly designed by Fra

[1] Vasari, IV, p. 219–220. The portrait of Alfonsina Orsini is to be found in the Collection of Cosimo I under the following heading: "un quadre pittovi Mada Alfonsina con adornamento dorato" (*Archivio di Stato di Firenze*, Guardaroba Medicea, 1554-1555, p. 31).

[2] On the other hand it is very difficult to believe Umberto Gnoli's supposition that is is by Perugino (*Pietro Perugino*, 1923, p. 51).

[3] Emil Schaeffer, *Das Florentiner Bildnis*, 1904, p. 134. Cf. also Berenson, *The Florentine Painters*, p. 124.

Bartolommeo, *The Dead Christ*, in the Pitti Palace. From that time on he inclined sometimes towards Leonardo, at others towards Raphael, at others towards Michelangelo. He was a clumsy eclectic to whom we cannot attribute any portraits of importance. Crowe and Cavalcaselle were very reserved about him [1] and with good reason. One of his authentic works gives us the chance to place him, the one of which Vasari speaks in the following terms: "He made a copy of the picture in which Raphael had depicted Pope Leo, Cardinal Julius de Medici and Cardinal dei Rossi, for Cardinal Innocenzo Cibo. But in place of Cardinal dei Rossi he painted the head of Cardinal Cibo, which was more or less a success; and he spent a great deal of effort and industry over it". In this work [2] we find none of the qualities of the original; the face of the Supreme Pontiff is almost lifeless; the colour lacks brilliance, the gaze of the three people is fixed, especially that of Cardinal Cibo, which is rigid and dull. If Bugiardini did not know how to make a good copy, it may be easily assumed that he was incapable of assimilating the conceptions of painters of genius.

He painted some portraits, Vasari points some out, the most interesting and important from the iconographical point of view being the one in which he gives us the features of his master Michelangelo. He was commissioned to do this by Octavia de Medici, who asked him to do it in secret (and here Vasari's version has the air of a studio legend); Bugiardini succeeded in making Michelangelo talk for about two hours, and without the master suspecting it, must have drawn his portrait during that time; Michelangelo must have then made a strong criticism of the drawing, not finding it in any way like the original, and showing surprise that his pupil had drawn it "with one of his eyes in his temple". Bugiardini must have declared that nothing was nearer the truth; he must thus have been able to finish the portrait with Michelangelo's consent [3]. This anecdote shows how little Michelangelo esteemed Bugiardini as a portrait painter.

---

[1] Crowe and Cavalcaselle, XI, p. 14 and following.
[2] National Gallery of Rome (Corsini).
[3] Vasari, VI, p. 206.

The result of the numerous discussions about this work seems to be that the original picture by Bugiardini is the one in the Casa Buonarotti, and not, as Crowe and Cavalcaselle imagine, the one in the Louvre. It is of great documentary interest because it shows us an ardent and vigorous Michelangelo who had complete self-assurance. The face is so sculptural that Bugiardini has rendered it sculpturally, and although the modelling has not the vigour one might expect, there is in this likeness something of the indomitable will of the sitter[1], and it is quite a different Michelangelo from that in the Chaix d'Est Ange Collection where he has the appearance of being discouraged and almost prostrate.

According to Vasari, Bugiardini was also the painter of a portrait of Francesco Guicciardini, executed at the time when the latter, on his return from Bologna, was writing his *History of Italy*. Vasari says it is a good likeness and adds that "it was much admired". It is still in the Guicciardini Palace in Florence. We must place it, if Vasari's particulars are correct, between 1534, the time when the Florentine historian gave up the government of Bologna, and 1540, the time of his death. The model is here represented against a very dark background and in an attitude which recalls that of Leo X by Raphael, a work which was, as we have just seen, familiar to Bugiardini. The modelling of the face and hands lacks strength: this face, compared with any other portrait by Raphael, seems the poor attempt of an hesitant pupil.

Bugiardini liked to follow Raphael's inspiration in his portrait and the result is never very successful. A painting in the Jacquemart-André Museum, which is entirely in his style, awkwardly reproduces the pose and even the features of the *Woman with the Golden Chain* in the Uffizi. Another portrait in the Decorative Arts Museum (also clumsily carried out) seems to have been painted under the same influence or under that of the *Mona Lisa*. These tentative efforts by a mediocre artist show to what extent Leonardo's and Raphael's conceptions became fashionable in the course of several years and how slavishly they were imitated.

---

[1] It is by no means impossible that Michelangelo made a drawing for this portrait so as to help his friend in his difficult venture. It was, according to Steinmann, the drawing in the Louvre.

Andrea del Sarto.
30. *The Sculptor.* (National Gallery, London)
31. and 32. *Drawings for the above.* (Uffizi)

Andrea del Sarto.

33. *Portrait of Lucrezia del Fede.* (Kaiser Friedrich Museum)
34. *Portrait of a Woman* (detail). (Prado)

It is likely that Granacci or Sogliani, of whom we have no authentic easel portraits, followed the same path. In his *Entry of Charles VIII into Florence* [1] Granacci made of what should have been a pretext for beautiful portrait studies a dull and lifeless procession; with similar painters the fifteenth-century tradition was gradually fading out; but on the other hand one does not see in their work any very lively understanding of the new principles. In contrast, however, there were some who drew inspiration from them and knew how to combine them in a fairly succesful manner with the principles bequeathed to them by the teaching of the older masters. This applies especially to the work of Ridolfo Ghirlandaio, the son of the great fresco painter of Santa Maria Novella.

Mr. Bode speaks of this painter with a certain disdain [2]; he could not conceive how Morelli could have recognised any talent in him and even have gone so far as to attribute to him a work of Leonardo's youth like the *Annunciation* in the Uffizi. Mr. Bode's judgment seems too severe if we consider the series of portraits which form the best part of Ridolfo Ghirlandaio's work. In truth it is these second-rate painters who faithfully reflect the essential tendencies of a period, not slavishly but sometimes even with a certain originality.

The two pictures in which his talent shows to the best advantage are the *Miracle* and the *Funeral of Saint Zanobius* [3] which were commissioned by the Company who had this saint as patron, to set off an *Annunciation* painted in 1510 by Albertinelli. Therefore we must not be surprised to find here the latter's influence. There is something of a monumental style in these two paintings, the human forms appear to fill the frames, the colours recall those in Albertinelli's *Visitation* and are even cruder.

But Ridolfo Ghirlandaio did not forget his father's teaching while taking

---

[1] Uffizi.
[2] *Gazette des Beaux-Arts*, 1889, II, p. 605.
[3] Uffizi. The two pictures are later than 1510 and before death of David Ghirlandaio, that is to say, 1525 (Vasari, VI, p. 537).

notice of these new ideas; the funeral was solemnised in the Piazzi di Duomo, between the Baptistry, the Campanile and the façade of Santa Maria del Fiore; one tower of the Palazzo Vecchio can be seen, drawn with great clarity. The procession is made up of Old Canons with expressive heads, which are, as in the great religious scenes of the fifteenth century, portraits of contemporaries. The spirit of Domenico Ghirlandaio survived in his son. In the *Journey to Calvary*, which the latter painted for the Church of San Gallo, Vasari finds "many handsome heads taken from nature and treated with loving care". Ridolfo acquired great reputation from it. "He depicted his father and several boys who were with him and among his friends Poggino, Scheggia and Nunziata, whose faces are very much alive". It is certain that if this tradition of portraits in frescoes was entirely lost—in spite of the teaching of Leonardo and of Savonarola—it was to some extent due to the influence of Ridolfo Ghirlandaio. As he was the painter of a good number of sixteenth-century portraits, it is doubtless due to him that a certain amount of life was kept in the principles of the past generation.

The *Miracle* and the *Funeral of Saint Zanobius* contain two or three physical types which resemble slightly some of those easel portraits which show Raphael's influence *(Plate XIII, fig. 26)* *The Old Man* in the National Gallery is very like one of the figures which looks towards us in the middle of the funeral procession; it shows the same arched, shaped lips, the same detailed study of wrinkles and important lines. This picture is one of those in which the spirit of Ridolfo Ghirlandaio is still imbued with the principles taught him by his father; but it also proves that he had seen the portrait of the Mona Lisa, that he had appreciated the way the pose helped the physical and moral study of the model and that he admired the charm of a lovely landscape background.

This portrait of *An Old Man* which Morelli with reason attributes to Ridolfo has the interest of all pictures which are painted with a true regard for realism. It must have been a good likeness. The white hair is done in a simple style; the dress is severe black. The face, which is not quite full view, has a sharp, piercing gaze. Under heavy eyebrows the eye sockets are deep and given value by the rose tones of the lids, which is one of the interesting characteristics of Ridolfo's style. The lines from the nose are very definitely drawn, the cheek bones very prominent and the hollows accentuated to give irregularity to the oval of the face; and a sarcastic mouth strengthens this impressive head. It is a striking head [1] of a cultured Florentine with sparkling wit and intelligence, showing that, faced with a model full of life, even an artist of the second rank can sometimes rise to a level well above his usual standard *(Plate XIII, fig. 27)*.

A balustrade separates the portrait from the background; it is a remainder of the fifteenth-century tradition which did not often dare to unite these two elements of art. The delicately drawn landscape has rather vague lines; the hills have indefinite contours and some rather tenuous trees; nothing characteristic about it. There is a curious contrast between this listless landscape and the extraordinarily vital features of the model. This gives interest to the picture, which Ridolfo must have painted at almost the same time as the *Miracle of Saint Zanobius*, at the period when he was developing a new technique and new ideas, parallel with the methods handed down to him by his painter father.

Ridolfo Ghirlandaio was more affected by the influence of Raphael than of Leonardo to begin with, because Raphael was his friend, and later because it came more naturally to him to imitate quickly and easily the latter's manner, which was less moving than Leonardo's. It was in his company, Vasari tells us, that he copied (like many painters of the time and later on) Michelangelo's cartoon, of which very little trace can be found in his work. When Raphael was called to Rome by Julius II, Ridolfo, at his request, finished a Madonna commissioned by some Viennese noblemen. It seems then that Ridolfo must have been an excellent imitator; his own personality became gradually submerged, like that of every eclectic artist.

His portraits showed his enquiring frame of mind and the facility with

---

1 We do not know whom this portrait represents. According to one conjecture it is Girolamo Benivieni (*L'Arte*, 1904, p. 500), and according to another Bernado del Nero. Cf. Berenson, *Une Exposition des Maîtres anciens à Florence* (*Gazette des Beaux-Arts*, 1900, II, p. 82).

which he entered into the spirit of others. In the Hermitage there is another *Old Man* [1] seen three-quarters view, studied in detail like the one in the National Gallery, but this time against a neutral background; this also brings to mind certain profiles in the *Funeral of Saint Zanobius*. Even a photograph gives the impression that it is by Ridolfo, evoking Raphael's types by the immobility of the face; the model has this time the gravity of an *Angiolo Doni*.

This influence is equally obvious in a picture in the Johnson Collection in Philadelphia [2], which represents an old man with a high forehead and a long grey beard, looking straight in front of him, holding a glove in his right hand and in his left a letter; he is very simply dressed and his head stands out against a neutral background. It is so much like his earlier works that we must attribute this to Ridolfo Ghirlandaio.

We can recognise this painter's style finally in the *Portrait of a Woman* in the Pitti Palace; clothed in a red dress she seems at first sight like an ugly edition of the *Maddalena Doni (Plate VIII, fig. 17)*. It is a careful, I would say almost relentless, study of the features; the eye sockets are powerfully drawn as well as the nose with its dilated nostrils; nothing is omitted which can bring out the lack of charm of this model. Maddalena Doni is herself rather heavily featured, but Raphael gave her freshness of colouring and gave atmosphere in the landscape. There is nothing like this in Ridolfo's painting; he certainly knew Raphael's picture, but the tendency for realism was not yet dead in him, and here it is not even tempered by the delicacy of the landscape as it is in the National Gallery picture. The first of these portraits which are almost certainly by Ridolfo Ghirlandaio was painted in 1509 [3]. It shows Raphael's principles influencing a strong nature which hesitated to accept the new formulas.

---

[1] Cf. *Catalogue Hermitage*, 1891, p. 140–141 (attributed to Raphael, considered formerly as the portrait of Sannazar). Cf. Waagen, *Die Gemäldesammlung in der kaiserlichen Ermitage zu Saukt Petersburg*, 1664, p. 44.

[2] Berenson, *Catalogue of the Johnson Collection*,   I, p. 41 (the other portrait which Mr. Berenson attributes to Ridolfo does not seem so certainly to be by him).

[3] Mr. Gronau found trace of it in the inventory of Della Rovere's *Inheritance*, who went in 1631 from Urbino to Florence (*Rivista d'Arte*, January-April 1912, p. 55).

But we can soon discern in this artist a clear and decisive evolution which was to lead him to create some portraits imbued with a different spirit, where nevertheless characteristic elements appear which do not hide the origin of his works. They reveal a wider conception of life. Ghirlandaio advances towards a more powerful study of physical features and devotes himself with more enthusiasm to give a more psychological impression. In spite of this, he did not give up using the three-quarter view which gives his portraits a family likeness. *The Unknown Man* of the Corsini Gallery has the same style of face as that in the National Gallery; Ridolfo lets the eyes come freely into view under the prominent eyebrows; he favours also a sinuous quality of line of the lips and prominent cheek bones. The two portraits certainly have points of resemblance; but the one in the Corsini Gallery has more seriousness and gravity in the gaze, which is almost sad. *(Plate XIV, fig. 29)*. This emaciated face seems tortured by an inward sorrow. The study of the features is, much more than in the picture in the National Gallery, the reflection of a state of mind.

It is thus strange to see a painter improving himself by degrees and succeeding in studying what is least physical, what is most difficult to analyse in a face. A charming *Unknown Man* in the Uffizi, for some time attributed to Piero di Cosimo, is almost the younger and more attractive brother of the two models in the Corsini Gallery and the National Gallery; might not one consider them the *Three Ages* expressed in three related heads? In each of these portraits the dress is very simple, dark in its entirety, lightened only at the base of the neck by a thin slip of white material; the pupils, placed in exactly the same place in the circle of the eye, flash a sharp look in the first two, softened in the third; the latter, entirely in Ridolfo's style, has a youth and charm which is lacking in the two others. It is modelled with less precision; the eyelids are broadly shaded as well as the left cheek; in certain parts this picture is a study in chiaroscuro and recalls not only the art of Raphael, but also that of Leonardo. Ridolfo varies his effects; and it is remarkable to see these three related heads, with the same gaze and the same oval face, leaving three different impressions.

On one hand Ridolfo kept a taste for characteristic portraits inherited from his father; he took great interest in portraying them, and even attains a harsh realism to the point of being abnormal [1]. He has, Vasari tells us, painted for the Florentine monastery of gli Angeli, where one of his brothers was living, a history of Saint Benedict in which "the best face was that of a dwarf who was guarding the door of the monastery".

Nevertheless the other tendency is just as much alive. It was to follow this tendency that he created one of the most curious works of the fifteenth century in Florence, the one wrongly called *The Goldsmith (Plate XIV fig. 28)*. It is no more a goldsmith than the Medici of Botticelli is a maker of medals. It was gradually becoming a habit not to be limited any longer by a profile or half-length portrait in posing the model. One of the most natural poses is that which shows the sitter taking an interest in something. The greater the space occupied by the portrait, the more the vital element of the pose preoccupied the artist's mind.

The Young Man attentively looking at the jewel which he has in his hands [2] is a picture showing Leonardo's influence. It is handled very skilfully. The light, coming from the right, illuminates the right side of the face, part of the neck, a fold of the white shirt and the hands. The study of chiaroscuro is very clever. The two hands are treated with delicacy; slim and aristocratic, they form, thanks to the high-light which accentuates the modelling of the fingers, two centres of light. It strikes an original note in this work. The technique is indeed very different from that employed in the *Old Man* in the National Gallery, but it is not so very different from the one used in the portrait of a *Young Man* in the Uffizi; there is a strong similarity in the balance of light and shade. Another decisive element is the landscape, very much the same in handling as that which stretches behind the head of the *Old Man* in the National Gallery; the lines are indecisive, architecture appears rarely, the tones go from grey to sepia; a single big tree, a bridge and

---

[1] Vasari, VI, p. 537—238. This picture, Milanesi says, has disappeared in the rebuilding of the Monastery.

[2] Pitti Palace.

a few figures: it is gaunt nature as expressed by his brush. Note also the dark-coloured costume and the left hand where the veins are drawn in the same way as in the portrait in the Corsini Gallery. Here then are the different elements which go to corroborate the attribution.

It is very important to see a painter imbued with the fifteenth-century traditions arriving at such a different conception from that of his youth. This last portrait of an *Unknown Man*, which we can without hesitation place between 1510 and 1520, gives us an idea of the power with which these new principles made themselves felt. Whereas most painters hesitated between the manner of Raphael, Leonardo and Michelangelo, Ridolfo's art ended by being above everything Leonardesque; and the facial expression in this portrait of the *Man with the Jewel* rather reminds one of the *Man with the Medal* by Botticelli.

What is certain is that painters had definitely abandoned the theme of impassivity which the contemporaries of Piero della Francesca considered as inseparable from the conception of a portrait. In the evolution of Florentine painting, it is one of the most characteristic, I might almost say the most moving, moments when one sees the features of a face becoming thoughtful or dreaming. It was gradually going to create a form of art where one only rarely finds the memory of past ideals; the face of the model was to be a reflection of its interior life. It is a principle which is already expressed in Ridolfo Ghirlandaio's work and its influence was bound to spread; painters were to be particularly tempted by the study of human sensibilities, whose different aspects they translated by new expressions of depth, allure and mystery.

CHAPTER V

LEONARDO'S INFLUENCE ON ANDREA DEL SARTO

Reasons for the sadness of Florentine portraits at the beginning of the sixteenth century. The troubled history of Florence. The sensibility of Michelangelo and of Leonardo da Vinci. Portraits in Andrea del Sarto's frescoes. His self portrait. *The Young Man* in the Pitti Palace. His melancholy. *The Sculptor* in the National Gallery. *Lucrezia del Fede.*

Among the painters who were attracted by Leonardo's theories there were some like Piero di Cosimo, or even Ridolfo Ghirlandaio, who in their turn exercised a good influence over their pupils. Neither must we leave out Albertinelli and Fra Bartolommeo, who, though seldom painting portraits, nevertheless helped to enlarge the conception of portraiture in the sixteenth century. As many painters who were their disciples are now going to take our attention, we must not be surprised at the position they hold in the evolution of this style.

Imperceptibly, painting changed; studying nature in minute detail no longer held the same value in the eyes of the artists who, carried away by Michelangelo's fire, saw men larger than life-size and represented them all powerful and majestic, as though they were gods. Fra Bartolommeo and Albertinelli have an almost superhuman conception of art; Bartolommeo's apostles are huge painted statues, which with the aid of chiaroscuro give the illusion of sculpture. As for Albertinelli's *Annunciation*, so different from that of Lorenzo di Credi's, which is almost contemporary, it opened the way to monumental painting and makes one anticipate Academic painting on the grand scale. The two inseparable friends had thus independently, and at the same time as Michelangelo, created a movement towards "grandiosita". The peaceful assemblies in the fifteenth-century frescoes and the finely modelled and lovingly painted scenes of the time of Pesellino and Botticelli were out of date; this calm of past times contrasted with the religious passion let loose by Savonarola; and accounts for the future tendency to take a more solemn view of humanity.

This was not without its influence on portraiture; the sitter was taking up a larger part of the picture, painters were more willing to study the general bearing than the physical details of the model, a very modern conception which G. B. Morono used later on in the north of Italy with extraordinary brilliance.

But this development towards the full-length portrait did not come about quickly; the fifteenth-century feeling was always there. In the first half of the sixteenth century there was an interlacing of the most varied influences. Besides Fra Bartolommeo's influence there is Leonardo's and Michelangelo's. Some painters clung to the influence of the painter of the *Mona Lisa*, others to the "terribilita" of the painter of the Sistine Chapel.

To understand the character of most of these works we must not forget the circumstances in which their creators lived. It was a period in Florentine history which had neither grandeur nor gaiety. There was no longer, as in the fifteenth century, any ease of mind in pleasure; the Medicis had played the happy role of giving to a people who loved all kinds of amusements and picturesque spectacles all they could desire in this domain. But the advent of the French in Italy had marked the beginning of a painful era; Savonarola's preachings had plunged Florence into a religious crisis which had the strongest repercussions on people's hearts. The misfortunes which followed contrast with the carefree atmosphere of almost the whole of the fifteenth century. Groups fought together violently until the time when one of the descendants of the Medici came to absolute power; and nothing was so unhappy as those thirty or thirty-five years following Savonarola's death, during which time Florence was in the agonies of seeking political stability.

The portraits of the masters who dominated this troublous period, Leonardo and Michelangelo, were themselves full of sadness. When we consider the one of Michelangelo by Bugiardini, there is nothing beautiful about the work, but it is one of the most sincere impressions of the great master that is left to us. The face, with the nose broken by Torrigiani, is so expressive that, through the mediocre craftsmanship of his interpreter, something of the torment which was ravaging his soul still remains. A torment which he himself bitterly defined one day in a letter to Vasari: "non nasce in me pensiero che non vi sia dentro sculpita la morte" [1]; the idea of death obsessed him in a sinister way; in moments of great despair he spoke of it as a possible deliverer from the evils of the world; at other times he was afraid of it, he was in terror of it and begged God to deliver him; it made him feel so far from Him and so near to oblivion! This sadness at the end of his life, which he expressed in a most moving way, was the melancholy of his whole existence [2]. Michelangelo's pessimism has its origin in his manner of thinking and feeling; he has left his tragic stamp on the faces of his heroes. It is the price he had to pay for his solitude.

In spite of the smile of the *Mona Lisa* and of *John the Baptist*, Leonardo has a conception of life which, without being so dramatic, is nevertheless devoid of joy and confidence. When Leonardo said "e se tu sarai solo, tu sarai tutto tuo", he expressed the same distrust as Michelangelo for mediocre humanity, and if we often find among his works unfinished paintings it is proof that he was stricken with another kind of pessimism, that which comes from the discouragement felt by an artist unable to reach the high level of his inspiration.

Here again, for want of the painter's evidence (one might say that Leonardo had modesty of feeling, and his manuscripts hardly ever refer to his intimate thoughts) it is his own face which reveals his character, as so often happens; it is the self-portrait at Turin which represents him already lined and old, with his beautiful prophet's beard. The corners of his mouth are folded in a slight smile, whereas the brows, dividing his bare forehead in a strong line,

---

[1] *Le lettere di Michelangelo Buonarotti* (ed. Milanesi, 1875, p. 538).
[2] *Die Dichtungen des Michelangelo Buonarotti* (ed. Carl Frey, 1897, especially page 62 and following, p. 141).

emphasise the handsome, analytical eyes which have tried to penetrate all the secrets of nature and which express an infinite melancholy. It is the fixed look of a man who has doubtless had moments of great enthusiasm, but who has suffered a great deal from his wandering life and uncertain destiny since the fall of Ludovico il Moro. Leonardo's pessimism is not like Michelangelo's, inherent in his temperament; it is the result of experience, but it is none the less real and powerful.

One can well understand from this emotion that artists following their lead received no comfort whatsoever from them nor from the course of events. This explains why the smile was gradually disappearing from the portrait. Domenico Ghirlandaio and Benozzo Gozzolo had represented patrician Florentines, contented and leading a life of opulence. Their calm assemblies, where discussions were carried on without violence or bitterness, belong to another period. For there now appears a kind of "mal de siècle" such as tormented Lorenzo de Medici in the course of his adventurous life. The murderer of the first Duke of Florence, was, so Filippo dei Nerli tells us, melancholy by nature, very pale of face, endowed with plenty of acid wit; he was not lacking in a certain solemnity of bearing, so much so that the young men of his time, among whom he showed himself so full of finesse and gravity, gave him the nickname of Philosopher. Many artists of the sixteenth century had, according to Vasari, a similar temperament. For instance, Pontormo, Francesco Salviati and Sogliani, who was the "personification of melancholy" [1].

In the course of the first half of the sixteenth century we cannot be astonished at encountering so often these dreaming and sad faces. As far as it is possible to generalise on such a personal topic as portraiture, one can affirm that the gaze loses its serenity and the features their repose. This evolution was not due to the artists' temperament alone; it was also connected with the great moral issues of the century. In fact it is not unusual that portraits should express the thoughts and cares which have given anxiety to a whole gener-

---

[1] Vasari, V, p. 123.

ation. It is so with the portraits of Philippe de Champaigne and also with Louis David. It is the same story with the Tuscan painters when they were seeking a master.

Besides, it is worth noting that most artists of this period had only modest talent compared with those of the fifteenth century; but they rise above mediocrity when they represent the living model. It is an oft-repeated observation that portraiture becomes, in periods of artistic decadence, the refuge of sincerity and originality.

The variety of influences which were felt at the beginning of the sixteenth century explain sufficiently well the character of paintings such as Andrea del Sarto's, and more especially his painted heads. He was one of those who willingly reflected the school of the greatest, such as they were. His supple talent modelled itself easily on that of more gifted artists and in his work one is reminded of Leonardo, Fra Bartolommeo and Michelangelo.

It was, to begin with, through Piero di Cosimo that he absorbed the ideas of Leonardo da Vinci [1], that Piero di Cosimo who could soothe the eyes with the "sfumato" of a work like *Perseus and Andromeda*. The first frescoes of Andrea del Sarto in the Portico of the Santissima Annunziata in Florence (1509-1514) present a singular contrast with the fresco of the *Nativity* by Baldovinetti, painted in the same building but at an earlier date. In this painting one sees very precise drawing in spite of the bad state of the work. In comparing the two frescoes many of Leonardo's principles can be seen revived in the latter work.

We are already familiar with a few of these principles. Only the faces which are very close to us can have definite outlines. The foreground thus appears clearly defined, in contrast the dominating feature of the rest of the picture is not contributed by the profiles "spediti crudi" but by a vague finish (un finito fumoso) [2]. As objects get further and further from the eye

---

[1] Vasari, V, p. 7.
[2] *Trattato di pittura*, I, p. 176.

so their outline becomes less and less distinct. And Leonardo arrived at the conclusion that distant objects should offer an indistinct shape in which actual details disappear; faces or objects which are far away from us should only be unfinished marks without definite limits [1]. "One sees", says he, "artists painting towns and other things in the distance, such as architectural backgrounds, as finished as though they were seen close at hand and this is contrary to experience" [2]. Leonardo's conception of perspective makes the precise and vigorous drawing of the fifteenth century Florentine painters seem henceforth out of date. Besides, to linear perspective is added aerial and colour perspective and this contrast of colour is a means of showing the distance of objects.

Andrea del Sarto was already, in part, applying these new conceptions in his frescoes in the Santissima Annunziata where the contours show a certain softening, but not to the point of breaking entirely with fifteenth-century tradition. In his religious pictures Leonardo analysed feelings or ideas without caring to evoke the features of known personalities: the essential thing for him being the psychological value of a scene or of a face. Well, Andrea del Sarto had not to a great extent departed from similar tendencies, for according to Vasari certain of his frescoes contain some portraits.

In the *Death of Saint Philippe Benizzi* he has painted Girolamo della Robbia, son of Andrea, with whom he was on the best of terms. In the *Distribution of the Clothes of the Saint,* the old man in red with head to one side and holding a staff in his hand represents Andrea della Robbia; his son Luca is also shown [3]. It is certain that there are several portraits in the *Procession of the Kings,* and it is again Vasari who points out the most important: that of the painter Jacopo Sansovino, with whom he was linked in close friendship, and of the musician Francesco dell'Aiolle [4]; Sansovino

---

[1] *The Literary Works of Leonardo da Vinci*, p. 285.
[2] *Trattato di pittura*, I, p. 434.
[3] Vasari, V, p. 13.
[4] Vasari, V, p. 16. Borghini, *Il Riposo*, ed. 1584, p. 418. Cf. Baldinucci, *Notizie dei professori del disegno*, ed. Ranalli, II, p. 77.

is seen three-quarters view looking straight in front of him, whereas Andrea del Sarto raises his arm in the direction of the spectator and behind him one can see, clearly drawn, the head of the musician.

In the portico of the Annunziata, Leonardo's and Fra Bartolommeo's influence predominates. While he was a pupil of Piero di Cosimo, Andrea showed more enthusiasm for copying Michelangelo's cartoon than Leonardo's; but it was only later on in the Frescoes of Scalzo that Michelangelo's influence was felt. On the other hand, in his *Nativity* there are signs of Domenico Ghirlandaio's influence; the grouping of the scene makes one think of the fresco on the same subject in the choir of Santa Maria Novella. It is purely a superficial resemblance, for the technique has no connection with that of the preceding period. With reference to this we should turn to the accentuated features with which the contemporaries of Piero della Francesca modelled a portrait. This almost mathematical precision was accompanied by a complete sense of repose. On the other hand, with the new tendencies, the softness of the contours tried to give whatever the outline of a head had in the way of emotion, spontaneity or whatever was indefinable.

Andrea del Sarto understood the importance of certain of Leonardo's precepts; for him, as for the great Florentine, emotion had something musical in it which expressed itself in the more personal way in which he studied a head. Andrea's magnificent drawings have in this respect a good touch of originality; to the rather dry line of the contemporaries of Domenico Ghirlandaio was added, through the teaching of Leonardo da Vinci, a fuller, more subtle line where an attractive softness enhances the modelling of the forms. This tendency reveals itself also in portraiture. One finds there the elements of a more refined sensibility than in the fifteenth century, in many respects almost decadent. It shows anyway a feeling more modern and further removed from the *Profile of a Woman* in the Poldi-Pezzoli Museum than the frescoes of Andrea del Sarto in the Santissima Annunziata are from the *Nativity* of Baldovinetti.

Nevertheless Andrea del Sarto was commissioned to carry out a similar work to that which had been given to Andrea Castagno and then to Botticelli.

On the façade of the Palazzo del Podesta he had to paint the captains who had fled from Florence at the time when Charles V besieged the town in 1529. He thought at first that he would give the work over to one of his pupils, Bernado del Buda, then he decided to do it himself; "he carried out the faces", says Vasari, "in such a way that they seemed to be living and natural" [1]. He had to represent, as well as the felonious captains, ordinary citizens who had in the same circumstances left the town in haste, and these latter "in piazza" on the façade of the Mercanzia Vecchia. But already in Vasari's time these paintings were difficult to discern. Those on the Mercanzia Vecchia had been whitewashed, and the others were very much spoilt. It would have been interesting to see how Andrea del Sarto had been able to treat such a subject, so alien to his style; all the more because it seems that he had very little help with the work. Vasari is insistent on this point: "he finished the pictures entirely by his own hand" [2].

The drawings in the Uffizi, where are to be seen the first rough outlines of these condemned men, are remarkable studies in movement, but the actual faces are lost in the whole effect of the sketch. Andrea del Sarto scarcely indicated them and it is impossible to judge from these rapid notes [3] the realism with which he had reproduced the features of the felons, represented with their heads upside down; he must have tried to make them terrifying as far as his temperament, never very vigorous, would allow him to give such a character to a face.

It seems that the Signoria of Florence would only have confided this mission of vengeance to artists of great talent and established reputation. Andrea del Sarto enjoyed then considerable prestige; and when Octavian de Medici wanted a copy of Raphael's Leo X, "just as beautiful as the original", he went straight to Andrea.

---

[1] Vasari, V, p. 53—54.

[2] The names of the Florentines appearing in these pictures have been kept; they were Alessandro Corsini, Taddeo Guiducci, Pier Francesco Ridolfi and the captains Cecco Orsini, Jacopo Antonio Orsini and Lucca Giovanni da Sessa.

[3] Berenson, *The Drawings of the Florentine Painters*, II, p. 5. F. di Pietro, *I desegni di Andrea del Sarto negli Uffizi*, 1910, p. 94.

We know the curious story which Vasari tells on the subject of this copy. Frederick II, Duke of Mantua, visiting Florence to pay homage to Pope Clement VII, was struck by the beauty of the famous portrait in the Medici Palace where Leo X is represented seated, having at his side Cardinal Julius de Medici and Cardinal dei Rossi. This work pleased him "extra-ordinarily", and he longed to become its owner. He made a request for it to Clement VII who hastened to fulfil his desire. Octavian, the tutor of Hippolytus and Alexander de Medici, received the order to send the picture to Mantua. While being astonished at the casual way in which the Pope had disposed of a work which was one of the most magnificent ornaments of the Medici Collection, he promised to conform to his wishes, but he made excuses for the necessary delay, so that he should be able to change the frame which was in a bad state and said he wanted to order a gilded one; as soon as it should be ready he would send off the precious picture to Mantua. It was a means of gaining time for Octavian de Medici.

He got in touch then with Andrea del Sarto begging him to make a copy of *Leo X* in all haste, to send to the Duke of Mantua, whereas Raphael's work would be hidden jealously. "Andrea, having promised to do the best he could, carried out in secret at Octavius' house a picture of the same size; he took so much trouble with it that when the copy was finished, the other, great connoisseur of art that he was, could not distinguish it from the original". When Frederick II received it the illusion was complete. The Duke expressed great satisfaction with it; Giulio Romano believed that he saw the original picture and praised it greatly. It was not until much later that the forgery was discovered when Vasari, going through Mantua, explained what had happened [1].

According to Vasari then, Andrea del Sarto was a very clever copyist; he had assimilated Raphael's style to such an extent that even a pupil of the Roman painter, a very experienced judge, was misled by it. Also it is not surprising that in the course of the nineteenth century the whole question was raised again. Vasari tells us that the original remained in the Medici

[1] Vasari, V, p. 41–43.

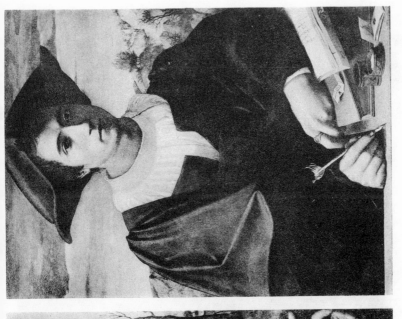

Franciabigio.
35. *The Man with the Gloves.* (Uffizi)
36. *Portrait of a Young Man.* (Kaiser Friedrich Museum)

37. Florentine School of the Sixteenth Century (1515-1530). *Portrait of a Young Nobleman.* (Kaiser Friedrich Museum)

Collection, and he in his turn had given it to Cosimo de Medici. It is obviously the picture now in the Pitti Palace. As for Andrea del Sarto's copy, it is very likely the one in the Museum at Naples [1]. The differences between this latter and the original have been noted in minute detail; the picture in Naples has kept its colour very fresh, in contrast to the one in Florence where some of the colours have become blackened as happens so often with Raphael's work. The colours are, generally speaking, warmer; the bodies less solidly constructed and the modelling a little less strongly brought out. These differences correspond well enough with the two painters' differing temperaments. Besides there is no reason to doubt Vasari's account. The only question remaining to be solved is how Andrea del Sarto's painting went from Mantua to Parma into the Farnese Collection: data which is missing to complete the history of the picture. In revealing Andrea del Sarto's craftsmanship, considerations of style compensate for this obscurity and solve the problem with a great degree of certainty [2].

Octavian de Medici's commission to the Florentine master shows us in what esteem he was held in his time, that a brilliant connoisseur should have considered him capable of accomplishing this "tour de force", of making a copy of a Raphael which would have defeated the most experienced of copyists. It was doubtless in homage to his talent; it also proves that he was considered to have a deep knowledge of this master's work and that he had really assimilated its basic elements [3].

Well, perhaps there is some similarity between the portraits of Raphael and Andrea del Sarto insofar as they both show the influence of Leonardo da Vinci; but the faces have not the same expressions and there is a great

---

[1] At Parma in the Palazzo del Giardino: it is said to be by Raphael.

[2] This question has been very much discussed. Cf. Baldinucci, *Notizie dei professori del disegno* (ed. Piacenza) II, p. 437. D'Arco e Braghirolli, *Archivo storico italiano*, series III, vol. VII, 2, p. 175 and following. In his catalogue (*Guido del Museo di Napoli, Pinacoteca*, II, p. 214 and following), Mr. de Rinaldus suggests for no apparent reason the name of Giulio Romano in place of Andrea del Sarto.

[3] Vasari tells us besides that Andrea carried out for this same Octavian a painting of an isolated head of Cardinal Julius de Medici, who later became Pope under the name of Clement VII, in imitation of the one by Raphael, and that it was "very beautiful".

difference in methods of construction. Raphael's Florentine portraits, as well as those of his Roman period, exude calm and self-confidence. This is perhaps the most characteristic thing in the two Pontifical portraits. It seems as if nothing should trouble their serenity; the two Popes are motionless in their attitude as masters of the world: one always finds with Raphael this healthy sense of moral values, this perfect balance of mind. Andrea del Sarto didn't see nature with the same eyes. What constitutes the originality of his portraits is that he expresses a rather complex state of soul. In portraiture the artist's personality appears much more strongly marked than in his other works which show a variety of influences. The Scalzo frescoes, which he worked on over a long period, tell us the history of these influences [1]. *The Baptism of Christ*, which is obviously one of the earliest, is still fifteenth century in certain aspects, although from others it shows the influence of Michelangelo and Leonardo. The one which shows the powerful profile of Dante has even some resemblance to an engraving of Dürer's; certainly on this occasion the German artist must have inspired the Florentine painter [2].

But in Andrea del Sarto's portraits one doesn't find a similar subservience. This type of painting rather than any other allowed him self-expression. He shows himself to us to begin with as one of the most gifted of Florentine draughtsmen; and also as a personal and sensitive portraitist. He was familiar with Leonardo's portraits and he imitated them; but he gave a new and distinctive mark to his own. His melancholy is very impressive; his models are not, like almost all Raphaels, full of calm; they carry with them the thoughts and cares which sadden their gaze. Let us first study his self-portrait which shows no signs of anxiety. According to Vasari's evidence he has painted himself in the fresco of the *Magi* in the Santissima Annunziata (he was then quite young); his features are strongly marked; later on in the *Assumption* in the Pitti where he appears in the background, alone, his face is rounded and has thickened. It is the same face as that in the Uffizi portrait, equally thickened by

---

[1] Vasari, V, p. 32.
[2] Fritz Knapp, *Andrea del Sarto*, 1907, p. 44.

age[1]. The colours have not the same warmth as in other paintings by Andrea del Sarto: the tints are almost dead. In spite of this there is no doubt that it is a self portrait. Vasari speaks of it as one of the works of his maturity. The historian's account is not lacking in imagination. As, after having drawn the features of a servant (commesso) of the Vallombrosa monks, he had some colours left over, Andrea thought of painting his wife Lucrezia del Fede; then, the latter being unwilling, he painted himself on a slate. In Vasari's time this picture was still in the possession of Lucrezia; it is today in the collection of the "autoritratti dei pittori"[2]. The interesting thing about it is that we have here an Andrea already aged; and although his face is not very different from the one in the *Magi* fresco, the facial expression has hardly altered; in their general style these two heads are exactly like the engraving which Vasari put at the head of his *Lives of the Painters*[3].

These perfectly handled self-portraits, which reveal a certain tranquillity of soul, are not the most characteristic of Andrea's works. There are others which are more interesting and which help us to define his style more exactly. One is in the Pitti and the other is the one generally called the *Portrait of a Sculptor* in the National Gallery.

The Young Man in the Pitti[4] is perhaps Andrea del Sarto's most typical portrait: it set a fashion. And without having such a wide influence as the *Mona Lisa* we must recognise here one of those master works, which, by the quality of its inspiration and style attracted artists and centres of culture. The painter has here eliminated all accessories: between the head and the rather dark background there is a blurred harmony which shows that the painter wanted to envelop his model in hazy atmosphere; the tones are softly graduated; none of the colours stands out; the effect of diffused light is

---

1 Cf. Crowe and Cavalcaselle, XI, p. 102.
2 Vasari, V.
3 Vasari, *Vite*, edition 1568, II, p. 149.
4 The Uffizi has a replica of this picture which has been put in the "autoritratti dei pittori" collection although the features do not in the least resemble those of the painter. M. Knapp claims that both these two portraits are poor copies (*Andrea del Sarto*, p. 74).

concentrated on the neck and beginning of the chest; a piece of white material is the only part which has a little intensity. The dress is beautifully simple; a dark cap partly covers the thick hair which falls on to the neck. Posed to face us, the model has powerfully drawn eyes (but scarcely visible draughtsmanship); the gaze is mysterious and troubled. In this head, where no feature is strongly pronounced, the only striking thing is this profound expression of sadness. A portrait like the *Mona Lisa* offers a multiple interest: the line of the bust, the pose of the hands, the grandeur of the landscape, have almost as much importance as the features of the face. But here there is only the strange beauty of the gaze and it is seldom that such dreaming melancholy has been treated so profoundly. To understand the exceptional quality of this work it suffices to compare it with a canvas in the Cook Collection at Richmond which is only a mediocre imitation [1]: it represents a young man with chestnut hair, dressed in black, which is very much like that in the Pitti Palace; but the whole effect and style is mannered and almost sickly; the lines of the face are more strongly marked and all the depth of expression has disappeared; in spite of the two entwined A's with which Andrea del Sarto signed his paintings, it is certain that it is a studio work which shows nothing of the beauty and distinction of drawing of the master.

The portrait in the Pitti Palace, with its dull complexion and melancholy gaze, admirably expresses the state of mind of some of the cultivated youth of the time. Besides it belongs to a period when Andrea del Sarto was already in full possession of his talent [2].

It marks an important date in the evolution of portrait painting, because from this time onwards his influence was added to that of Leonardo's works. This sad expression was to become classic; the best pupils of Andrea del Sarto, Franciabigio and Puligo, were to conceive humanity in this form. It was a

---

[1] *A Catalogue of the paintings at Doughty House, Richmond, and elsewhere in the collection of Sir Frederick Cook*, v. I, Italian School by Tancred Borenius, 1913, p. 38.

[2] It is likely that this picture is of 1513 or 1514, earlier at any rate than those where Franciabigio tried to express the same feelings. M. Wölfflin (*Die Klassische Kunst*, 1899, p. 170) believes it to be a little later and almost contemporary with the *Disputa* (1518).

new aspect of artistic sensibility where we can recognise a subdued reflection of the sadness of Michelangelo's heroes.

Although less characteristic, *The Sculptor* in the National Gallery is nevertheless conceived in a similar style [1] *(Plate XV, fig. 30)*. If in general we can only find in the pose of the model the attitude which pleased the painter, this time, nevertheless, it is reasonable to respect tradition; the block which the figure is holding between his hands symbolises the basis of life which he is going to give to the natural spectacle, which attracts him and which holds his constant and penetrating attention. The pose does not lack originality or novelty. Andrea del Sarto considered it thoroughly before deciding on it; four drawings in the Uffizi bear witness to his hesitation; one of them is only a rough note where the idea is forming: the block is scarcely indicated and the model is represented with his head inclined. The painter then had the idea of posing the model full face, the arms firmly leaning on the block; then almost in profile and in a similar attitude, and finally another drawing, the same pose as in the National Gallery, almost back view with the head turned to a profile [2] *(Plate XV, fig. 31, 32)*. All this indicates a long study in elaboration. Far from giving his models always the same pose, Andrea tries to find the one which would show the essential character of the face and the keenness of the gaze to the best advantage. The preparatory drawings as well as the finished work give the model, to a lesser degree, the same air of lassitude as is found in the *Young Man* in the Pitti Palace.

In a dark costume, against a dark background, this head is set in profile against neutral tones. As in the preceding portrait the white of the shirt and of the neck, and the grey-blue of the sleeve stand out strongly. The paint is laid on freely here with strokes of the brush still visible in the fingers of the right hand. In contrast to the handling of the *Young Man* in the Pitti, where the strength of the features stands out, here he has accentuated the modelling, playing skilfully with light and shade, and lighting up the face with it where

---

[1] This portrait is signed A.A. (Andrea d'Agnolo); it is obviously of a painter rather than a sculptor as the catalogue suggests.

[2] Cf. Berenson, *The Drawings of the Florentine Painters*, II, p. 4. — Di Pietro, op. cit., p. 26. — The date fixed by Mr. di Pietro for this portrait in the National Gallery is about 1517.

the tones of the flesh go from pink to pale yellow; under a brilliant forehead he has strongly shaded the eyes in their sockets.

In this expressively drawn face you see the arch of the nose accentuated, the dimple in the chin and the mouth with pronounced lips; one finds the same elements in the portrait in the Pitti, as far as one can compare the treatment of a profile with that of a full face or three-quarters view. It is not impossible to suppose that this is the same person of whom we have two paintings at two different periods of his life; in the National Gallery picture, age has accentuated the essential character of the face, has slightly emaciated it, whilst keeping the depth and intensity of the gaze. The skilful way in which the painter has distributed the colour makes one believe it to be one of the important works of his maturity; one can date it about 1520. The general effect seemed to please him, for in other pictures and frescoes of Andrea del Sarto's are to be seen figures in this position, including the Saint Michel in the group of Saints in the Uffizi, and the one which represents Jacopo Sansovino in the Annunziato in the *Procession of the Magi*.

In any case, these two paintings are among the most characteristic of Andrea del Sarto's works; their sensitive handling raises them well above the level of his other paintings. It is clear that Michelangelo's influence was felt in these works; Andrea del Sarto is the type of painter who hesitates, in his interpretation of the inner feelings of a model, between the style of Michelangelo and of Leonardo. In the Johnson Collection in Philadelphia there is another portrait, which, according to the beautiful reproduction of it in Mr. Berenson's catalogue, seems equally worthy to be attributed to Andrea del Sarto. It is a knee-length portrait of a seated young man; the right hand is raised; he seems about to speak; nevertheless he lets the left hand fall heedlessly on the arm of a chair. As in the Pitti and in the National Gallery, the background is dark in colour, which gives sufficient relief to the face and the feelings which it expresses. Mr. Berenson says that if this work were in a better state it would be one of the most beautiful creations of Andrea del Sarto in particular, and of Florentine art in general [1]. The picture was painted at a

---

[1] Berenson, *Catalogue of the Johnson Collection*, I, p. 44.

time when Andrea was attracted by Michelangelo's feeling for tragedy and was painting the fresco of *St. John Preaching in the Wilderness* in which appears the admirable portrait of Dante.

But if in the Scalzo cloisters Andrea del Sarto tries a monumental style and accentuates physical characteristics, it is without grandeur. He was more fortunate in portraiture where, while inspired by Michelangelo, he showed that he was not impervious either to the charm of Leonardo or to the religious expression of Fra Bartolemmeo, nor to the colour of Perugino. His figures move about in a refined, delicate atmosphere; the softness of the drawing tempers the feeling of Michelangelesque strength; and these combined qualities merging together give a peculiar charm made up of delicate sadness and restrained emotion to his portraits of men.

When Andrea del Sarto painted portraits of women, he was more directly inspired by Leonardo da Vinci. The most beautiful is certainly the one in the Prado, which represents according to the catalogue Lucrezia del Fede [1] *(Plate XVI, fig. 34):* a conjecture which has for a long time been accepted and which seems to have no foundation. It is Vasari and Baldinucci who must guide us here; both of them give us precise and valuable information on the authentic portraits of Lucrezia del Fede.

Vasari affirms that Andrea del Sarto was so much in the habit of painting his wife that he began to give her features to every woman he painted. She was in fact very charming to look at ("piacevolissima"), and her husband was madly in love with her. Without exaggerating to the extent of Vasari, who does not seem to have had favourable recollections of her, one can take it for certain that the painter, naturally placid, allowed himself to be dominated by his young and seductive wife. In the first edition of *The Lives* Vasari even considered her influence pernicious; She made it particularly felt when Andrea went to work in France; he soon felt homesick and responded without hesitation to Lucrezia's call [2], in spite of his promises to the King.

---

[1] De Madranzo, *Catalogo de los cuadros del Museo del Prado*, 1920, p. 28.
[2] Vasari, V, p. 28–31.

On the other hand Baldinucci tells us that when Jacopo da Empoli came in his youth to study and copy the best parts of the *Nativity of the Virgin* at the Santissima Annunziata, he saw Lucrezia one day, already very old, stop to look at his work and show him the figure for which she had posed [1]. There was therefore a portrait of Lucrezia in this fresco. For his part, Vasari points out another which is a profile of the Magdalene kneeling beautifully draped in *The Disputa* [2] in the Pitti Palace. It is unfortunately difficult to compare a profile portrait with another where the model is shown full face, to the extent that the most reliable documentation on this matter is still the central figure in the *Nativity of the Virgin*.

Well, there is an obvious similarity with the lovely *Portrait of a Woman* in the Kaiser Friedrich Museum, treated with a spontaneous technique (*Plate XVI, fig. 33*); and this latter recalls in its turn a drawing in the Uffizi where the model is painted almost half-length [3]. Both of them are doubtless likenesses of Lucrezia del Fede; and if one thinks of the great similarity between these features and those of *Faith* in the Scalzo, it is not impossible that this fresco in *grisaille* gives us another portrait of Andrea's wife.

But none of these paintings is similar to the one in Madrid, which is a longer and less full oval [4]. Besides, what is more interesting even than the identity of this portrait is the charm of composition. Andrea del Sarto, remembering Leonardo and the Leonardo-inspired portraits by Raphael, has kept his own personal style; from certain aspects it recalls the seductive drawing of Correggio. A smile, lightly veiled with melancholy, lights up the regular features of this young woman which the painter, as in his other portraits, brings out against a neutral background; shadow falls on the neck and on the right cheek, whereas the rest of the face is in full light; the frank gaze of the eyes is an even more brilliant element. The chestnut hair is covered up with a piece of oriental material where the white is set off by maroon-coloured

---

[1] Baldinucci, *Notizie dei professori del disegno*, ed. Raualli, III, p. 66.

[2] Vasari, V, p. 28.

[3] Di Pietro, op. cit., p. 35 and following.

[4] The opinion of Mr. G. Frizonni, I capolavori della Pinacoteca di Madrid (*Archivio storico dell'Arte*, 1893, p. 313).

and black and yellow stripes, like the one Raphael painted in the *Virgin of the Chair*. The dress is ample and flowing, the bodice is very short with a deep-cut neck as in the *Nativity of the Virgin*. The arms drop heedlessly, but, in contrast to Leonardo and Raphael, Andrea has not completed them by a study of the hands. We find here, then, a little modified, the procedure that was dear to him. The features are less pronounced, more clearly drawn; he gives more gaiety to a woman's portrait and gives it an expression of softness. But he always tries to make it a study of the soul.

Thus with him the portrait evolved even more clearly towards a living analysis of the moral character of the model. Paintings like those in Madrid, the Pitti Palace and the National Gallery should please as much as those of Leonardo or Raphael. We do not know what has happened to some other portraits by this painter: the portrait of a Canon of Pisa, for instance, or of a certain Cosimo Lapi, of Baccio Bandinelli, and, in France, of the eldest son of Francis I[1]. Nevertheless he does not seem to have been, like other painters, overwhelmed with commissions of this type. He was above all a prolific painter of religious pictures, and in this respect he ended by falling into monotonous mannerisms. On the contrary, it is as a portrait painter (and he was only this occasionally) that he painted his greatest masterpieces, those which exercised the most felicitous influence on his contemporaries.

---

[1] Vasari, V, p. 30.

CHAPTER VI

THE DISCIPLES OF ANDREA DEL SARTO

Andrea del Sarto's influence on Franciabigio. The two *Portraits of a Man* in the Berlin Museum. Franciabigio's monotonous poses and facial expressions. Characteristics of Puligo's art. His "sfumato". Portraits in the Desborough Collection. Andrea del Sarto's art becomes mannerism with his disciple. The distortion of the spirit of Andrea's art. Antonio del Ceraiuolo. Bacchiacca; his *Portrait of a Woman* in Berlin.

The tendency which we noticed in Andrea del Sarto's work became more defined in the art of his two disciples: Franciabigio and Puligo. Perhaps neither of them carried the analysis of the human soul so far. Nevertheless they both painted pictures which for some years were thought to be not only by their master, but by Raphael himself. Their rather less pronounced personality remained interesting whenever they gave up the traditional grouping in religious pictures to look at a living face and to interpret its profound significance.

In contrast to Andrea del Sarto, Franciabigio seems to have been a portrait painter from choice. "He made", says Vasari, "a great many very beautiful portraits from life; working at everything with enthusiasm and application, only having a very modest idea of his own powers, he spent his whole life in Florence" [1]; he never wanted to leave the town and having linked up very early with Andrea del Sarto, his art developed along similar lines. It was not only the latter who inspired him, but also Albertinelli,who was his first master and whose influence can be traced in the *Annunciation* in Turin. Like Andrea del Sarto he had the greatest admiration for Leonardo and Raphael; and by temperament he remained completely outside the style of Michelangelo.

[1] Vasari, V, p. 198.

On many things, and particularly in portraiture, he held the same ideas as his friend. Faithful to a conception which was to become more and more defined, Franciabigio rarely reproduced in his religious or profane paintings known personalities. In a picture in the Uffizi,nevertheless, he painted a self-portrait in the guise of Saint John the Baptist [1]: this is a rare example because all his works are conceived in such a way that it is grouping and mass that predominate rather than individual heads. His Madonnas are classic: the one in Vienna, as far as the physical type is concerned, keeps very closely to Raphael's style.

Franciabigio is distinguished from Andrea del Sarto by the importance he gives to landscape in his portraits. Andrea preferred neutral backgrounds, whereas it is seldom that Franciabigio gets away from the style of Leonardo and Raphael in this respect; and if sometimes he deviates, it is obviously due to his master's influence.

Unfortunately we only have a few of Franciabigio's authentic portraits left; they are signed and dated: the *Young Man* in the Uffizi which bears the date 1514 and its author's monogram of the three letters F.R.C.; the one in the Kaiser Friedrich Museum, where, written on a sheet of paper by the desk is the inscription "1522 li 24 octobre" and a complicated monogram FRACR, which is an abridgment of his baptismal name Francesco di Cristofano as Milanese has established it [2]; and finally the one in the National Gallery where there is an inscription "Tar ublia chi bien eima" followed by the painter's monogram. It is then from these works, whose authenticity is indisputable, that we can assess Franciabigio's talent.

The picture in the Kaiser Friedrich Museum [3] is rather successful in places. The overcrowded effect of the foreground with the desk, the manu-

---

[1] Uffizi, *Madonna surrounded by Saints* — Cf. Vasari, V, p. 191 — Borghini, *Il Riposo*, 1584, p. 440. The work is signed F.R.C.: it was formerly above the high altar in the church of San Giobbe.

[2] Vasari, V, p. 189, On Franciabigio's monogram, Cf.Nagler, *Die Monogrammnisten*, 1860, II, p. 729.

[3] In the same museum there is a *Head of a Man* wearing a cap, against a black background, attributed by Crowe and Cavalcaselle (XI, 35) to Franciabigio, but it does not seem to be by him. A certain solidity in the construction of the head rather indicates a work of the Roman School, too poor nevertheless to be by Sebastiano del Piombo,as was first thought. Besides this picture has been very much repainted.

script and the sheets of paper, which is clumsily handled and spoils the effect of the whole, will have escaped no one's notice: the strong hands of the model, although confidently drawn, especially the left hand, are too much in evidence. But with these reservations the portrait shows originality of conception. The pose is almost full face, half of the head being in shadow; the modelling of the face is brought out without too great contrast, the right cheekbone is hardly pronounced, the chin stands out from the neck without sharpness; thus Franciabigio emphasises the lines of the face without bringing them out too violently, just as Andrea del Sarto does in his *Portrait of a Young Man* in the Pitti. But he adds an element which gives this head a profound life of its own by contrasting the side in shadow with that in the light; a contrast which loses its intensity as it reaches the brilliant tones of the shirt, which is a little too pronounced *(Plate XVII, fig. 36)*.

The colours in this portrait are often earthy and dull, indeed they help to give the face that sad and morose expression which has the same significance as in Andrea del Sarto's portraits of men. The effect sought after by the painter is completed by the background where the sky is reddened by the setting sun. Perhaps the painter had in mind a link between the melancholy of the model and the ending of the day. The background is flooded with a light that is seldom found in Florentine pictures. The countryside is of tender green merging into grey; all is peaceful; two people are walking towards some houses on the right; there are some slender trees, one of which is quite bare; these twisted dry branches are often seen in the backgrounds of Franciabigio's portraits and the vegetation is characteristic of many of his pictures [1].

It is quite natural to compare this portrait with another in the same room in the Kaiser Friedrich Museum which the catalogue also attributes to Franciabigio *(Plate XVIII, fig. 37)*. There is certainly some resemblance between the two. But how much more obvious are the differences! To begin

---

[1] Milanesi in a note to his edition of Vasari's *Lives* has made the suggestion that this portrait is of Matteo Sofferini, one of Franciabigio's intimate friends (V, 197). But there is nothing to support this identification and besides Sofferini is nothing but a name to us.

with, the pose of the second strikes us as being similar to the one of *Angiolo Doni*. The hair attractively frames the three-quarter-view face; Raphael liked this attitude which he thought gave more life to a portrait and which he used in the lovely drawing in the Ashmolean Museum at Oxford, which is undoubtedly a self-portrait. We must then give first place to Raphael's influence; an influence which in no way detracts from the originality of the painter.

If, as in Franciabigio's picture, the material of the shirt is brilliant, it is less obvious and besides produces a completely different effect; it is not contrasted here with cold tones, but harmonises with the more brilliant colours; the colour of the face is alive and the lines of the lids are emphasised by light touches of pink; the fair hair frames the face with rare distinction. Besides, the painter has not modelled the face in the same way as Franciabigio. Nothing here recalls the melancholy which Andrea and his friend liked to study. The lips are sensual, and disillusionment, almost morbidness, mixes with a love of life in the expression of the eyes.

If there is any resemblance between this portrait and the one of Angiolo Doni it is, as we have said, entirely formal: it can only be seen in the pose. Whereas Raphael's portraits always show a good moral balance, the *Young Man* in the Berlin Gallery has a decadent air; he is dressed in a sumptuous garment, decorated with dark grey fur, where the beautiful, flowing brocade takes its full value. Look particularly at the nervous hands, of an elegant and fine nobility, which the painter has made deeply expressive.

The landscape is more subtle than Franciabigio's, the slender trees with light foliage animate it and give it a strange life; it is a broken landscape without the moving romanticism of Leonardo, but it is original and unexpected. The magnificent graduation of tones of green in land and sky, separated by the light strip of rose violet of the twilight, is of delicate colouring. So many aesthetic elements which, apart from the idea of the setting sun, are lacking in Franciabigio's pictures!

There is in the last analysis an important fact. It is the skilful balance of this composition which is full of distinction. The artist has perfectly represented the nonchalant attitude and the detachment of a young and blasé patrician. Who is the artist? It is obviously not Franciabigio as in the museum catalogue; nothing reminds us of his backgrounds, his often dull colouring, his delicately but often stiffly drawn hands; he never attained a like mastery. M. Philipps suggests Rosso Fiorentino [1] but this suggestion—which is perhaps interesting—has no solid foundation. For there is nothing more rare than a portrait by Rosso Fiorentino; nevertheless we know that he produced a large number of them. "In Florentine houses", says Vasari, "there are many beautiful portraits and pictures by him" [2].

It is unfortunate that there are no other precise indications by which we can study Rosso's talent as a portrait painter [3], for he seems to have had modern and aesthetic preoccupations. The historian of the *Lives* tells us that he had a grave way of speaking and that he was an excellent musician; he "put a great deal of poetry into the composition of his figures" [4] and he liked subjects which were in some ways "extravagant". As well as this he gave his people "certe arie crudeli e disperate". He was therefore an original artist who could express his personality very vividly in his work.

However attractive Mr. Phillips' conjecture may be (which goes as far as to suggest it as a self-portrait of Rosso), it is better to recognise that there is nothing to serve us as a point of departure or as a point of comparison. The picture which bears the closest resemblance to the work in the Kaiser Friedrich Museum is the *Man with the Jewel* by Ridolfo Ghirlandaio; but as the expression is entirely different the resemblance is only superficial.

Franciabigio was already thirty years old when in 1514 he painted the *Man with the Gloves* [5]. The one in the National Gallery is almost contemporary with it: painted in 1516. There is a certain similarity between these two, the second being moreover of a softer technique. The *Man with the*

---

[1] Claude Philipps, *Il Rosso by himself* (*Burlington Magazine*, XX, p. 140).

[2] Vasari, V, p. 158.

[3] Mr. Berenson (*The Florentine Painters*, p. 180) believes he has found two of them: a *Portrait of a Young Woman* in Siena and a *Portrait of a Man in Red* seen in profile in the Academy in Venice.

[4] Vasari, V, p. 156.

[5] Uffizi (This picture was in the Pitti until 1919).

Gloves has certain features reminiscent of Raphael *(Plate XVII, fig. 35)*: but this influence is only general in its scope, for the expression is no longer the same. The face, with rather elegant features, is framed with dark gold hair. Here Franciabigio has sketched out a theme which he was to develop eight years later in his portrait in Berlin [1] contrasting one half of the face lighted up with the other half almost in shadow. In the picture in the National Gallery the thoughtful air is tempered by a disillusioned smile. The colours are less dull here; it is true that we do not see the original colours, as the picture has been much repainted. There is nothing unexpected in Franciabigio's composition, which is rather clumsy; the pose of the hands, which are drawn without emphasis, is unnatural. Nevertheless Franciabigio has succeeded in obtaining in this case, more than in the painting in the Kaiser Friedrich Museum, the unity of interest; and the whole effect is atmospheric and reminds us of Andrea del Sarto.

The landscape is treated with more delicacy than in the portrait in Berlin; the trees are slender, rather as Perugino liked to paint them; here are the bare, leafless trees which pleased Franciabigio so much; then the brownish tints of the hills and houses which can be seen softening into blue and ending by losing themselves in the blue of the sky. With Franciabigio then the background relieves the weakness of the foreground; without this delicate countryside the *Young Man with the Gloves*, with rather vacant eyes, would be a mediocre work.

And this is even more true of *The Knight of Malta* in the National Gallery. Since this picture, before going to London, formed part of the Fuller Maitland Collection, its owner considered it to be by Raphael, on the grounds that it resembled the *Young Man leaning on a Parapet* in the Louvre, which many critics regarded at that time as an authentic work of the Roman painter. Well, nothing is less certain than this last conjecture; it would have been better to assess them inversely; the picture in the Louvre is in many ways like the

---

[1] The portrait in Berlin was one of his last works. According to Vasari, Franciabigio died in 1524 at the age of 42.

one in London and the one in Florence, and as these two latter are by Franciabigio it is very likely that the first is by him as well.

The Knight of Malta keeps rather more closely to the conception of the *Man with the Gloves:* the dark cap and costume with the pronounced white line of the shirt; the face, rather weakly modelled; the landscape, with its large trees, stretches out to form a strip of blue. Franciabigio has given his model the same expression as in the portrait in the Uffizi, a little sadder perhaps, but a sadness which the inscription "Tar ublia chi bien eima" explains.

But one does not feel with this artist the same power of innovation as one does with Andrea del Sarto; of a less inventive mind, he is content to imitate the poses of Raphael's models, being attracted as well by the mysterious charm of some of Andrea's faces [1], especially the *Young Man* in the Pitti where he did not think of adopting a different formula. The fashion was then for dreaming faces; and he conformed to it. His works give the impression that his originality has been diminished by this.

Nevertheless the portrait in the Louvre is more successfully approached. It is really a fortunate combination of the portraits in Berlin, Florence and London; we find here the principal elements of Franciabigio's art. The influence of the *Mona Lisa* is at least as obvious as that of Raphael: it is especially noticeable in the treatment of the hands, which by their drawing are similar to those of the *Young Man with the Gloves;* but their pose is more natural, Leonardo having fortunately on this occasion influenced the artist. The modelling of the face recalls the pictures in the Uffizi and in Berlin; the colours are dull and without brilliance, as so often happens with Franciabigio; there are finally in the landscape and the sky passages which are worthy of him; we find here the bare tree which he loved to draw. One might say that it was by a pupil of Raphael who, having admired the portrait of the *Mona Lisa* had also seen the one of a *Young Man* in the Pitti by Andrea

---

[1] In a portrait in the Benson Collection which represents an artist painting, Franciabigio scarcely modifies the attitude of *The Sculptor* in the National Gallery (*Catalogue of Italian pictures collected by Robert and Evelyn Benson,* 1914, p. 71).

Puligo.

38. *Portrait of a Young Man. (Pitti Palace)*
39. *Portrait of Pietro Carnesecchi. (Uffizi)*

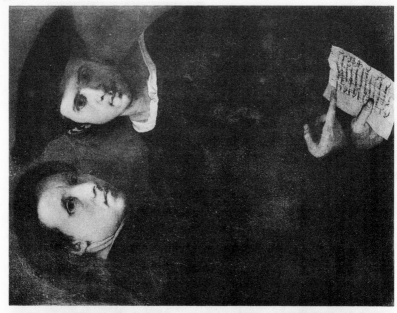

Pontormo.

40. *Portrait of an Engraver.* (Louvre)

41. *Portrait of Two Friends.* (Paolo Guicciardini Collection, Florence)

del Sarto. The conclusion would seem to be that it is the most characteristic and best composed work of Franciabigio, one in which the artist has expressed with the finest sensitivity the tendencies of his art.

This picture is of almost the same period as those in the Uffizi and the National Gallery; it has even a more attractive softness. The one in the Kaiser Friedrich Museum is in contrast of a harder technique and of a less harmonious presentation; to explain this difference we must not forget that Franciabigio was familiar with Dürer's engravings, which were then in circulation in Italy, and influenced the technique of some artists to the extent of making it less gracious and more sharply in contrast [1].

Franciabigio understood very well how to translate faithfully and with a refined distinction the state of mind of certain people of his time, who, thinking of the vanity of worldly things, regarded them with detachment and complete scepticism. It is in his portraits as in some of Andrea del Sarto's that we see again the deep intensity of this "mal de siècle" which so often goes with troublous times. Some of his drawings are inspired by the same spirit; they are in a florid style, sometimes uncertain, but always sensitive and delicate [2]. Nevertheless the faces have not here the same charm as in his paintings; in contrast the touch of vitality is here more spontaneous and is brought out with a less uniform impression.

As a generalisation Franciabigio varies his poses very little; his portraits are nearly always painted full face, half length and have a rather vague expression. The one in the Gallery at Windsor was executed on these principles. It is probably this work Vasari refers to as the portrait which Franciabigio made of "fatorre (Bailiff) de Pier Francesco dei Medici" in the palace of St. Geronimo at Fiesole. This *Young Farmer*, in a similar pose to that of the *Young Man* in Berlin, is heavier, more stocky, he is lost in the dark colours across which shines the white of the shirt; on a stone parapet can be seen the "palle

---

[1] Vasari, p. 197.

[2] In the example in the Wicar de Lille Museum, which has something frank and direct about it, the attribution to Franciabigio is much more likely than the conjecture of Oskar Fischel who assigns it to Raphael, but nothing in this work recalls Raphael's impeccable certainty of drawing (*Raffaels Zeichnungen*, II, 69, p. 91).

d'oro", the arms of the Medicis. This is a kind of fantasy of Franciabigio's, one of those studio follies which painters liked to produce, something in character, meant to impress contemporaries, and it did impress them, because it is one of the few portraits by Franciabigio to which Vasari refers [1]. As for the *Portrait of a Man* in the Lichtenstein Gallery which is dated 1517 [2], it adds nothing to that which those in the Louvre and the Uffizi teach us. As in the case of the *Bailiff* in Windsor Castle it appears against a neutral background; we find again Franciabigio's range of colours: the sober greys, the browns, the greens; the face has the arch of the brows very pronounced and treated in chiaroscuro. This portrait, although undoubtedly the work of Franciabigio (besides it bears his monogram), is one of the least characteristic. It also shows how stylised Franciabigio's art was; the pose of his models is set, almost stereotyped: they have nothing of the vivacity with which the *Sculptor* of Andrea del Sarto in the National Gallery looks at the spectator [3].

Andrea del Sarto's influence was felt even more strongly by Domenico Puligo than by Franciabigio. The work of master and pupil have often been confused; it is for this reason that a *Magdalene* in the Borghese Gallery, Rome, which is certainly by Puligo has for a long time been attributed to Andrea del Sarto. Nevertheless it is easy to distinguish between the work of the two artists, Puligo's drawing being softer and the expression of the face less individual. Vasari has clearly defined the character of his art, and his information

---

[1] Cf. *La Collection Royal des peintures de S. M. Edouard VII, Château de Windsor*, pl. LXIV.

[2] W. Bode, *Die fürstliche Liechtensteinsche Galerie in Wien*, p. 73.

[3] We must also mention a portrait in the Corsini Gallery, Rome, representing a man of already advanced years, turning the pages of a book, recalling in his pose the *Bailiff* of Pier Francesco de Medici. But here the resemblance ends and if we mention it it is on the authority of Adolfo Venturi, who attributes it to Franciabigio (*La Galerie Nationale*, II, 116); the construction of the face has no resemblance to Franciabigio's technique, or the landscape composed of trees in the mass which is very far removed from the charming and light countryside such as we find in the background of most of Franciabigio's portraits. This picture of a fat man of florid aspect, pleased with life, does not even seem to be a Florentine work, and the attribution to Garofalo would seem more probable than the former conjecture.

helps us to recognise his works[1]: he was "gracious in colouring", he painted softly with no harshness, he thought that the best way to give grace and relief to his paintings was to make the distance appear as though bathed in mist; his faces with their vague contours have an air and a colour meant to please; he never modified this way of painting and "he was much esteemed for it as long as he lived"[2].

Thus it is not surprising that one Puligo resembles another. In short his technique is inherited from Andrea del Sarto. In Ridolfo Ghirlandaio's studio, where he spent some time during his youth, he had certainly not yet found himself; it was only when he knew Andrea that he began to use an ideal feminine type, closely related to that of his new master. It seems that he was on very intimate terms with the latter, who gave him much advice and corrected his sketches and paintings: Andrea's influence was complete and Puligo did not come under any other.

Among Florentine painters of the first half of the sixteenth century he is unique. He was not ambitious for glory but simply wanted to earn his living in a pleasant way[3]; for he loved the company of musicians and courtesans. Bored with the pleasures of life, he understood the decadence and morbid spirit of society of his time and he knew how to express, in perhaps a more direct manner, the melancholy and disillusioned dreams which tormented some of the models of Andrea del Sarto and Franciabigio.

Vasari tells us that during his apprenticeship in Ridolfo Ghirlandaio's studio he painted many portraits, some of which went abroad. He continued in this way and became a fashionable portrait painter, which proves once more that his contemporaries liked these faces, where the life of the soul presented itself veiled in a certain sadness. One of his patrons was Pietro Carnesecchi, a curious type of young Florentine of the period, of whom he has left us a charming portrait in a picture which was for a long time attributed to Andrea del Sarto (Plate XIX, fig. 39). Well, there is not only Vasari's text, which is

---

[1] Vasari, IV, p. 463—464.

[2] Cf. also R. Borghini, Il Riposo, 1584, p. 395. "Il suo dipignere fu con dolcezza non molto tinto, ma come da una certa nebbia velato con grazia e relievo."

[3] Vasari, IV, p. 466-7.

catagorical; these is also the striking resemblance between this portrait and the features of a young man in the foreground of Vasari's fresco where Hyppolitus de Medici is raised to the dignity of a Cardinal: it is, says Vasari, in his *Ragionamenti*, Pietro Carnesecchi, former secretary of Clement VII, which he had painted when he was very young [1].

Pietro Carnesecchi was born in 1508; he was then nineteen years old when Puligo died [2]. So it was in fact the face of an adolescent which he had drawn. According to what we know he was attractive and gracious, "dotto e gentile" says Claudio Tolomei, slim of figure with an almost feminine bearing and with a sickly complexion [3]. This young man of poor health and very cultured mind, who perished tragically because he clung to heretical doctrines, lives again graciously in Puligo's painting. The construction of the face obviously resembles the method Andrea del Sarto liked, not entirely three quarters, not entirely full face, but the play of shadows is quite different: they are light and give softness to the chin. Besides the understanding of colour is very individual, the yellow of the hair, the rose of the lips—very pure rose—and the little touch of violet which appears very discreetly on the chest which is draped in a dark coat, are charming harmonies. There is no clashing of colours and the tones are very delicate and enveloped in the "sfumato" which Andrea del Sarto taught his pupil and which the latter treated with a real delicacy of touch.

Painted at the end of his life, and representing perhaps the most typical of Puligo's faces, this picture is one where the technical method and the character of the model harmonise perfectly; his art is then an effeminate art, his portraits are without vigour or brilliance, but they give delight by their subtle charm.

Vasari only mentions one other portrait besides the one of Pietro Carnesecchi. "Puligo", says he, "painted the Florentine Barbara, famous courtesan

---

[1] Vasari, *Ragionamenti*. . . . (Milanesi ed.) VIII, 167.
[2] According to Vasari Puligo was fifty-two when he died in 1527.
[3] Agnostini, *Pietro Carnesecchi e il movimento valdesiano*, 1899, p. 53.

of the time, very handsome and much loved for her beauty, her distinguished manners, and also because she was a good musician and sang divinely". In this picture he must have wanted to symbolise his own tastes and way of living where music and love had great importance and which recalls a little Giorgione's life in Venice. According to Raffaello Borghini this picture must have undergone some modifications during his lifetime; its owner, a certain Giovanni Battista Deti, had had the pages of music which the model was turning over changed into the emblem of Santa Lucia [1].

Now in Lady Desborough's Collection at Panshanger, Mr. Carlo Gamba says he has found the portrait of the courtesan Barbara [2]. Because of its resemblance to the pose of Lucrezia del Fede in Berlin, Crowe and Cavalcaselle had attributed it to Andrea del Sarto [3]. But in its fundamental handling of technique it resembles that of Pietro Carnesecchi: the drawing is in no way pronounced and loses itself in the soft contours; the shading is delicately graduated in the manner of Puligo and the landscape has not the same precision as in Andrea del Sarto's and Franciabigio's pictures. Is it, as Mr. Gamba says, Barbara's face? It is an attractive conjecture; the model, who has a cold gaze, a tight mouth and a haughty air, turns over a sheet of music; not far from her a Petrach lies open. But then what becomes of Raffaello Borghini's statement where the whim of a collector had changed the attributes of the musician's craft? Perhaps they cleaned the picture and removed Santa Lucia's emblems.

Whether this identification is certain or not, it is interesting to see Puligo trying to paint the features of a woman of almost masculine type; he who also knew how to study the feminine aspect of a boy's adolescent face. One of the most fortunate passages is the grace of the delicate and slender hands. It is natural to compare them with a portrait in the same Desborough Collection, placed in the catalogue under the name of Pastore di San Marco [4].

---

[1] R. Borghini, Il Riposo, p. 396.
[2] C. Gamba, Di acuni ritratti del Puligo (Rivista d'arte, Jan.-Feb., 1900).
[3] Crowe and Cavalcaselle, XI, p. 145.
[4] Crowe and Cavalcaselle attribute it to Andrea (XL, p. 146).

Let us consider the shape of the drooping hand; it is almost identical in structure and movement with the left hand in the so-called portrait of Barbara. Pastore's clothes recall those of the *Bailiff* in Windsor Castle. The picture is well preserved, the colours still fresh, subdued and delicate, the modelling of the face being a little more emphasised than in the portraits in the Uffizi and the Desborough Collections, but the "sfumato" being just as expressive. The face is comely, with its serious and grave expression, which tempers a lightly suggested smile. It lacks perhaps the alluring quality of Carnesecchi, but Puligo has tried to give it a more masculine, more energetic expression, succeeding up to a certain point, although his technique is more suitable to other characters and other faces.

In a portrait in the Pitti of the same tonality, the expression is even more grave than that of Pietro Carnesecchi, it is a charming young head with fair hair, and although the face is a little less refined it may be of the same person *(Plate XIX, fig. 38)*. The background resembles that in the Pastore di San Marco, plain grey on which the shadow of the model falls. The hands stand out against an ample black coat; they are perhaps without elegance, but strike a brilliant note of light. For all his monotony Puligo makes the discoveries of a real artist, and this beautiful splash of white becomes the original note in the picture.

There is less charm and a less adaptable handling in another painting in the Desborough Collection which is supposed to be a self-portrait of Andrea del Sarto, although the face is entirely different and the technique is exactly that of Puligo's. The face is amorphous and without life, the pose stiff and awkward; the hands are rather ineffectively modelled and have not Puligo's usual delicacy. It seems rather more like a studio work; and yet the text of the letter on the table is very clear and does not allow any doubt "8 dicembre Mastro Domenico assai mi chiamoso (disfat) to verso di voi avendo ... strato propinquo ingegno per dimostrarmi qual proprio sono ... tanto obrigato 1523 Andrea". The work is dated and this "Mastro Domenico" which gives such satisfaction can obviously only be Domenico Puligo.

In a final analysis all the portraits we have of Puligo show a strong family likeness[1], their personality is translated into a melancholy smile of a certain feeling of gravity. Their author could not, like Puligo, leave his own ineradicable stamp on the fundamental characteristics of a face. The "sfumato" of Andrea del Sarto becomes with him a sort of formula, and in spite of their charm the faces he has painted only seem to express themselves in a rather artificial way. His capacity is limited and his work lacks variety.

Andrea del Sarto's influence ended then in impersonal mannerism. Vasari tells us the names of other artists who were his pupils at the same time as being important portrait painters: Antonio del Ceraiuolo, for example, about whom we have no precise data and to whom is attributed without great certainty a drawing in the Uffizi. After having worked under the direction of Lorenzo di Credi, he became the friend of Puligo in Ridolfo Ghirlandaio's studio. He excelled, says Vasari, in giving life to portraits; he made remarkable likenesses; but their drawing was not sure and often shows distortions almost amounting to caricature[2].

Now we sometimes find portraits where Andrea's influence or that of his school is apparent but which, although having a certain physical life, lack charm of colour and expression: such as two paintings of women in the Pitti. One has a badly constructed face and listless eyes; the other, who is holding a missal in the left hand, has curved lips and a rather distorted nose (according to Vasari, Ceraiuolo used to draw noses and lips rather badly). They are perhaps two portraits by a studio friend of Puligo's; but they would seem to give a rather indifferent idea of his lack of distinction and awkward handling.

It is again in the circle of Andrea del Sarto and Franciabigio that an interesting artist, Bacchiacca, appears who was fundamentally only a reflection of different masters he had studied or known. He was to begin with a pupil of Perugino's, as his *Christ Preaching* indicates in Christ Church, Oxford.

---

[1] Among the known portraits which have the characteristics of Puligo's art we must also mention a portrait of a prelate, a little soft in technique, which is in Naples and which used to be attributed to Andrea del Sarto. Mr. de Rinaldis prudently says that it is of the sixteenth-century Florentine school (*Pinacoteca del Museo Nazionale di Napoli*, 1911, p. 41).

[2] Vasari, IV, p. 463.

Then he painted in the manner of Andrea del Sarto or Franciabigio[1], imitated even Michelangelo and Dürer; thus a painter's style was formed which only shows individuality in a few portraits; they are interesting to study because they show the decadence of what had been the ideal of Leonardo and Andrea del Sarto and sometimes give us the effect of caricatures of powerful and well-conceived works.

Vasari does not mention any of his painted portraits. Nevertheless comparison with his other works helps us to discover some of them. Let us consider the *Scenes from the History of Joseph* in the Borghese Gallery, which served to decorate that famous room of Pier Francesco Borgherini where the most celebrated artists of the period worked. The tones have no charm; blue and a crude green predominate; the colours are flat and without brilliance; the hands are elongated and from the point of view of structure have a slight similarity with Puligo's. The landscape is treated without imagination; it is even almost shapeless; the trees are crudely drawn, placed at random over the hills; the painter takes pleasure in adding architectural features and a scene of some sort.

This is the kind of landscape in the background of a portrait in the Cassel Museum, representing an old man with very pronounced wrinkles, who gently bends his head. A work of youth no doubt; the features here are again very clearly drawn, a little in the style of Ridolfo Ghirlandaio. This portrait seems to have a symbolic value: a skull, an hour glass and in the background the triumph of death. This is how deep feelings are expressed by an artist with neither soul nor talent.

When Bacchiacca was guided by Andrea del Sarto his contours became less defined, he painted his *History of Saint Joseph* in this way. What never seemed to alter was his colour, which always remained crude. The *Magdalene* in the Pitti gives us a good idea of this clumsy art; the head is elongated, the chin narrow, the hollows of the cheeks very pronounced; the green of the background and the red velvet which covers the sleeves are jarring in their harshness. A tiny little picture in the Berlin Museum of a *Woman*

---

[1] Vasari, VI, p. 455.

Stroking a Cat resembles this *Magdalene*; there is a fleeting vision of Leonardo's and Raphael's art, but it is only diffused and vague. The hands are treated roughly, the colours lack distinction and depth; the puffed sleeves still further enlarge the breadth of the shoulders thus making the body appear out of proportion with the head. Compared with the works which inspired it, this picture is almost a caricature. There is nothing left of the poetry of Andrea del Sarto or Franciabigio, nor of the charm of Puligo. Bacchiacca clumsily interpreted the art of these two painters; there are obvious traces of Dürer's style in his work and there is something Germanic about the bearing of his models.

His rather heavy handling is to be found again in certain works of the beginning of the sixteenth century, which must certainly be attributed to him. There is no doubt that the *Young Woman with a Necklace*, a drawing in the Uffizi thought to be by Sodoma and even Leonardo, is really by Bacchiacca [1]. The hands are drawn in exactly the same way as in the *Portrait of a Woman* in Berlin; the contours of the face lack elegance and harmony; Mona Lisa's smile is changed into an ugly grin. It is surprising that in front of such a second-rate work anyone could think of the great Florentine. Giovanni Morelli was rightly inspired when he thought (even with reservations) of the name of Bacchiacca.

Let us also consider the portrait in the Corsini Gallery in Florence of a *Young Man* represented standing by the statue of the *Boy with the Thorn* [2]. The crude green of the landscape, the love of odds and ends, the woolly drawing of the hands and face, the expressionless head, the awkward pose, are all elements of Bacchiacca's style assembled in one portrait, which is doubtless one of his last works and where can be seen on this occasion an unskilful imitation of Pontormo and Bronzino. Thus Bacchiacca never un-

---

[1] Cf. G. Morelli, *Della pittura Italiana*, 1897, p. 107. Berenson (*The Drawings...*, II, 137) attributes it to Pontormo, who never drew such rough hands nor a face so lacking in character. Luzio (*La Galleria dei Gonzago venduta all'Inghilterra nel 1627-1628*, 1913, p. 236) says it is Isabella d'Este by Leonardo: a completely false conjecture.

[2] The picture is dated 1540; it is attributed wrongly to Bronzino by Mr. Schulze, *Die Werke Angelo Bronzinos*, 1911, p. IX.

derstood how to assimilate the spirit of those who influenced him and he could only produce gross travesties of the work of others.

Leonardo's theories which so successfully inspired painters of melancholy were no longer understood. Their feeling was distorted and the interest lost. Portraiture evolved slowly towards a different conception. Fortunately Pontormo was about to look for new formulas, which would frequently reveal Michelangelo's influence; it is hard to find anything more interesting than the accomplishment of this original and sincere painter who succeeded in leaving his mark on the history of Florentine painting in so vigorous and assertive a manner.

CHAPTER VII

ANDREA DEL SARTO'S INFLUENCE ON
MICHELANGELO PONTORMO

Andrea del Sarto's influence on Pontormo's first portrait. *The Engraver* in the Louvre. The portrait of Cosimo the Elder. Its importance. The study of facial character. Portraits of his maturity. *The Adolescent* in the museum at Lucca. *Alexander de Medici* in the Johnson Collection. Portraits of women. The beauty of costume. *The Adolescent* in the Trivulzio Collection. The influence of Michelangelo and Sebastiano del Piombo on Pontormo. *The Cardinal* in the Borghese Gallery.

Pontormo had an original nature; left an orphan when young, he had no restraining influence when his character was forming; while still young he followed a vocation which seemed to manifest itself very early and all the more naturally because he was the son of a painter. "His *Annunciation*", says Vasari, "must have astonished Raphael before the latter's departure for Rome"; if this fact be true it is the proof of an extraordinary precocity [1]. Now it is important to know that Pontormo was tormented while so young by the demon of painting. Apprenticed to Mariotto Albertinelli, he does not seem to have stayed there long; after that he studied under Piero di Cosimo and Andrea del Sarto. These were the first influences he felt at the same time as that of Fra Bartolommeo and to a lesser degree that of Leonardo. To begin with, his style showed a great variety of tendencies, which does not in this case indicate a malleable temperament but rather a seeker, an artist already very inquisitive and desirous of knowing everything and gathering from other people ideas which would most easily intensify his personal gifts.

He is distinguished by a certain independence of thought added to a strong

---

[1] Raphael having left Florence for Rome in 1508,   Pontormo, born in 1494, was hardly fourteen years old.

independence of character. Vasari, who was a little astonished at his habits, describes him as a strange man caring little for the company of his contemporaries, living in a house so simple as to be almost a hut. He was very shy; and although he had quite a number of friends and pupils and was very much appreciated by them he always liked the solitude which he used to find "a faithful friend to study" and which brought him a natural melancholy. It is not surprising then if in some of his portraits certain aspects of his troubled temperament are expressed.

In the evolution of his talent there was an early period which did not last very long when he came under the influence of Andrea del Sarto. Being himself also commissioned to decorate the cloisters of the Annunziata, he was inspired by the famous scenes in the history of Saint Philip, which pleased him inordinately. According to Vasari, it was from the teaching of Andrea that he so rapidly acquired his remarkable craftsmanship. *The Visitation* in the Annunziata is in fact partly painted in the spirit of Andrea del Sarto; it is composed with skill, and among his feminine types is one which is very similar to the portrait of Lucrezia del Fede; the pose of several of the figures has a brilliance and freedom which does not fail to recall Michelangelo, whose *Battle of Cascina* Pontormo copied. There is also expressed that fertility of mind, that inventive faculty which astounded his master and apparently must have caused him a certain bitterness, almost jealousy.

From this early period come the portraits where his individuality is already established but where nevertheless he has not entirely broken away from Andrea del Sarto's influence. From this point of view the most interesting is perhaps *The Engraver* in the Louvre *(Plate XX, fig. 40)*. The figure represented is ready to work on the jewel which is shown beside him on a table; it is then really the portrait of an engraver and not, as so often happened at that time, that of a model taking up the appropriate pose; but as for identifying it as Giovanni delle Corniole, a contemporary of Pontormo, it is pure conjecture whose importance even Villot himself does not stress [1].

---

[1] F. Villot, *Notice des tableaux exposés dans les Galeries du Musée Imperial du Louvre*, 1858, 1st part, p. 86.

The colours have darkened very much; the dress and the background are today almost the same colour; but in spite of these changes it is easy to find the source of this work. Pontormo was inspired by *The Sculptor* of Andrea del Sarto, of which we have seen a replica of a sort by Franciabigio in the Benson Collection. The theme is identical; the face full view whereas the body is threequarters; the model looks at us with keen attention; and, it is here that the original gift of the artist is expressed; the eye socket is already executed in an individual manner: it is round rather than elliptical in shape and gives the gaze a strange expression. This anatomical peculiarity was to remain one of the most interesting elements in his portraits; it animates the faces and gives them a very personal character, which lends even fuller value to the contrast between the parts in light and those in shadow. If finally we look at the drawing of the right hand, we see it is firm and vigorous; the pads of flesh are heavily modelled; it is the same technique that Pontormo used in the *Madonna Surrounded with Saints* in the Church of San Michele Visdomini in Florence.

It is then almost certain that we have here one of Pontormo's earliest portraits, at any rate the earliest of those which still exist. It is a new interpretation of a theme which had attracted Andrea del Sarto; beginning with an identical pose, the artist imparts into the model's eyes the enthusiasm of youth. But his melancholy is not the same as that of Andrea del Sarto or Franciabigio; it has a new essence; it is accompanied by fever and enthusiasm for work. It is really Pontormo's own character coming out as Vasari describes it: "quite young he was already melancholy and solitary". His curiosity, open on to the universe and ready to seize all originality of feeling or movement, can be seen in these eyes.

Of the same date is a *Portrait of a Woman* in the Uffizi, formerly attributed to Andrea del Sarto although it shows all the characteristics of the nascent talent of Pontormo. The young woman is seated three-quarter view; she takes the pose which since the the time of *Mona Lisa* is more or less consecrated to feminine portraits; it also bears a resemblance to the Andrea del Sarto in Madrid. But the fullness of the drawing of the sleeves, the shoulders and the head is striking; there is besides less intensity in the brilliance of the colours; the tones are rather washed out: the greens are paler than with Andrea; the eyes are rounded and almost like those in the Louvre portrait, and the hands are of a similar structure; the gaze is troubled; the upper part of the face is saddened by it whereas the lips suggest a smile which recalls the *Mona Lisa* or *Lucrezia del Fede*.

Such is the starting point of Pontormo's art in portraiture as in his other works; it has the attributes of the work of Andrea del Sarto, had he drawn forms more powerfully and analysed not the gravity of melancholy, but the troubles of mind and heart. The two portraits in the Louvre and the Uffizi are thus of very great interest because they establish for us the exact moment when Pontormo began to express his own individuality in a new way.

In the catalogue of Pontormo's paintings drawn up by Mr. Clapp, which is meant to be quite complete, there is no mention even among the paintings of doubtful attribution of the *Portrait of a Musician* in the Uffizi [1], whose authenticity is however almost certain. Note to begin with that we must undoubtedly give the same value as that of *The Sculptor* or *Medal Maker* which were often given because of the pose and setting of the figures. This music book is undoubtedly only there to make the pose look more natural; it may also indicate the tastes of the model. Now, in studying the face of this dilettante one is struck by its technical resemblance to *The Engraver* in the Louvre. Besides, it has suffered from the same changes; it is very much blackened and the colours of the flesh have become almost livid. It was painted at a time when the young Pontormo in his indefatigable curiosity of mind might have used certain of the chemical mixtures so dear to Leonardo da Vinci. In spite of this the portrait is still a beautiful work; Pontormo's style is recognisable in the shape of the eyes, which look out with infinite sadness from a face where the mouth is folded in bitterness. Here the touch of melancholy is more moving than in an Andrea del Sarto and more emphasised than in *The Engraver*.

---

[1] Attributed by the 1920 catalogue to Andrea del Sarto and thought to be the portrait of the musician Francesco dell'Aiolle.

This picture, like the others, shows us a Pontormo who with invariable regularity places his heads against a neutral background to make the hands and the character of the face stand out. He broke away then from Leonardo's influence much more completely than from Andrea del Sarto's. Being interested only in human beauty, muscular power, in the grace or violence of movement, his conception of painting was the same as Michelangelo's; he found himself being more and more drawn towards the creator of the cartoon of the *Battle of Cascina*. By temperament he was to remain most often faithful to the Michelangelo principle which maintained that to paint a landscape was a task unworthy of a great painter [1]. Also, we shall see the luminous and colourful landscape disappearing entirely from portraits influenced by Pontormo. From this time onwards the background was to be neutral and cold, showing a more pronounced taste for the actual face. There was no more divergence from this. It was the features only that had to be studied and also the pose, the natural attitude. Furthermore, conventional or familiar surroundings were sometimes added. This shows a similarity with the modern idea; perhaps what was lost in the way of poetry was gained in power of analysis. We have already noticed this tendency with Raphael while he was in Rome; it was also apparent in Andrea del Sarto's work. With Pontormo it became a rule from which he was never to depart. From this point of view Leonardism was completely dead for him.

When he finished the *Visitation* in the Annunziata (1516) Pontormo was already well known; commissions flowed in; he worked with enthusiasm; he had his helpers and among them was Giovanni Antonio Lappoli, native of Arezzo, whose biography Vasari wrote. This Lappoli one day painted his own portrait by means of a mirror; but his master, not thinking it a sufficiently good likeness, corrected it for him, to such an extent and so well that he perfected it and gave it a real vivacity of expression. In Vasari's time this

---

[1] Cf. Francisco de Hollanda, *Quatre dialogues sur la peinture* (translated into French, 1911, p. 28—29).

portrait was still in the possession of Lappoli's heirs [1] but it was no longer there in Bottari's time and today we do not know where it is. Vasari's account shows what careful attention Pontormo paid to getting a resemblance and the effect of life; if he corrected one of his students' works it was in order to give it the touch of truth which was missing.

In the years which followed the completion of the *Visitation*, that is, between 1516 and 1520, "he painted", says Vasari, "two of his intimate friends in the same picture". One was the son-in-law of Becuccio "bicchieralo" and Vasari has forgotten the name of the other; "it's of no importance", he adds very rightly, "it is sufficient to know that it is by Pontormo's hand" [2]. These are undoubtedly the *Two Friends* in the collection of Count Paolo Guicciardini in Florence; One is shown three-quarters view and is holding what seems to be a page of Latin verse; the other is full face: the two heads stand out against a dark background and above black clothes the artist has succeeded in bringing out the relief of the features by crisp drawing, which emphasise the gaze of the eyes from their deep sockets (*Plate XX, fig. 41*). The expression of the heads is very beautiful and the whole of a deep seriousness. The painter has here concentrated his skill on studying character. If in his drawings, which are among the most beautiful in the Florentine school, he is haunted by originality of movement, its vigour or its suppleness, in his portraits it is the individuality of the face which holds his attention.

According to Vasari it was some time after he finished this double portrait that he painted *Cosimo the Elder*. Between times he had worked, as did most great painters of his time, in the decoration of the nuptial chamber of Pier Francesco Bogherini. "He painted", says Vasari, "for Goro de Pistoia who was then secretary to the Medicis, the Magnificent *Cosimo the Elder*"; and he painted it almost knee-length; it is a work really deserving of praise (*Plate XXI, fig. 42*). In Vasari's time this *Cosimo the Elder* belonged to the son of Octavian de Medici, Alexander, who became Pope under the title of Leo

---

[1] Vasari, VI, p. 259.
[2] Vasari, VI, p. 260.

42. Pontormo. *Portrait of Cosimo the Elder.* (Uffizi)

Pontormo.

43. *Portrait of a Young Man.* (Pinacoteca, Lucca)

44. *Head of a Young Woman.* (Uffizi)

XI; In the eighteenth century it was transferred from the Uffizi to the cell of the Monastery of San Marco,which Cosimo used to take so much pleasure in visiting. Then in 1912 it was brought back to the Uffizi and an indifferent copy left in its place at San Marco.

In spite of certain obvious faults this portrait remains one of the master-pieces of Pontormo's youth. The red coat lined with black fur is undoubt-edly rather disagreeable to the eye, so are the branches with bright green leaves round which is entwined the inscription from Virgil,"Uno avulso non deficit alter". In general Pontormo's colour lacks charm, and on this occasion it is very crude and spoils the powerful expression of the face. This picture is rather an exception among his works; posed in profile it recalls by this pose the type of portrait usual before the time of Botticelli. It is quite natural, because in order to paint this portrait Pontormo had to make use of infor-mation from medals of Cosimo. We must not forget that it was at the request of Goro Gheri,the secretary of Lorenzo de Medici,that he painted this por-trait, and he must most certainly have given Pontormo all the necessary documentations from his master's collection [1]. The fact that Pontormo had painted this portrait from a medal allows us to measure exactly the distance which separates such a profile from those we are accustomed to find in the fifteenth century. In the fifteenth century,the face was drawn very precisely against a landscape or a neutral background; it was wonderful from the point of view of craftsmanship but fixed in expression; on occasions some grace was expressed and often much coldness. Now with Pontormo the idea is quite different. If he gives us a profile portrait it was from necessity, because he had to draw his inspiration regarding the features from the model that was given him. But the body is facing us; Cosimo is seated; his hands are very much emphasised and become an essential element in the picture: the hands are very powerfully drawn, as becomes a conscientious pupil of Michelangelo; certain portions such as the joint of the forefinger are rather distorted,which

[1] Cf. Trapesnikoff, *Die Porträtdarstellungen der Mediceer des XV. Jahrhunderts*, 1909, p. 2 L. — A. Heiss, *Les médailleurs de la Renaissance,Florence et les Florentins de XVe au XVIIIe siècle*, 1st part, 1891. — A. Armand, *Les médailleurs italiens des XVe et XVIe siècles*, 1883—1887, vol. II, p. 23—24.

makes the whole effect more expressive. Besides Pontormo has found means of bringing life to the chill profile of the medal, emphasising the projections and hollows of the face, making it look thin and almost emaciated. By stressing the cheek bones and the lobe of the ear, he has given a striking air of overwhelming sadness to this face, rendered ugly by the awkward curve of the nose and the prominence of the lower lip. He has drawn the eye socket exactly as in his full-face portraits; it is deep and the gaze has something sinister about it. Cosimo had reached that period in his life when the ills of the body and moral suffering were overwhelming him.

The imagination of the painter sees him almost as Machiavelli described him to us in the years which preceded his death. The death of his favourite son, John, had deeply affected him; and he saw his other son Piero stricken in health and ill-suited to govern the state. As for Cosimo, gradually conscious of his increasing infirmity, he could no longer direct affairs with the same enthusiasm as formerly; at times even he was assailed with doubts as to the value of his political work [1]. It is of this Cosimo, melancholy and sickly, that Pontormo has left us an impressive portrait.

Actually it is not in this manner that he was painted by Bronzino, who had to derive inspiration from medals. The portrait he left of him in the Medici series in the Uffizi shows a man who has still plenty of intellectual health and lively power; the face is less troubled and the elements which make the face ugly with Pontormo are scarcely indicated by Bronzino. Pontormo has purposely exaggerated everything which could emphasise the idea of physical and moral suffering. In the features he has tried to express those which will give the sensibility and depth of character of the face. It is an interpretation of the ego of the model painted in a spirit of affliction. Even if it is not a good likeness it gives the portrait a life and deep unity. This Cosimo the Elder makes us think of Michelangelo, broken and old in the Chaix d'Est-Ange Collection. He belongs to the race of great fighters who have worn themselves out in a life of activity. We can understand in

---

[1] Cf. Machiavelli, *Istorie fiorentino*, libro VII, 4–7: "tutte queste cose gli fecere passare gli ultimi tempi della sua vita inquieti".

seeing it how far its author is removed from Andrea del Sarto and has finished by being drawn towards the full and monumental conceptions of Michelangelo. The world and humanity appear to him in a tragic aspect. He sees them through his own temperament; for this reason he does not hesitate to deform the features of a face to give more power and expression.

The picture of Cosimo can be compared to a head in the Pitti Palace which is of remarkable character and power. The very pronounced profile has something fifteenth century about it; but the modelling is like that of Cosimo; the cavity of the eyes is constructed in the same typical way; the cheek bones are very pronounced; the light and shade are in conflict on the lower half of the face, the line of the chin is thus very apparent and dented. The dark tone of the costume brings out all the austerity and energy of the face.

With regard to this picture [1] Mr. Schaeffer has thought of a possible identification. There is in fact, in Vasari's fresco in the Palazzo Vecchio, *The Entry of Leo X into Florence*, a head which bears a strong resemblance to this latter. And in one of the "Ragionamenti" where Vasari analyses the immense series in the Palazzo Vecchio, he tells us who is the thin old priest who bears the Pope's cross: "Francesco da Castiglione, Florentine Canon, beside whom are walking all the pope's secretaries" [2]. Unfortunately we have no precise data about this Francesco da Castiglione and it is difficult to say whether the likeness is accidental or real. But it is quite impossible to date this work as being at the beginning of the artist's career. Mr. Schaeffer's conjecture is a direct contradiction of the almost indisputable fact that Pontormo was to begin with a pupil of Andrea del Sarto.

Neither is there any reason for placing this among his mature works between 1534 and 1535 as Mr. Clapp suggests. There is nothing in the technique to prevent its being contemporary with the portrait of Cosimo the Elder. On the contrary, of the two paintings one has certainly inspired the other. Pontormo was still attracted by the successful idea he had in interpreting a

---

[1] Pitti Palace. Cf. Schaeffer, *Ein Bildnis Pontormo im Palazzo Pitti* (Monatshefte für Kunstwissenschaft, 1910, p. 115).

[2] Vasari, *Ragionamenti...*, (VIII, p. 142).

medal profile and it is likely that he went back to this procedure to give the features of a man with a very pronounced and impressive face. One of the reasons Mr. Clapp gives for fixing the date much later is that according to him such a strong work could not have been painted during the time when its painter was under the influence of Andrea del Sarto. Now it is obvious that when Pontormo drew the likeness of Cosimo he had entirely abandoned Andrea's manner. The decoration of the Poggio a Cajano, later in date by two or three years, has nothing to recall the painter of the Scalzo. It is natural then to date the picture in the Pitti at the time when the artist is fumbling his way and discarding those he had followed up till then. Moreover he seems to show a new influence as well as that of Michelangelo, who little by little ended by conquering him. Vasari tells us that a short time before Pontormo worked in the Certosa d'Ema (1522), many of Dürer's prints were in circulation in Florence[1]. Pontormo, whose inquiring mind was indefatigable, was struck by the revelation of an art so different from the one he loved: everything about it was powerful and strong; grace was lacking. There are obvious traces of the influence of this in the frescoes in the Certosa d'Ema. And it is not impossible that in the portrait in the Pitti, there is a recollection of the implacable firmness with which Dürer emphasised the slightest physical detail and gave the relief a strong accent.

What is then important in this portrait is to see a new tendency which was to manifest itself later in the head of Cosimo. Pontormo tried to express his own character and that of the model powerfully; it is the work of a painter who from choice took the theme of masculine energy.

We are now between 1522 and 1524—a time in the painter's life when he knew how to bring an original note into the conception of portraiture; he showed great precocity, since at twenty-seven or twenty-eight years he had created such impressive works as the frescoes of the Villa at Poggio a Cajano, the portrait of Cosimo and the one in the Pitti Palace. But very soon Pontormo lost the influence of Dürer's art in his work; his

---

[1] Vasari, VI, p. 266.

style tended to become more sober. He shows something of the influence of the powerful masters of the fifteenth century; the Castello frescoes recall in certain ways the grandeur of Masaccio or Mantegna. He still admired the powerful technique of Michelangelo; but he had now a stronger personality to counteract this crushing force. There was some measure in his brilliance and he controlled the tumult of his imagination.

If in the *Martyrdom of St. Maurice* (Pitti) and in the *Deposition of Christ* in the Capponi Chapel in the Church of Santa Felicita, we find a style of grouping the figures which is strange without attaining the extravagance to which Vasari so often refers, there are on the contrary other works which are of a less troubled tendency: *The Madonna* in the Corsini Palace, the one in the Louvre, and the *Birth of Saint John the Baptist* in the Uffizi. It is during this period, from about 1525 to 1535, that almost for certain some portraits very different from the earlier ones were painted, revealing a much more serene and balanced vision of human nature.

A charming drawing of a young girl is characteristic of this new state of mind. There is no seeking after effect here and if the expression is a little astonished and troubled, it is due to a large extent to the shape of the eyes which, as nearly always, are round. The pose is calm; the position of the hands recalls the *Mona Lisa*; it is a free and personal imitation of the great portrait by Leonardo; it shows Pontormo coming back suddenly to the conception which had been so popular in the beginning of the sixteenth century.

This restless genius had been dreaming for some time of less sad and more comely faces. What we might call the rejuvenation of his sensibilities took him momentarily far from Michelangelo's influence. We find again the pupil of Andrea del Sarto. According to Vasari it was a time when he must have painted many portraits; he indicates several of them: for Ludovico Capponi who commissioned the *Deposition from the Cross* in Santa Felicita he painted a portrait of his daughter (who was very beautiful) as the Magdalene; he also painted those of Francesco Guardi; of Alexander and Hyppolitus de Medici, of Giovanni Guidicionni, of the Bishop Nicollo Ardinghelli and of Carlo Neroni [1]. In many cases these people are nothing but names to us; besides Vasari does not describe any of these pictures except the one of Francesco Guardini, dressed as a soldier, and he fixes the date as the Siege of Florence [2].

Now we have at least two portraits of soldiers by Pontormo; one black line drawing where the model, in a natural pose, is represented almost full face with his hand on his sword, the head lightly bent to the right [3]. The other is a picture which belonged to Princess Matilda [4]. The shape of the eyes is Pontormesque; the hands, especially the one resting on the halberd, are executed in that strong and plump manner which had become peculiar to the artist ever since he painted the portrait of Cosimo the Elder. They are two contemporary works. The body and the pose have the same suppleness; the expression is almost identical, younger and more carefree in the painting, more wondering in the drawing.

Is Francesco the halberdier? or is he not rather the man with the sword? Mr. Berenson believes it to be the latter and Mr. Gamba the former [5]. It is almost impossible to decide. Let us rather take interest in the painter's new tendencies. The faces of his sitters are lax; there is a feeling of a more simple and less agonised conception of the world.

One of his most beautiful portraits, the best painted and the most alive, dates from this period; it is the *Young Man* in the museum at Lucca [6], a painting in which the colours have kept a surprising brilliance *(Plate XXII, fig. 43)*. The impression of youth that Pontormo wanted to give is expressed in various ways: the yellow, almost gold, of the spongy flowing hair, the slightly startled eyes; a face pink and round in its simplicity, a thin neck, a slim body lost in its ample clothes; such are the elements which the painter

---

[1] Vasari, VI, p. 272–275.

[2] "Che fu opera bellissima" says Vasari.

[3] Cf. Berenson, *The Drawings . . .* , II, p. 138. — Clapp, *Les dessins de Pontormo*, 1914, p. 106.

[4] *Princess Matilda Collection*, 1904, p. 39.

[5] C. Gamba, *Pontormo* (piccola collezione d'arte), p. 11.

[6] This picture has been given the title of *Julius de Medicis Duke of Nemours*, without any justification. It is not in fact in any way similar to the famous painting by Raphael, a copy of which is in the Uffizi.

has stressed and added to this the freshness of warm colour intensified by a lovely light. The rather stiff silk of the coat with pronounced folds has high-lights which disappear into a most subtle range of colours going from rasp-berry to soft pink. The general bearing, though composed, is relaxed. In the face, which is rather precisely drawn, the shape of the eyes is modified and is not so conventional as formerly; they become elliptical and thus the gaze is not so strange. Its vivacity successfully completes this portrait of an elegant, slim adolescent, which is certainly the most spontaneous and the most charm-ing of Pontormo's creations: unexpected as well, for this painter did not seem to be made to express in this unforgettable and unusual way the candour of youth.

His imagination no longer allowed him to be carried away by distortions which are perhaps sources of beauty but which hinder a real likeness. This desire to be more natural is also to be found in a painting in the museum at Bergamo, which seems to be of a real Florentine plebeian[1]. The painter, clearly facing the model whose gaze sparkles with animation, has rendered spontaneously his face full of vivacity and his cap carelessly placed on his head[2]. His pose and costume are almost identical with those of an unknown man in the Uffizi, which has the features of a mature man. But this latter lacks lustre. If there were not such a strong similarity between the two pic-tures one might be induced to believe it one of his disciples' work. The artist forced himself to be more measured, more reasonable. Even the drawing has lost vigour; the modelling is less apparent and it is difficult to find in this work the principles which inspired Pontormo in his *Cosimo the Elder* or in

---

[1] Frizzoni, *La Galleria Morelli in Bergamo*, 1892, p. 18.

[2] According to Frizzoni it is a portrait of the uncongenial Baccio Bandinelli. But is there not a chance likeness between the picture at Bergamo and the engraving which Frizzoni has taken as a basis for his comparison? For to be exact this attribution would have presupposed, given the age of the model (20—22 years old), that the date of Pontormo's work is 1510 or 1515, according to which Baccio Bandinelli's date of birth is 1488 or 1493. Then this must be a work of Pontormo's youth, almost adolescence. Now the technique of this portrait recalls the *Young Man* at Lucca. It is certainly later than 1525, that is to say then the time when Baccio Bandinelli was over thirty. For Frizzoni's conjecture to be correct, Pontormo must have painted this portrait from an earlier sketch, which is very improbable.

the powerful profile in the Pitti; under the uniformly stretched skin no single anatomical detail is visible, thus making these works less powerful and less profound than those of his youth.

But this new style often has its charm. It is expressed successfully, as well as in the museums at Lucca and Bergamo, in a portrait in the Tolomei-Baldovinetti Collection in Florence which recalls by its pose the *Unknown Man with a Beard* in the Uffizi and the young Florentine in the Morelli Collection. It is an expressive face with rather a questioning gaze. The face is elongated, the forehead wide; the eybrows are curiously raised; the nose is thin and the mouth intelligent. Everything here expresses calm, balance and intelligence. The headgear, a sort of high stiff beret, is very full and accentuates the delicacy of this arresting head; less dark in colour than the clothes, it adds to the value of the pure fresh tones of the face.

The portrait of Alexander de Medici, which both Clapp and Berenson say is to be found now in the Johnson Collection at Philadelphia [1], was painted in his maturity. It is the only one we know anything about of the three that Pontormo painted. The first, of Alexander when young, had been painted when the latter had come to Florence with his cousin Hyppolitus, sent by Clement VII and accompanied by Cardinal Silvio Passerini; it was Octavian de Medici, to whom the Pope had strongly recommended them, who had them both painted by Pontormo; Hyppolitus represented with his favourite dog, Rodon, was a particularly good likeness. We do not know where the two works are today which, according to Vasari, were contemporary with *The Madonna* in the Louvre and show strongly the effects of Dürer's influence [2].

On becoming Duke of Florence, Alexander had himself painted a second time by the same artist whose portrait of Amerigo Antinori, a young patrician very well known at that time in Florence, he had admired. He was already represented in a small picture, as tiny as a half sheet of paper, which must

---

[1] Berenson *Catalogue of the Johnson Collection*, p. 45. Clapp, *Jacopo Carrucci da Pontormo*, 1916, p. 170. — *Rassegna d'arte*, 1913, p. 63.

[2] Vasari, VI, p. 273—274.

have been a very careful and precisely drawn work, since Vasari, in praising it, says that no miniaturist ever painted so minutely or in such detail [1].

"Taking this as a point of departure Pontormo painted a larger portrait of the Duke who was holding a pencil in his hands and drawing a woman's head; Alexander then made a present of this picture to Taddeo Malespina, sister of the Marchesa di Massa". The documents of the Florentine Archives, published to begin with by Gualandi and excellently commented upon since by Carnesecchi, added some details to Vasari's text. Really it was to one of his courtiers, Ansoldi, that Alexander gave this portrait as a recognition of his faithfulness; it was only later on, after the Duke's death, that one of Marchesa Massa's daughters, Taddea Malespina, received it as a present from Ansoldi. In the end Cosimo I expressed a desire to possess it, and Ansoldi, hearing about it, set about finding it. The picture had got into the Prince of Massa's Collection. Ansoldi was not able to get possession of it and wrote a letter to Francesco de Medici in 1571, where he explained the fruitless results of the steps he had taken and described the work in the following terms: "This portrait was executed by Jacopo Pontormo, famous artist, in Florence at the Pazzi's house at the time of Pope Clement VII's death; the duke is here represented full face and half-length, clothed in mourning, in front of a table; only speech is lacking"[2]. When Alexander had himself painted in this position, it was in the house of the Pazzi, where he was always happy to find the two "marchesine" di Massa, Riccarda and Taddea Malespina, the latter finally inheriting the work which had been painted before her eyes.

This information is valuable because it allows us to date the work exactly: 1534, the year of Clement VII's death, when the Duke was in mourning. Besides, the brief description given completes that of Vasari; and there is no doubt that it exactly fits the portrait in the Johnson Collection. According to Berenson the model wears dark clothes and a curious cap from which fall

---

[1] Vasari, VI, p. 278, and V, p. 91. In Vasari's time this little picture, now lost, hung in the Guardaroba of Duke Cosimo.

[2] Gualandi, *Nuova raccolta di lettere*, 1856, III, p. 62. Carnesecchi, *Rivista d'arte*, 1909, no. 1. – *Rassegna d'arte;* Clapp's article, 1913, p. 63–66. *La lettere d'Ausoldi* found in the National Archives of Florence (*Carteggio medico del Principato, filza* 567, 187 and 225).

two panels of cloth; seated in front of a table, he holds a white sheet of paper in one hand in the other a pencil with which he is drawing a profile. The features are quite characteristic; we recognise the sensual mouth of Alexander and his anxious and disturbing eyes. The relationship is obvious between this and a portrait at Bergamo painted by Bronzino as well as with another of uncertain authorship in the Ionides Collection in the Victoria and Albert Museum.

Pontormo has given a melancholy air to Alexander de Medici, enigmatic figure of the Florentine decadence. He is a tired dilettante; incapable of thinking of serious things, and living for pleasure and the joys of life. He is engaged in drawing; he likes above all the company of pretty women, the sight of whom gives a brilliance to his restless and sparkling eye. This shows clearly the character of the prince, a heedless and vicious aesthete, as history has described him. Since, besides this, everything tallies with the brief descriptions of Vasari and Ansoldi, it is almost certain that the portrait in the Johnson Collection is the one which Cosimo tried in vain to acquire for his Gallery.

This time the painter took pleasure in representing his model surrounded with objects familiar to him and following an occupation dear to him. This Medici, of whom he might have made a great sceptic if he had been in the state of mind of his twentyfifth year, is drawing in a Florentine interior. Less and less Pontormo's figures give us the impression of being plunged in thoughts of agonised sadness. Their mind is scarcely brushed by a touch of melancholy.

The portrait of the *Woman with a Dog*, in the Städel-Institut at Frankfurt also shows a new conception *(Plate XXII, fig. 45)*. It was for some time attributed to Bronzino; and it was Mr. Berenson who first saw it as a Pontormo. In fact Bronzino's art was of a different nature; in all his works, which are quite varied in spite of their reputation of uniformity, there is nothing so direct, so speaking as this face without charm or grace but where the liveliness of intelligence makes up for all the missing qualities. Pontormo has become a realist who no longer studies the sensibility of his models to the point of seeing there a reflection of his own, but who tries to make a speaking likeness which is full of life.

Already he has represented Hyppolitus de Medici with his favourite dog. He goes back to this idea: seated in a beautiful armchair, this young woman, richly adorned, has posed in front of the painter rather as we pose today in front of a photographer. The familiar surroundings are well arranged, probably at the model's desire. It is not the heedless abandoned theme of Alexander de Medici. The circlet of gold which binds the brown hair, carefully parted in the middle, the necklace of rich setting, the sumptuous jewellery and the dress, with its beautiful velvet sleeves: all these ornamentations indicate that the wearer is anxious to show herself at her very best.

Not so much importance was attached to dress in Leonardo and Andrea del Sarto's time. Here it is again imposing itself on the mind of the painter. Imperceptibly we are arriving at the time of the great state portraits of Bronzino. But without omitting any detail which might flatter the vanity of a young and elegant woman, Pontormo has exercised his psychological gifts to give force to her astute air, her malicious look and her quickly repressed smile.

The same pose of the head, seen three-quarter view, is often used in woman's heads and even in men's; the pose which is so charmingly rendered in a red chalk drawing in the Uffizi where the head is elongated and the features are fine and clear; a slight sadness is in the gaze, and the face, which has gentleness, expresses a calm resignation. The contour is very firm and the modelling delicately shaded *(Plate XXII, fig. 44)*. It is a rapid note but reveals an admirable talent for portraiture. This study was made, not perhaps for the Frankfurt picture [1], as has been suggested, but for a similar work, in the grand style, such as he liked to compose from that time onwards, placing the model in a setting appropriate to his tastes.

---

[1] It is Mr. Clapp (*Jacopo Carrucci da Pontormo*, p. 153) who has made this rather arbitrary comparison of which he himself knows the weakness: the expression of the two heads is in fact very different. We do not insist on the comparison which he made between the Frankfurt portrait and the drawing in the Uffizi; we have explained further back that this drawing could not be attributed to Pontormo.

In the portrait in the Oldenburg Museum a young woman, very richly dressed in green velvet, is represented seated; she has a diadem of gold on her hair, a great chain on her breast and around her neck a beautiful collar of pearls. Here the technique is looser; the pose is less stiff than in the Frankfurt example: the gaze has great vivacity; the movement of the arms is developed with ease. The fine and decided face discloses a character full of brilliance and liveliness.

Is it not obvious that it is of the same nature and spirit as the painting in Turin, which was attributed to Bronzino or better still considered to be a portrait of Eleanor of Toledo? *(Plate XXIII, fig. 46)*. Everything goes to indicate a picture almost contemporary with those of Frankfurt and Oldenburg. It is the same attitude, the same full hands with tapering fingers, the same enquiring and lively eyes; the folded lips, the quivering nose, the powerfully drawn temples; here are touches worthy of an artist who tries to seize the features which give character to the faces of his sitters. We are very far removed from the art of Bronzino, and this expressive face has so much kinship with the one in the Oldenburg Museum that it seems to be almost the same person.

During this fruitful period of his maturity, Pontormo's melancholy seemed to give place to calmer thoughts. Nevertheless, the expression of the gaze which, in the portrait at Oldenburg, has an eager feeling about it, is almost tortured in the example in Turin. The artist achieves real sadness in the face, of most expressive ugliness; of the *Young Man* in the Trivulzio Collection in Milan [1]. This last work is considered by Mr. Clapp as one of the best examples of Pontormo's art between 1521 and 1522; it would rather seem to be of a much later period; the pose of the head [2], the design of the

---

[1] This portrait used to be in the Rinuccini Collection before passing into that of Prince Trivulzio. But this is not a strong enough reason to believe, as Mr. Gamba does, that it represents a member of the Rinuccini family.

[2] We find this same three-quarters view in a portrait in the Corsini Gallery in Florence representing a man of mature age working at his table. Is is attributed to Pontormo by Mr. Gamba, but the weakness of the modelling of the face and hands and the uncouth colouring of the face seem to indicate a studio work.

hands, the richness of the dress, the manner of holding the book, show that it is contemporary with the two of a seated woman about which we have just spoken. There is, besides, in this face a return to anxiety; the eyes have that curious shape which easily gives a troubled expression; they seem to be enlarged by some painful vision and give a strange touch to this very young face which stiffens against emotion.

Pontormo thus comes back to that melancholy which is the basis of his character. The sadness of Michelangelo's heroes impresses him more and more. Even his originality suffers from the admiration that it awaked in him. In his nudes he was inspired by the full Michelangelesque forms to such an extent as to become a mannerist haunted by powerful anatomical lines and the crushing force of muscles. Besides, he was liked by the man whom he imitated. When Alfonso Davalos Marchese del Guasto had obtained from the great Florentine master a cartoon of *Christ Appearing to the Magdalene*, he wanted to have it copied, and it was the painter himself who advised him to go to Pontormo: "no one could serve him better". Another Florentine, Bartolommeo Bettini, did the same and conferred on the same artist the task of finishing a sketch representing a *Naked Venus embraced by Cupid* which was the work of the sculptor of the Medici tombs. The date of the Marchese del Guasto's commission being fixed by a letter of Figiovanni (1531) [1], we can conclude from it that at this time Pontormo was drawn more and more strongly towards Michelangelo's art. He underwent in Florence the same influence as Sebastiano del Piombo did in Rome [2].

From this time onwards Pontormo's portraits have more grandeur and majesty and are similar to the Roman style of which Sebastiano del Piombo was one of the most brilliant exponents. Besides it is probable that the Florentine did not ignore this Roman's art. Perhaps as Milanesi and Clapp claim [3] he spent some time in Rome; this conjecture is unnecessary to explain

---

[1] Carl Frey, *Die Dichtungen des Michelangelo Buonarotti*, p. 508–509 (Figiovanni's letter to Michelangelo).

[2] It was then that Michelangelo finished his principal work, the Chapel of San Lorenzo (1530–1531).

[3] Vasari, VI, p. 276–277. — Clapp, *Jacopo Carrucci da Pontormo*, p. 69.

the similarity which exists between the imposing style of the latter's portraits of Sebastiano del Piombo and the style of the Tuscan painter. It is enough to refer to the interesting passage of Vasari: "Sebastiano", says he, "painted the portrait of Francesco degli Albizzi, who was then in Rome on business, and he did it so well that it did not seem a painting but a living head; Francesco, full of joy, took the picture with him to Florence; and the whole of Florence admired the likeness of Francesco". A letter of Michelangelo to Sebastiano del Piombo and another one of Piombo's date this work which was so popular in Florence [1]: it was executed in 1525 and is today lost [2]. It must have been rather similar in technique to the lifelike *Portrait of a Man* represented knee-length in the Benson Collection, a true example of monumental portraiture. It is uncertain whether a painting of this kind could have immediately pleased Pontormo. But we must not forget that Michelangelo admired the Roman artist very much: and as he was on excellent terms with Pontormo right up to the end of his stay in Florence, it must have given him a pretext to admire the Michelangelism of Sebastiano.

Unfortunately we have very few portraits of the Michelangelesque period. The great work of the end of his life, *The Last Judgment* in San Lorenzo, is known to us through drawings, some of which are among the most beautiful that he created. One portrait, the one of the Cardinal in the Borghese Gallery, also belongs to this period. The Roman influence is here even more obvious than in the portraits of Frankfurt, Oldenburg and Turin. The Cardinal is seated in an armchair, the face turned to three-quarters. It is the same pose as the Julius II by Raphael, and Cardinal Reginald Pole by Sebastiano del Piombo. This portrait, which Passavant believed to be by Raphael and representing a Cardinal Borgia [3], is an authentic Pontormo. The pose

---

[1] Vasari, V, p. 575 — cf. *Le lettere di Michelangelo*, edition Milanesi, 1875, p. 445. — *Les correspondants de Michelange, Sebastiano del Piombo* (edition Milanesi), 1890, p. 32.

[2] Cf. P. d'Archiardi, *Sebastiano del Piombo*, 1908, p. 220. It is possible that there were other portraits by Sebastiano del Piombo in Florence. In the inventory of the *Guardaroba Medicea*, series 31, one, a portrait of Baccio Valori is listed. Perhaps this is the one Vasari referred to (V, p. 576).

[3] Passavant, *Raphael d'Urbin et son Père Giovanni Santi*, II, p. 358.

obviously recalls Raphael; the oriental carpet with geometric shapes of yellows, greens and browns on a red background is like the one which covers the table on which Inghirami writes: the engraved bell is like the one which Leo X has beside him in the painting by Raphael (*Plate XXIV, fig. 48*).

But all the rest is pure Pontormo: the colouring to begin with, which is so seldom good with this artist; the red and the white lack brilliance; the architectural background is of a washed-out green, which is dull. The hands are distinctly drawn with Pontormo's usual distortions, especially now that he is under Michelangelo's influence; in the right hand, the swelling below the thumb is very pronounced, added to slightly defective anatomical construction of the forefinger. Finally we have again the characteristic modelling of the eyes, and especially—and perhaps this is of most importance—that grave and sad expression which is even more profound than in the Trivulzio Collection. Again the face becomes agonised; and is this time tormented by thoughts similar to those which haunt the *Jeremiah* in the Sistine Chapel and which ravage the faces of Michelangelo.

An identification of the figures represented has been attempted. Mr. Venturi has noted that in the background of the picture a motif of ears of wheat tied together by a ribbon is repeated three times: which must be, according to him, the crest of the Spanocchi family of Siena, and the Cervini's; and as, in the list of Cardinals from 1470-1550, there was only one who had the right to use ears of wheat in his coat-of-arms; that is, Cardinal Cervini, who became Pope under the title of Marcelus II, and it is his name which Venturi evokes [1]. On the other hand Mr. Gamba sees the features of Innocenzo Cibo [2] and it is undeniable that there is a striking resemblance between the two faces [3].

However, it is certainly a work of the Michelangelesque period. The portrait is not, as was the case formerly, merely a study in psychology; the

---

[1] A. Venturi, *Il Museo e la Galleria Borghese*, 1895, p. 195.

[2] C. Gamba, *Pontormo*, p. 17.

[3] We must especially compare the portrait in the Borghese Gallery to Innocent Cibo which Bugiardini has represented in his copy of Leo X by Raphael (Corsini Gallery, Rome).

model is represented at home following a familiar occupation. At the same time the painter's temperament which, in the last years of his life, became more and more that of a hypochondriac and a hermit, shows through it; he goes back to those gloomy faces where he used to express most sincerely what was in him.

Having then begun by imitating Andrea del Sarto, he gave an original and profound form to the sadness which seemed to weigh on the Florentine generations during the first half of the sixteenth century. He had an equal desire to seek out new themes and thus to create paintings of deep character and assured psychology. Great variety is one of the most striking things about the portraits we have of his. His work helps us to understand the change brought about between his own art and that of Bronzino. Leaving the portraits of melancholy, he came under the influence of Raphael and Michelangelo and even Sebastiano del Piombo, in carrying out the portraits of great and beautiful bearing which impressed Bronzino in his youth and partly formed his genius. He understood how to interpret the expression of a face; against a neutral background (since under Michelangelo's influence he had decided to abandon landscape backgrounds), he set living faces, full of emphasis. Neither was he indifferent to the beauty of costume and adornment, and it is in this respect also that he inspired Bronzino.

As a final analysis, very diverse tendencies are to be found in Pontormo's work. This troubled spirit, enemy of monotony, was open to all new influences. Nevertheless there are shades and delicacies in rendering the human figure which escaped him. It is not without interest to note that it was another admirer of Michelangelo who understood how to study them. The followers of Leonardo's rival, not having had any examples of portraiture from their master, kept their own personality in the study of the face. This was the case with Francesco Salviati as well as with Pontormo.

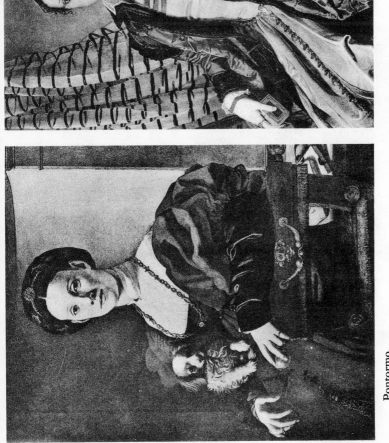

Pontormo.
45. *The Woman with a Dog.* (Städelsches Kunstinstitut, Frankfurt am Main)
46. *Portrait of a Woman.* (Pinacoteca, Turin)

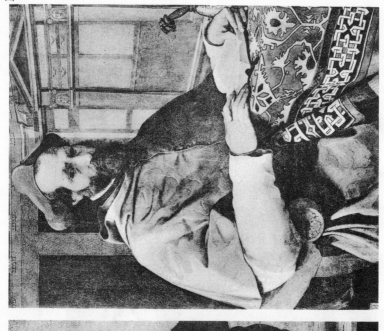

Pontormo.

47. *Portrait of a Young Man.* (Trivulzio Collection, Milan)
48. *Portrait of the Cardinal.* (Borghese Gallery, Rome)

CHAPTER VIII

FRANCESCO SALVIATI AND THE VENETIAN
INFLUENCE

Salviati's stay in Rome. Parmigianino's influence on his art. The portraits of the Roman period; what distinguishes them from Parmigianino's portraits. Salviati's stay in Venice. Its importance. The self-portraits in the Colonna Gallery, the Corsini Gallery and the Uffizi. The naturalism of Salviati's portraits. *The Adolescent* in the Poldi-Pezzoli Museum. *The Lute Player* in the Jacquemart-André Museum.

Salviati seems to have been more renowned than Pontormo. Domenichi puts him among the greatest painters of all time; when speaking with enthusiasm of the beauty of certain Sienese women, he considered that neither such great artists as Appeles, nor Michelangelo, nor Francesco Salviati could do them justice in their paintings [1]. Aretino goes almost as far in his praise of him; he describes in detail the qualities of this "glorious youth" who had urbanity, modesty, charm in conversation and so many gifts that the least among them seemed to be that of painting, which nevertheless he possessed to an admirable degree.

Salviati having painted the portrait of Aretino, the latter wrote to him that His Majesty King Francis I, for whom it was intended, had found it full of intense life and had had it placed among his favourite treasures, in the hope of being able to take into his service the painter of such a lovely picture. To this evidence of Francis I he added that of Titian and Vasari who were just as flattering [2]. The Florentine painter then had the friendship of this formidable writer Aretino, implacable critic in his aversions, but whose judgment was full of finesse and intelligence; those who had the good fortune to please him were certain that their fame would be increased by it.

Salviati was also esteemed by other critics of great authority, Annibale

[1] Domenichi, *Nobilita delle donne*, 1549, p. 249.
[2] *Il secondo libro delle lettere di M. Pietro Aretino*, 1609, p. 316.

Caro and Bishop Paolo Giovio [1]. The nature of the praise lavished on his talent has only been studied up to the present in a fragmentary way and it is nevertheless the more interesting and lively; this artist, who was so finished and so forced in his decorative compositions, knew how to forget, in front of a face that inspired him, all the discoveries of his cold technique, to find again a healthy tradition made from simplicity and naturalness.

The forming of his artistic training was varied. He spent his youth in Florence, where he was for some time in Andrea del Sarto's studio and that emphatic sculptor Bandinelli's. What is important is that when twenty years old he went to Rome where he became Vasari's companion. There he very much appreciated both the decorative sense of Raphael's disciples and the anatomical beauty of Michelangelo's creations. Neither was he insensible (and this to his credit) of the strange and attractive charm of Parmigianino's painting. When he went back to Tuscany he was thus affected by the Roman pomp and grandeur.

Now the nature of his talent must have been modified a little by his journey to Venice, very brief it is true, but it made a deep enough impression on his mind. The light in his pictures became clearer and less warm as a result. In the Chapel of the Confraternity of the Misericordia which is in Rome next to San Giovanni Cecollato, two of his frescoes show these successive influences [2].

One which represents the *Visitation* and is dated 1538 is entirely Roman in inspiration, nearer even to the art of Raphael than to that of Michelangelo; the forms, which are full, have a certain majesty, but the colour is dull and cold. The second, *The Birth of John the Baptist,* is later by thirteen years (1551), and on this occasion the painter has tried to please the eye with warm colours: the yellows and reds are Venetian in tone. It gives a quite different impression; the harmony of colour takes away from the heaviness of the masses and gives life to the whole.

---

[1] Bottari, *Raccolta di lettere...*, 1822, III, p. 200, V, p. 223.
[2] Vasari, VII, p. 16.

Thus in contrast to certain Florentine artists who did not like to leave their country and remained faithful to its artistic traditions, Salviati had travelled even when young; he was one of those easily affected by foreign influences, influences sometimes Roman, sometimes Venetian. His talent did not lose in originality by it. He does not give us the prodigious touch of a Pontormo but rather a naturalness and skill of handling which gives his faces a new charm. Salviati was, besides, one of those painters who could only confuse lovers of classification; so diverse, spontaneous and unexpected are his portraits.

According to Aretino his style is in some ways similar to that of Michelangelo [1]. In fact Salviati was also a disciple of the master of the Sistine Chapel; but only the technical methods can be seen in his work. In his frescoes or pictures he seems to want to solve a complicated problem of design and to believe that this complication itself is the essence of Michelangelo's art: this is shown in his *Charity*, kneeling and surrounded by children, where he had to achieve the feat of giving in a small space an impression of power and movement. It is in this way that movement becomes distortion; even the idea of Charity is lost in the artist's useless efforts at virtuosity.

It is rather difficult to say up to what point the influence of Michelangelo can be traced in Salviati's portraits. It would be striking, if it were true, that the Julius de Medici in the Holden Collection at Cleveland was his work, as Mrs. Mary Logan suggests [2]. But it would be perhaps reckless to consider this attribution as possible. It is rather from Pontormo that Salviati sought inspiration; thus he never left the circle of Michelangelo's admirers and his first sympathies did not change. There were some points of resemblance between the two artists' work; they were both interested in particular in the character of a face; a preoccupation which is obvious in the portrait of a *Man Seated* in the Pitti Palace, very similar to certain heads by Pontormo,

---

[1] "Il suo disegniar dotto", says Aretino, "e regolato mi rapresenta il giuditio, cona discretione Michelangelo distende, e tondeggia l'artificioso de le linee, e in somma le promesse, che ci fa il suo fare sono tanto certe, quanto grandi". Letter addressed 11th July 1539 to the sculptor Leone Leoni, *Il secondo libro delle lettere di M. Pitro Aretino*, p. 85.

[2] Mary Logan, *Rassegna d'arte*, 1907.

with wide eyes and a strange expression. Its creator is nevertheless gifted with a more subtle talent; the contours, the hollows and curves of the face are studied more subtly; the model's pose is more natural and more relaxed. It is here that a new state of mind manifests itself with this painter; little by little he is drawing away from the Michelangelo tradition, to be won over by different principles. Since that time he was more inclined to be influenced by Raphael, Parmigianino or the Venetians. But their influence on his art was only superficial; he brings out a very deep conception of the human face and is also very individual, in spite of striking reminiscences.

Already in his frescoes the principal, and perhaps the only, element of interest are the living and well placed portraits. How bored and theatrical they seem without the faces where the features of some of his contemporaries are reproduced with delicacy! In the Oratory of the Roman Confraternity of the Misericordia *The Visitation* arouses our curiosity by the presence in the foreground of two people, one which points out with a large gesture the scene unfolding in front of him; in this simple group there is more true animation than in the large crowd which looks on at the meeting of the Virgin and Elizabeth. These are obviously portraits and very expressive ones.

Now the one on the left recalls by its style another in the Patrizi Collection in Rome: a bearded man who holds in his beautifully drawn right hand a statute of Michelangelesque shape *(Plate XXV, fig. 49)*. This picture has, like that of the *Visitation*, a rather different distinction from that which characterised up till this time the creations of the Florentine painters. Obviously Parmigianino's influence is coming out in this work.

Salviati arrived in Rome in 1530 at a time when the impression created by the works of Correggio's disciple was still profound. This painter's art, the originality of which is a little deliberate and affected, has nevertheless an astonishing charm and it is easy to understand that he was accepted in Rome as if he had revived the graces of Raphael's art [1].

In a portrait by Parmigianino it is in the first place the colour which is attractive; it has kept a lovely freshness as in the costume of Anthea in Naples

---

[1] Vasari, V, p. 224.

where the yellows and deep pinks harmonise perfectly. His brush shows rare virtuosity and can suggest the indefinable shades of movement and expression of a face; the soft and penetrating gaze carries with it a touch of mystery. The *Giovanni Battista Castaldo* in Naples is characteristic of this style, so different from that which was until that time popular in Rome; the model is seated, a book in his hand, still moved by what he has been reading. In the face, brightly lighted from the right, charming contrasting tones are reflected; the white embroidery on the black garment, the elegant and fine hands are vibrant notes which emphasise the distinction of this seductive, melancholy and gentle person. Such dreaming and serious faces are often to be found among Parmigianino's portraits. It was by looking at these that Salviati developed a taste for paintings with a delicate expression, where the skill of his brush even went as far as to render the softness of the texture of the skin.

In the portrait in the Patrizi Collection, he added to these qualities a freer observation of the face; we feel here less of the research which in Parmigianino's portraits takes away from the spontaneity of the expression. The Tuscan artist's imagination created then a more direct feeling of life. It is even more convincing in the example in Vienna [1] and in the Florentine Collection of Marchese Carlo Niccolini where there are two portraits which obviously date from the period when the penetrating gaze of Parmigianino's faces was attracting Salviati. Now the differences between the style of the two painters are still more striking than their points of similarity. They appear to begin with in certain technical details; the fingers taper towards the end, just as the painter of Parma represented them. It is not in this way that they are painted in the Vienna picture, where the more bony drawing reminds us of Vasari's style: which would indicate a Florentine work of the sixteenth century painted towards 1540. On the other hand the naturalness of the

[1] Hermann Voss, *Italienische Gemälde des XVI. und XVII. Jahrhunderts in der Galerie des Kunsthistorischen Hofmuseums zu Wien* (*Zeitschrift für bildende Kunst*, 1912). The portrait in Vienna is the one next to the mutilated statue of an Amazon whose horse is being struck down. This statue was part of the Patrizi Collection where it still is (Salomon Reinach, *Repertoire de la statuaire grecque et romain*, 1897, II, p. 326). It is thus possible that the model was a member of the Patrizi family.

[2] Carlo Gamba, *Alcuni ritratti di Cecchino Salviati* (*Rassegna d'arte*, 1909).

pose is worthy of Salviati as well as the expression of the face; the colouring of the flesh slightly resembles Parmigianino's style which is of a more lively warmth; there is a fresh pink in the flesh tones which is native to Florentine art before it felt the influence of Venice.

These same elements are found again in a work in the Niccolini Collection; the verve of the painter is here even more astonishing; his treatment of the costume shows a remarkable understanding of the sheen on silk, and the illumination of the face characterised by the strong point of light on the right cheek, is the work of a sensitive artist who is at the same time a virtuoso. The structure of the fingers directly recalls here the style of Parmigianino and shows that there was a time when Salviati imitated this artist to a great extent; but the Florentine painter always kept that independence in the pose accompanied by lightness and elegance in rendering materials and also of a more balanced conception of the play of light.

His personality easily broke loose from these foreign influences. It could be seen in conflict, so to speak, with the attraction exercised on him by an original treatment of art. He was remarkably gifted for assimilation, and when he had come to know and admire the splendour of Venetian colouring, he was able to inspire himself from it in a very skilful way. His later portraits, though resembling those of the Roman period, have not the same appearance; his interpretation of life increased in freedom of expression and imagination.

In the Farnese Palace as in the Oratory of the Misericordia, Salviati's great compositions are of no value apart from some heads full of character. In one of these frescoes, dated about 1554, he represents Ranuccio Farnese receiving the Insignia of Captain of the Holy Church from Eugenius IV; and in the other of Pope Paul III conferring the same honour on Pier Luigi Farnese at the time when Charles V is seen approaching accompanied by Cardinal Alessandro Farnese and other noblemen "portrayed from nature" [1]. In studying this last group Mr. Gamba was able to do a most successful piece of identification; he recognised a bearded face which, seen in profile, is almost

---

[1] Vasari, VII, p. 32.

identical with a portrait in the Colonna Gallery, considered for some time to be that of Poggio Bracciolini painted by Girolamo da Treviso (*Plate XXV, fig. 50*).

There is no doubt that this picture is one of the authentic works of Salviati and one of his very best. The background is a beautiful colour: against dark red velvet two stripes each composed of bright yellow, blue and pink stand out; the face and hands are strongly illuminated by light coming from the right which sheds warm tones on the flesh, hair and beard with astonishing skill; reflected lights can be seen in the shaded portions and some hair falling on the lace collar is painted in a series of chromatic gradations very far removed from the Florentine conception. The brilliance of Venetian colouring, the attractive play of Titianesque colour, had left a deep impression on Salviati's mind and this is the most certain evidence of the skill with which he assimilated methods which he could not have picked up in Rome or even in Florence.

Besides, this portrait shows us how subtle the painter's talent had become and how he had developed that ease and spontaneity which already reveals itself in the paintings where he imitated Parmigianino. Often with Florentine artists we are struck by the affected, almost stiff, attitude of the model who is obviously posing, even up to the time of Pontormo, where in *The Cardinal*, although the pose is less fixed, there is an obvious seeking after effect. In contrast the subject of the picture in the Colonna Gallery does not make a gesture which is not perfectly natural; he holds a precious medal in his hand and it seems as though he is about to speak to his neighbour; the painter has caught the fleeting expression of the face in a snapshot. This admirer of Michelangelo, who in his frescoes has almost slavishly followed the lessons he has learnt from the powerful muscular figures of the Sistine Chapel, has understood how to break away from anything forced which might over-emphasize the anatomical aspect in these portrait studies. This simplicity and abandon, so often found among Venetian painters, is unusual in Florentine painting where artists were more willing to submit to definite traditional canons. Salviati want even further than Pontormo, who had already enlarged the conception of the portrait: he posed his model very naturally in the least affected attitude.

It is by this essential characteristic that we can recognise the faces he painted. There is one which is very similar in method and brilliance to the one in the Colonna Gallery; it is a young man, who, laced into a fashionable costume, looks straight in front of him with a meditative air; certainly one of the most lovely of Salviati's portraits. There are many points of resemblance between the two faces; the manner of treating the forehead and arch of the brows is identical; the shape of the face has similar characteristics. Is not the model in the Colonna the same as the one in the Corsini Gallery? Anyway it is quite easy to identify the first; the features are exactly the same as those in the engraving of Salviati in Vasari's *Lives*; they also resemble those in a mediocre portrait formerly in the Uffizi Library, with the following inscription: "Francesco Salviati Pittore". Far from its being a portrait of Poggio Bracciolini, it is a self portrait of the artist; and it is not unreasonable to suppose that the head in the Corsini Gallery is also his when younger; besides there is less ease in the general pose which points to an earlier painting than the one in the Colonna Gallery. The technique is still of a rare quality, the face and hands have a very virile appearance and form; the painter conceived them as lovely patches of colour to which the light coming from the right gives full value against the dark tones of the costume *(Plate XXVI, fig. 52)*.

Everything shows Venetian influence, and striking evidence of this has been claimed for a picture in Berlin, the copy of Titian's *Ranuccio Farnese* which is today lost. The little picture in Berlin can only have been a dull reflection of the splendour of the original; the colour is without life; since Salviati was familiar with Titian's work, he would certainly have expressed his admiration in a different way, rather as an enthusiastic learner than a clumsy copyist. In fact certain characteristics of his art explain themselves with difficulty under Titian's influence. We must also see the portrait of the young Ranuccio at Rome since the latter, having become Cardinal, conferred on him the task of decorating one of the rooms in his palace. There he found again the brilliance of colour, the naturalness and swing of the pose which are so beautiful in Titian's portraits and which had impressed him during his stay in Venice.

He was then profoundly influenced by his stay; most of Salviati's existing portraits bear its stamp. In the self-portrait in the Uffizi, the warm colours, especially the pinkish-yellow of the flesh and the white of the small collar, are in perfect harmony; everything else is dark except the red slash at the shoulder. The painter has studied this in detail: the hollow of the eyes, the wrinkles of the brow and the corners of the eyes are strongly marked; in his care with the precision of drawing he remains a Florentine, although his tones and colours are Venetian. The illuminated portions are treated with a sensitive technique able to render the slightest vibration of light on the delicate skin.

It is the charm of this technique which gives real originality to the *Portrait of an Adolescent* in the Poldi-Pezzoli Museum: there is an obvious resemblance between it and the pictures in the Corsini and Colonna Galleries; the highlights on the hair and those which brighten up the attractive colours of the shaded parts of the neck and the right cheek are significant; the brows are raised in an accentuated curve under which the elongated eyelids give a curious character to this attractively oval face. It recalls in its delicacy not, as Mr. Giovanni Poggi suggests, that of the young Cosimo I as he appears in a picture by Ridolfo Ghirlandaio [1], but rather that of his son Fernando; the little picture of him by Bronzino in the collection of the twenty-four Medicis gives him these delicate features and this penetrating gaze. Could the portrait in the Poldi-Pezzoli Museum be of the young Fernando de Medici? It is not an impossible conjecture. Salviati was not such a favourite with Cosimo as Bronzino, but nevertheless he received some commissions from him; Vasari and an inventory of the ducal collection dated 1554 mentions a painting of 'Giovanni delle bande Neri' as his work [2].

---

[1] Giovanni Poggi, *Rivista d'arte* (Aug.-Dec., 1906).
[2] Vasari, VII, 27. — *Archivio di stato di Firenze* (31, Entrata e uscita di guardaroba, 1554–5).

He was also commissioned to paint other members of Cosimo's family. It has even been said that in painting the young Fernando we have just been speaking about, Bronzino had in mind Salviati's *Adolescent* and wanted to give his picture a similar attraction. In fact there is no doubt that the other portraits of Fernando de Medici by Bronzino lack this dreaming expression and keep a set face.

No, to be exact, the head in the Poldi-Pezzoli Museum is, even more than a charming combination of colour, a fine psychological study; the background is dark as well as the costume, against which the crude white of the collar, with its carelessly knotted tie, stands out; the face is even more pronounced and in its features, where nothing is lost, we read astonishment and melancholy. The feeling here expressed evokes in this way the manner of the Florentine painters of the sixteenth century, and we come back to a certain extent to Andrea del Sarto's conception of the portrait. This is not surprising. Where could Salviati have learnt to look at the world with an optimistic smile? His irritable temperament, Vasari tells us, tended to make him sad. As for the masters which inspired him, most of them were of a troubled state of mind. It is then inevitable that his interpretation of a face should reveal this kind of sensibility.

The expression, at once gentle and melancholy, of the *Adolescent* in the Milan Museum becomes sadder and more gloomy in the two paintings in the Uffizi and Naples Museums which show Salviati's genius arriving at a harmonious synthesis of its component elements. It is strange that the one in Naples [1] should have formerly been attributed to Raphael. Passavant had already discovered this mistake and had suggested the name of Salviati [2]. All the evidence shows that this is correct; even a superficial comparison with the portraits in the Uffizi and the Colonna Gallery leave no doubt about it *(Plate XXVI, fig. 51)*. The face, brilliantly lighted, is modelled by the play of effects of light skilfully shaded at the temples; warm and delicate colours

---

[1] This portrait bears for some unknown reason the name of "Cavalier Tibaldeo". This attribution must be the result of muddling it with Raphael's picture, now lost, representing the poet Antonio Tebaldeo.

[2] Passavant, *Raphael d'Urbin...*, II, 368; Crowe and Cavalcaselle, *Raphaello*, 1891, III, p. 8.

stand out against the dark velvet of the costume; nothing is more characteristic of Salviati's style than this natural attitude to which the painter has given all his attention. The bend of the left arm is freely drawn and that of the right is impeccable. Florentine art rarely knew in the sixteenth century such virtuosity, such an arabesque enveloping the body with so much suppleness and lightness.

The portrait in the Uffizi, placed like the former against an architectural background, is certainly not so attractive; the artist's gifts are shown more in the construction of the face than in the freedom of the pose; in fact the general line has not the same elegance as in the Naples picture. Here it is the expression which makes the picture, a face with fine features, a melancholy gaze which has none of the tragedy of a Pontormo, but which seems to be near discouragement: this is what the artist has been able to analyse in a subtle manner. He has, however, rather neglected the drawing of the body and the study of the hands.

It is in this way that Salviati's talent for originality reveals itself; the various elements which made it up blended themselves gradually into a personal style which could vary in its technical methods, but found unity in its richness of inspiration and sensibility. Due consideration has not been given to the characteristics of his art when examining a delicate and harmoniously composed work in the Jacquemart-André Museum: the *Lute Player (Plate I, fig. 1).* It was at first attributed to Bronzino; then Emile Bertaux thought of Pontormo. Neither of these conjectures is satisfactory. The *Young Man* in the Museum at Lucca, where Pontormo gave the greatest feeling of youth, is still a little affected; the movement has none of the ease of the *Lute Player;* neither did Bronzino ever render with such freedom and simplicity a natural attitude. Everything about this picture points away from the art of these two painters and towards that of Salviati. Unfortunately repainting has changed the beauty of the whole; the costume and the modelling of the left hand have suffered very much from it. But the face and the right hand, which have hardly been touched up, have kept an accent and an expression which are revealing. They evoke the picture in the Poldi-Pezzoli Museum by the oval of the face with its delicate contour, and the one in the Uffizi by the shape of the brows, the ones in Naples and the Corsini Gallery by the lighting of the face and the virile drawing of the hands. The warm tones, which are striking in the brightly lighted passages, are easily explained if we think of the Venetian influence so usual with Salviati. He was perhaps thinking of the musicians which Giorgione's and Titian's contemporaries were so fond of when he was composing this picture, which has so much deep and intimate poetry. It is an almost unique touch in Florentine painting. Only Salviati could have given his model such an easy set of the head and shoulders, such a subtle movement of the arms and hands, and finally a gaze so full of musical feeling. The purity of Florentine draughtsmanship unites thus with the charm of Venetian colouring in this work which, it seems, expresses the best of Salviati's genius.

These same distinguished and elegant faces are to be found very much diminished in some portraits where his influence is obvious: a simple head in the Cook Collection at Richmond[1], freely posed, and another in the Platt Collection [2] of New Jersey, are certainly not by this artist but they are composed in a similar style. Salviati's imitators were struck by the ease of his technique. The *Two Architects* in the Naples Museum also shows very clearly the influence of the Tuscan painter: it must be attributed to one of his pupils and not, as was formerly thought, to the School of Andrea del Sarto or of Bronzino.

All these pictures recall the essential characteristics of Salviati's style; the naturalness of the pose and the subtlety of movement. Throughout the modifications of his technique, it finally became very close to the Venetian style; there is always the same care to avoid any forced attitude or any commonplace expression of the face.

---

[1] *A catalogue of the paintings at Doughty House, Richmond, and elsewhere in the Collections of Sir Frederick Cook,* I, p. 48.

[2] *Rassegna d'arte,* 1911 (article by Mason–Perkins).

CHAPTER IX

TASTE IN PORTRAITURE AT THE TIME OF COSIMO I DE MEDICI

In the sixteenth century painted portraits were preferred to sculptured busts. Discussions on the pre-eminence of painting over sculpture. The ostentation of new Florentine masters. Cosimo I and Eleanor of Toledo. Their influence on the evolution of the portrait. The portrait becomes a decorative element. Its important role in public ceremonies. The cult of the Sovereign and the Medici family. The Palazzo Vecchio, temple of Medici glory. Portraits in Vasari's frescoes. Their iconographical and aesthetic value. Portrait Collections. The one of Cosimo I inspired by Paolo Giovio. Cristofano dell' Altissimo.

The development of the State portrait marks the difference between the end of the fifteenth and the beginning of the sixteenth centuries, and the first sixty years of the fifteenth. Rich Florentine patricians now preferred a portrait in their own palace to one appearing on the wall of a chapel; in Andrea del Sarto's work several life-like heads can be recognised; but the features of many famous Florentines are no longer to be found there, as was usual in Botticelli's pictures or in a fresco by Ghirlandaio.

It is also clear that they preferred a portrait to a medal or to a bust, which from that time appeared less frequently. It was undoubtedly because, since Leonardo's time, sitters liked graceful attitudes and there was more liking for painting than for sculpture which is not perhaps capable of the same delicacy of analysis.

Besides, it was a very fashionable controversy in the sixteenth century to try to establish the supremacy of one of these arts over the other. Now from this purely formal discussion sometimes successful formulas resulted, which serve to explain certain characteristics of the artistic evolution. In his

Treatise Leonardo da Vinci made an apology for painting; this latter gave the first place to sculpture because it was the result of more subtle speculations which were unknown to the rival art. The great difficulty which the painter has to overcome is that he must absorb the spirit of nature and he must try to interpret every visible thing, which is impossible for a sculptor with his less rich and less varied technique [1].

Later, Pontormo expressed the torments of the painter, torments which came from his audacity; he wanted to imitate in colour everything that he saw in order to give it complete verisimilitude. But he was at times too bold; that is when he attempted to surpass nature, wishing to give life to a face drawn on a flat surface; if he had considered that since God created man, He did it in relief, he would not have attacked such a complicated problem, which required divinity and a miracle to solve it [2].

It was perhaps Vasari who expressed in the clearest way—and the most naive—the reason that made people prefer a painted portrait to a sculptured bust. After having shown that a good painter ought to understand drawing perfectly, be a good colourist, and understand just as well as an architect the laws of perspective, he must have besides, he adds, "the means of depicting living people from nature and making a good likeness; it is this which has provoked many confusions in our time, for example, the portrait of *Pope Paul III* when placed on a terrace in the sun so that the varnish should dry, was taken for the Pope in person and saluted by the passers-by; nothing of the kind would ever happen with a bust or a statue."

These discussions on a rather vain problem show that already the portrait was regarded as belonging essentially to the art of the painter, which could more easily than sculpture render the mobility of a face. At the time when a face was considered from the point of view of power and majesty, and the outline of the face held the attention, medal makers and sculptors

[1] *Trattato di Pittura....* (ed. Ludwig), I, 82, 484.
[2] Cf. *Due lezioni di Benedetto Varchi...*, 1549. It is at the end of the volume that we find the results of the enquiry made by Varchi on the problem of the pre-eminence of the two arts. Pontormo's letter is quoted from page 132 to page 135. The artist there claims that the most beautiful of Michelangelo's work are his frescoes in the Sistine Chapel, and not his sculpture.

were more in vogue, and it was natural that painters themselves had the ambition to make clear and precise profiles. But when with Botticelli and Leonardo the inner life of the model inspired the artist the problem was no longer the same. People wanted to be represented as capable of feeling, and the reign of gracious and melancholy women began. The feelings they wished to have attributed to them could only be expressed by the brush; from that time there was an ever increasing predilection for a painted portrait.

To these theoretic considerations we must add others which belong to history and have their importance. It is quite usual for political events to have their repercussions on the evolution of art. Now those which occurred during the first forty years of the sixteenth century tended to modify the mentality of the rich and cultivated classes. Through a series of crises Florence attained an absolute government; in 1531 the Duchy of Florence was created and later a Grand Duchy of Tuscany. The convulsions which had exhausted Florence after the Savonarola movement helped the establishing of a régime where the descendants of the Medici imposed by force what Cosimo and Lorenzo had been able to impose by persuasion. At the same time the face of Florentine society altered; a court was created which had very little in common with the centre of gracious simplicity in which Cosimo the Elder and Lorenzo the Magnificent had lived.

Alexander and Cosimo, the one the son of Lorenzo Duke d'Urbino and the other of Giovanni delle Bande Nere were still Medicis, but they belonged to a generation which had suffered the disturbance of the city and which had not the same conception of authority as in the fifteenth century; their contemporaries, dominated by the idea of a Machiavelli, considered power to be absolute and did not think that it could be shared. The Prince must reign by force; Guicchiardini himself, who apparently would have liked the Venetian form of government, was in favour of everything that could increase and consolidate the prestige of an imposed will.

The new tyrants wanted to be the centre of the State; and as such they wished to be honoured. In the fifteenth century it was often a case of the cult of the mind and energy, now it was a cult of the Prince and his power. There existed at the court of Florence an etiquette, a very great care over dress, a need for display, which could not fail to have an influence on the artists who in their portraits expressed to some extent the manner of life and way of thinking of their contemporaries.

The Master of Florence was from the year 1537 Cosimo I de Medici; in 1539 he married the daughter of the Viceroy of Naples, Eleanor of Toledo. This couple exercised a kind of fascination over painters, there was hardly one who had not painted their portraits; the Duke had a great liking for portraiture and even, as we shall see, for collections of portraits. Both he and the Duchess Eleanor had an indisputable influence on the evolution of this type of painting: Bronzino's art would be difficult to understand without realising how these two both had a taste for luxury and display.

Ridolfo Ghirlandaio and Pontormo have both left us interesting portraits of the young Cosimo. In Ghirlandaio's, which Mr. Poggi discovered at Castello, characteristic features are easily recognisable. It is the "beautiful and lifelike" work to which Vasari refers where the son of Giovanni delle Bande Nere was painted as a young boy [1]. There is a calm and indifference in the still childish face, and nothing in it reveals that implacable will which Pontormo analysed so effectively.

This latter, having been commissioned to decorate the first loggia at the entrance of the Palazzo of Castello, included a portrait of the young Duke, as well as of his mother Maria Salviati. Two preliminary studies belong to this commission, a painting and a drawing in the Uffizi representing Cosimo I; the drawing especially is one of Pontormo's best [2]; the profile is hard and already brutal, the penetrating eye of an inquisitor keeps the characteristic shape so dear to the painter; the repressed mouth, the tight lips, the prominent chin, are striking features of a graceless and clean shaven face which

---

[1] Vasari, VI, p. 545. Cf. Giovanni Poggi's article (*Rivista d'arte*, Aug.-Dec., 1916). This portrait is now in the Villa Petraia near Florence.

[2] This drawing is in the store room at the Uffizi. Cf. Gamba, *Rivista d'arte*, 1910, p. 125–127.

Salviati.
49. *Portrait.* (Patrizi Collection, Rome)
50. *Self-Portrait.* (Colonna Gallery, Rome)

Salviati.
51. *Portrait of a Man.* (National Museum, Naples)
52. *Portrait of a Man.* (Corsini Gallery)

express firmness, violence and obstinacy. The painted portrait is less lifelike than the pencil sketch, where Pontormo has quickly caught the features of his young model, exaggerating perhaps his grave and serious character. It was from these sketches, more than from a medal like the one of Domenico di Polo where he is also represented young and callow, that Vasari drew his inspiration when representing his sovereign in the Cosimo I hall in the Palazzo Vecchio.

Later on the Duke allowed his beard to grow and it made him look even more formidable. In his bronze bust, Benvenuto Cellini lost nothing of his implacable brutality; the medium helped to accentuate the hard character which the Venetian Ambassador Vincenzo Fedeli[1] defined with unusual psychological penetration: he shows him to us at forty-two years old, in flourishing health and of a very solid physical aspect, completely preoccupied with keeping his dignity of bearing; his gaze at will became frozen and frightening: "governa gli stati suoi con un grandissimo rigore e spavento". He sometimes took part in amusements with those around him and on those occasions could be approached; but apart from these pastimes he pretended not to recognise any of his companions; "and not one among them had the courage to be in the least familiar with him; the Duke hedged himself in with his habitual severity". Perhaps rather than severity it was arrogance.

He wanted to live opulently. Already in Ridolfo Ghirlandaio's portrait he is represented richly dressed. This taste for beautiful materials and sumptuous garments only tended to increase and the Duchess of Toledo fostered it. He was, says Mellini[2], magnificent in his manner of living and splendid beyond belief in all the details of his existence; he wanted his house and his court to be maintained "con grandezza" and that in everything they should respond to the idea of his own power. He nearly always took his meals in public; he used to sit "in testa di tavola, col dossello sulla testa": the duchess

---

[1] Albèri, *Relazioni degli ambasciatori veneti*, 1839, series 2,   I, p. 337-338, 348 and following.
[2] Domenico Mellini, *Ricordi intorno ai costumi, azioni et governo del Serenis Gran Duca Cosimo* (published in Florence in 1820), p. 3–5.

was on his right. Thus a very severe Court etiquette was established which Eleanor helped to impose.

The latter, daughter of the Viceroy of Naples, Don Pietro, came from a country where despotism was ferocious and merciless: being, besides, Spanish by birth and education she brought to the Medici Palace at the Via Larga, when she came into her sovereignty, habits of luxury and ostentation which must have very much surprised Cosimo's simple and retiring mother, Maria Salviati; she surrounded herself with Spanish ladies and numerous pages. And when, in 1540, Cosimo transferred his Court to the Palazzo Signoria, the display was even more sumptuous.

The painters who had such models in front of them did not find there any of the feelings which up to that time had given charm to the Florentine portraits. The newcomer showed them an icy, impenetrable face; she would not consent to be represented in a simple setting without pomp, in an easy and familiar pose; she always kept up the role of Duchess, daughter of a Viceroy, descendant of one of the most noble Spanish families, and used to living according to the strictest etiquette.

She loved beautiful dresses and sumptuous jewels. At the baptism of her son Don Grazia, she had over her dress of white velvet a very beautiful bodice in cloth of silver: "she was so covered in jewelry as to make a magnificent spectacle". "I heard many people say", said Bishop Jacopo Cortesi, "that she wore 300,000 crowns worth of jewels"[1]. In fact she had numerous goldsmiths in her service. Benvenuto Cellini received important commissions from her; he made her a golden girdle, "tutto gioiellata" in low relief, with masks and other lovely ornamentation, and a pendant which he had begun and finished with his own hand, where he represented among other things two little figures and delicately worked animals; he had set a diamond in it which the Duke had bought for 24,000 crowns, a ruby to the value of 3,000 crowns and numerous pearls[2]. The Duchess had a passion for precious stones. She caused negotiations to be made in Genoa to obtain pos-

---

[1] Anna Baia, *Leonara di Toledo, duchessa di Firenze e di Siena*, 1907, p. 62.
[2] B. Cellini, *Vita* (ed. Guasti), p. 434.

session of a pearl which was more splendid than any of her own, which were nevertheless of rare beauty [1].

Now it seems that Eleanor had a great influence over her husband [2]; the Venetian Ambassador Priuli says that after the death of the Duchess he did not live with the same pomp and splendour. She did everything she could to encourage Cosimo's inclination for a luxurious life. The new formal Court of Florence was to a great extent her creation. Both realised that an attractive ornament of this Court was a circle of good intellects; the Prince's prestige added to it; if Cosimo was like his ancestors, a Maecenas, it was because he thought it essential to protect artists in a state which sacrificed much to pomp and display [3].

Besides, he agreed with Eleanor that painters ought to be the architects of his glory, and that one of their principal functions was to perpetuate his features and those of his near relatives. Thus family portraits became fashionable, the family portraits which did not interpret a state of mind but the conception of a social function.

The glory of the Medici was never celebrated with such brilliance. Great public ceremonies were a pretext to show off the increasing magnificence of the Duke and his ancestors. Painters commemorated them, not only in pictures as Franciabigio had done with *Entry of Leo X into Florence* but in the course of these events themselves, place was found for glorifying important happenings in the lives of the Medicis. On reading the account left us by Pier Francesco Giambullari in a letter to Giovanni Bandini, Envoy of the Duke of Florence at the Court of His Imperial Majesty, concerning the fêtes given for the entry of Eleanor of Toledo into Florence [4], we see how everything was arranged for the crowning glory of the two sovereigns.

[1] Albèri, *Relazioni degli ambasciatori veneti*, series II, vol. I, p. 465 (relation d'Andrea Boldu à la Cour de Savoie).

[2] "Essa poteva assai sull'animo del marito", says Galluzi, *Istoria del Granducato di Toscana*, ed. 1781, II, p. 46.

[3] Cf. Guido Manacorda, *Benedetto Varchi* (*Annali della R. Scuola Normale di Pisa*, 1903).

[4] *Apparato et feste delle nozze dello Illustrissimo Signor Duca di Firenze e della Duchessa sua Consorte*, 1539.

The new Duchess was to meet Cosimo between Leghorn and Pisa, and the couple made their entry into Florence on June 29th, 1539, by the Porta Prato, which was decorated with a magnificent triumphal arch. The Spanish Princess, sumptuously dressed in crimson satin embroidered with gold, was able to assess the grandeur of her adopted family at the very moment of entry into the city where she was to rule; for everything on this triumphal arch proclaimed the glory of the illustrious father of Cosimo, Giovanni delle Bande Nere "ever victorious" and brilliant in arms. Further on in the Piazza San Marco, the same hero appeared seated on a "ferocious" horse, holding in his right hand a heavy iron mace ready to strike. The execution of this statue was entrusted to Triboli, and on the base Bronzino had represented in bronze colours two episodes in the life of the rider; one where he was attacked in the Marshes near Pavia by numerous enemies, whom he succeeded in repelling with courage and great honour; the other where he was making incredible carnage of an enemy battalion near Abbiatigrasso [1].

But it was in the great courtyard of the Medici Palace that the past was most sumptuously evoked. Vasari tells us that Triboli was again the great decorator here, and that he had the collaboration of the best young painters of the time; among others, Bronzino, de Vacchiacca and Battista Franco [2]. He mingled Greek and Roman themes with the history of the Medici family [3]. On the Eastern side it began with the successful return of Cosimo to his country, then the journey of Lorenzo the Magnificent to Naples on behalf of the safety of his country, the entry of Leo X into Florence, the taking of Abbiatigrasso by Giovanni delle Bande Nere, the Coronation of Charles V by Clement VII, a Medici, and even the unhappy days of the decadence summarised in a picture where the numerous difficulties encountered at Naples by Duke Alexander were shown.

The west side of the courtyard was consecrated to Cosimo, still young and already famous. They depicted him at his "fortunate birth", which

---

[1] *Apparato....*, p. 16. Cf. Vasari, VI, p. 38.

[2] Vasari, VI, p. 87.

[3] *Apparato....*, p. 22.

marked the beginning of a new order, as the inscriptions said "magnus ab integro caeciorum nascitur ordo"and "redeunt saturnia regna". Then followed his election to the Ducal rank and afterwards the taking of Montemurlo. In another picture he is seen receiving from the hand of the Emperor all the insignias of his rank; and finally is depicted the Marriage by Procuration at Naples between the Duke and Eleanor of Toledo.

Neither was this all: in the Loggia several portraits of famous ancestors had been placed: a Cosimo the Elder "naturalissimo" dominated the centre; then there was a Leo X accompanied by two Cardinals, Julius de Medici and Luigi dei Rossi, which must have been a copy of Raphael's work, and as a pendant to it Clement VII with Hyppolitus and Alexander de Medici.

Such was the important place given to portraiture in a great official cere-mony. The cult of the family imposed itself on the new chief of Florence as a necessity; never had so many portraits of the Medici been painted as from this time when one of their descendants became in a definite and lasting way the Master of Tuscany. Some years later in 1566, when Johanna of Austria made her solemn entry into Cosimo's capital and when they celebrated her nuptials with the heir to the ducal crown, Francesco de Medici, there was no less splendour; in the decorative scheme designed by Vincenzo Borghini, portraits played an important part, and again on this occasion the Medici fam-ily were much glorified.

The procession was welcomed as in 1539 at the Porta Prato, by Giovanni delle Bande Nere, surrounded by celebrated Florentines among whom ap-peared Pippo Spano, Farinata degli Uberti, Piero Capponi and many writers and artists. Domenico Mellini in his long description of this ceremony [1] emphasises these portraits of celebrated men which were almost all made from others "painted from nature". The organiser of this beautiful festival wanted the great Condottiere, reflection of Florentine power, to be ac-companied by those who had brought honour on their country in all spheres,

---

[1] Descrizione dell' entrata della Sereniss. Reina Giovanna d'Austria et dell' apparato fatto in Firenze nella venuta et per le felicissime nozze di S. Altezza et dell' Illustrissimo et Eccellentiss. S. Don Francesco dei Medici, Principe di Fiorenza et di Siena, Scritta da Domenico Mellini, 1566.

and especially in those of the intellect. Thus Florence and the Florentines was the first glory to be offered to the newcomer.

It was also the apotheosis of the ducal house; and this apotheosis took the form of a crowd of portraits or commemorative pictures where, without a break and to excess, the celebrated ancestors were depicted; if in 1566 they insisted more on the past glory of the town and its great men than in 1539, they also gave more space to living Medicis and those who had lastingly conquered power; we have got a long way from the idea of ancestors who were seldom portrayed and who apppeared modestly in a procession or assembly of saints. They even acquired the habit of depicting members of the ruling family in ceremonies which were not especially consecrated to them. When Archbishop Altoviti made his entry into Florence, "he went into the Archbishop's chamber, which was adorned with a number of marvellous tapestries of great price, and also with numerous portraits of the illustrious house of Medici, painted from nature"[1].

These latter were also represented in the huge catafalque standing in the church of San Lorenzo for Michelangelo's funeral[2]; one of them shows Lorenzo the Magnificent welcoming the young sculptor into his garden of antiquities, in another Michelangelo is receiving from Pope Clement the commission for the new Sacristy and the San Lorenzo Library. Besides this catafalque there was, in the first chapel beside the high altar, a huge painting, where they had imagined Michelangelo in the Elysian Fields, surrounded by celebrated painters of the past and Florentines. It would be tedious to describe, after Vasari, the scenes which recalled the important moments in the life of the sculptor up to the occasion when Stefano Pieri, a pupil of Bronzino, had represented him seated beside Duke Cosimo, having a discussion with him. It is interesting and curious to see all these occasions in which they took the opportunity to perpetuate the faces of living people. Portraiture had become a real element of decoration; if its importance had thus increased

---

[1] *Igresso dell'arcivescovo Antoni Altovi a Frenze* (15 May 1567) published by Pietro Faufani (*Spigolatura fiorentina*, 1868).

[2] Vasari, VII, p. 296 and following.

it was obviously due to the influence of the court of the Medici, which contributed so much to the development of the cult of the sovereign at the same time as the cult of great men.

Cosimo I de Medici had a greater ambition than to have his exploits recounted in ephemeral decorations of state ceremonies. He dreamed of making the Palazzo della Signoria the temple of his glory and to fix in frescoes for all eternity the memory of his brilliant reign. He conferred on Vasari the task of carrying on this imposing work.

The historian of the *Lives* was unfortunately a painter without power or brilliance. When quite young, in 1524 (he was then thirteen), he came from Arezzo to Florence, brought by Cardinal Silvio Passerini, and the studios he frequented were those of Andrea del Sarto and Baccio Bandinelli; he had even, according to him, known Michelangelo at this time, who was working at the Medici chapel in San Lorenzo. In 1528, Rosso, visiting Arezzo, where he found the young Vasari, helped him with advice on the technique of drawing. An even more important event in his career was the journey he took to Rome in 1531 when twenty years old, with Cardinal Hyppolitus de Medici; there he was able to dedicate many long months to the art of painting. In company with Francesco Salviati he untiringly copied the noted works in the Vatican [1]. The Sistine made a deep impression on him and he became an ardent admirer of Michelangelo. Later on he copied with great care Raphael's *Leo X* [2]. This is sufficient to prove that he was irresistibly drawn towards the Roman conceptions. He soon had the ambition, like Michelangelo, to decorate huge spaces. But the mind and strength of this artist underwent strange distortions on entering into his art, which was no more than a set of vacant formulas. In his historical frescoes, in which figure important collections of portraits, he tried to unite the grandeur of Michelangelesque attitudes to this need to characterise individual faces, which was a thing that Michelangelo could not endure.

---

[1] Vasari, VII, p. 653–654.
[2] Vasari, VII, p. 662.

Now he had no very great qualities as a portraitist. In his *Life*, written by himself, he tells us that he painted at almost the same time (1533) *Alexander de Medici, Catherine*, future Queen of France, and *Lorenzo the Magnificent*[1]. We do not know what has happened to the second picture, but the two others are in the Uffizi; neither is impressive by its lifelike rendering or power; they make us at times think of the works of Le Brun, organiser of the Glorification of Louis XIV.

The author himself explains his intentions. He surrounded the young Duke with everything which suggested his role and power in the State. He wanted to make a symbolic portrait of it. Clothing him in brilliant armour he showed that he was ready, for the love of his country, to take in hand the defence of every public and private interest. Behind his shoulders columns and ruined buildings recall the Siege of Florence in 1530; ruins which show up in contrast the town enjoying the benefits of peace under the serenity of his sky.

The courtier painter ended by exaggerating the place of symbolism in portraiture and by falling into puerility; the red cloth covering the throne indicates by its colour the bloodshed of those who had refused to accept the domination of the house of Medici; a piece of this cloth covering the thigh of the duke shows that the Medicis themselves were struck by the death of Julius and the wounds of the old Lorenzo. The stem of laurel, which takes on a new life, is the ducal family which was to have numerous offspring and a brilliant future. As for the helmet on the ground consumed by fire, it is the symbol of eternal peace which "due to the good government of the Prince enabled his people to live in joy and amity"[2]. In the midst of all these allegories the artist has neglected the portrait itself; in the one in the Johnson Collection and even in the other heads of the young duke of Florence there remains something of his strange and troubled mind. With Vasari on the other hand he is the personification of good government; there is great contrast between the insignificance of the face and the complacent care with

---

[1] Vasari, VII, p. 657.
[2] Vasari, VIII, p. 241-242.

which he has arranged the symbols; the personality of the model is lost in the dullness of design and colour.

The *Lorenzo the Magnificent* reveals a like care to give philosophical and historical importance to the work, which could not help detracting from the realism and strength of the picture. Besides, in the letter which he writes on this subject to Alexander de Medici, we can see that he thought less of the physical and psychological resemblance of the portrait than of the objects which surrounded it: on a marble pillar he has drawn a face of falsehood which Lorenzo uncovers with his hand, and beneath it a very ugly mask representing Vice, under a vase full of roses and violets on which is hung another very beautiful mask which symbolises Virtue, with a crown of laurels and this inscription: "proemium virtutis" [1].

In this way he describes with hollow symbolism the glory of Lorenzo. This very conception is an admission of weakness; the artist, incapable of rendering by technical methods the character of his model, thus evades the difficulty; he makes us a commentary and this commentary becomes almost the entire portrait. It was fortunate that this tendency did not spread and that Vasari himself abandoned it. The abuse of allegory would have hastened the death of this kind of painting which was the only one in which Florentine artists had not lost contact with life, and they would have lost it if Vasari had founded a school.

But he had not a strong enough personality to impose a style of art. He was even in his eclecticism inspired by the Venetians; his self-portrait in the Uffizi by its characteristics and pose is reminiscent of Titian [2]. At times he approaches the fifteenth-century style. Being commissioned to decorate the refectory of the Monastery of San Michele in Bosco at Bologna he painted, among other scenes, Saint Gregory at table in a Monastery served by monks; it was simply a gallery of portraits in which he gave to the reigning Pontiff

---

[1] Cf. Vasari, VIII, p. 240. On the vase full of roses these words are written: *virtus omnium vas*.

[2] Vasari does not seem to have considered these portraits as very important works. He speaks of them with some detachment. "Ne de ritratti fatti da me, che pur sono assai, faro menzione alcuna, che sarebbe cosa tediosa: e per dire il vero, me sono difeso, quanto ho potuto, di farne" (Vasari, VII, p. 638).

the features of Clement VII; and among the people which surround him we can easily recognise Alexander de Medici and many Brothers of the Monastery [1].

Nevertheless it was unusual for Vasari to be inspired by the living model in his religious pictures. On the other hand he made prodigious use of them in his historical paintings, which he derived great pleasure in composing and in which he considered himself worthy to be compared to the great decorators whom he had so much admired during his progress to Venice: Correggio at Parma, Giulio Romano at Mantua. His first great series of frescoes were those in the Palazzo Cancelleria in Rome: a task which was conferred on him by the good offices of Paolo Giovio.

On the end wall Vasari painted the two most important stories; on one side Pope Paul III appears as protector of the arts and on the other he does homage to the art of some celebrated men, including Sadoleto, Bembo, Contarino, Giovio and finally Michelangelo himself, who can be seen in the recess of a door [2]. It is a curious blending of life and fantasy and the symbolic figures are rather crushing in their size. Also, these frescoes, made to unite a beautiful collection of portraits, swamp them into insignificance and artificial imitation. The religious pictures, in which a gathering of patricians and great ladies would seem out of place, give a much better impression of life. Besides this, the fire of Michelangelo, which inspires the allegorical figures, does not seem suitable to scenes which should demand a more serene and harmonious composition. This lack of balance between the nature of the subject and the means of expression is already an obvious sign of decadence.

After having celebrated in this declamatory way Paul III in his role of Maecenas, he was commissioned to honour the glory of Cosimo I. It was in 1555 that Vasari became Administrator of Art to the Duke of Florence [3]. Having at first begun by decorating the Chambers of the Elements dedicated to the Celestial Gods, he then had the idea of making a companion to it under

---

[1] Vasari, VII, p. 664-665.

[2] Vasari, VII, p. 679. — Cf. Ernst Steinmann, *Freskenzyklen der Spätrenaissance in Rom* (*Monatshefte für Kunstwissenschaft*, 1910).

[3] Vasari, VII, p. 698.

the title of the Terrestial Gods—the illustrious house of Medici. Wishing to please his master, he contrasted the two in rather doubtful taste, which must, however, have very much flattered the last representative of the ancient Florentine family. Vasari himself tells us that if he placed the Hall of Cosimo the Elder beneath that of Ceres it was because the great ancestor seemed to have been a kind of New Ceres always ready to fill his city to overflowing with all kinds of riches.

He held these frescoes in great esteem; he has left us a long commentary on them [1] under the form of a conversation between Francesco de Medici and himself: a dialogue which has its uses, for the allegories at times are lacking in clarity and the portraits are so numerous that a guide is necessary in the midst of this important gathering.

In the first conversation, on the second day, the young Prince was astounded that it was possible to get together such a collection of portraits and Vasari explained his sources, which were particularly the fifteenth-century sculptors and great fresco painters whose religious pictures were full of portraits. At the request of the Prince he made a complete and detailed analysis of all this collection, without omitting any of the faces which he had chosen to record. It would be of little interest to follow all the painter's commentaries. But what is worth noting is to see the cult of the sovereign and his ancestors reaching its zenith.

Let us for example take the Hall of Cosimo the Elder; it is in the five panels into which the ceiling is divided that some typical scenes of his life are painted: the departure into exile, the interviews between artists and learned men, Brunelleschi's presentation of the plans for San Lorenzo, the conversation with Santi Bentivoglio, whom Cosimo advised to take power in Bologna, and finally the return from exile. In the court of intellectuals and artists surrounding Cosimo, Vasari has been lavish in portraits; we see

---

[1] *Ragionamenti di Giorgi Vasari sopra le invenzioni da lui dipinte in Firenze ner Palazzo di Loro Altezze Serenissime.* These dialogues were almost entirely written in 1558, except for the last one dedicated to the Hall of the Five Hundred which is dated 1563. They were published in 1588 by Giunti in Florence: they were republished by Milanesi in Volume VIII of his edition of Vasari (p. 1-231).

there Marsile Ficin offering his works and by his side Paolo Toscanelli, Donatello with his characteristic "cappuccio", Brunelleshi, Fra Angelico, Luca della Robbia, Filippo Lippi in profile, Ghiberti, Andrea del Castagno and, talking together, Pesello "excellent painter of animals" and Paolo Uccello "great master of perspective".

For Vasari these frescoes had no value apart from forming part of an allegorical series; and that is why he includes such figures as Eternity, Renown, Prudence, Courage, Guile, Religion, Vigilance and Daring. To all this he adds medallions painted on the walls and representing members of Cosimo's family, his father and his three sons. The hall of Lorenzo the Magnificent is arranged in the same way; it is again by symbolic attributes that the painter wants to express the loftiest virtues of the illustrious protector of the arts who in an important scene dominates, as does Cosimo the Elder, a great assembly of eminent minds.

To be the worthy descendant of Lorenzo, Cosimo I also had to have his court of intellectuals and artists; this is why in the hall of his name he is represented seated in the midst of architects and engineers, such as Tribolo and Tasso, sculptors such as Ammanato and Bandinelli; beside these Benvenuto Cellini is holding a discussion with Francesco di ser Jacopo, the administrator of the Duke's buildings. The paintings of the Duchess and her sons, Francesco, Giovanni and Garzia, painted on the walls are portraits without character, like almost all those which Vasari has placed in the medallions on the walls he was commissioned to decorate. Nevertheless, in the Giovanni delle Bande Nere room he has had a more successful result: Piero Francesca de Medici and Catterina Sforza appear both in profile and are not without attraction. Her hand on her breast, her head erect and proud, this latter has the hard and haughty bearing of a virago. It is one of the few faces which leaves a strong impression in this interminable gallery of portraits.

The central scene in the Clement VII chamber is the one in which crowds predominate; the artists has here commemorated the crowning of the Emperor Charles V by Clement VII: a solemn and magnificent ceremony watched by a large number of prelates. "I was present there", says Vasari "when

I was still young and I have taken pleasure in recalling this event". But he had great difficulties to overcome, the greatest of which was the smallness of the space "which was sixty ells and ought to have been a hundred thousand". From this time onwards painters turned their attention to feats of this description.

There was no life whatsoever in these crowds, not even as much as Salviati had given to his portraits. As for Francis I and Charles V, they had awkward attitudes and feebly drawn features. In the Hall of Leo X *The Entry of the Pope into Florence* remains, in spite of certain qualities of composition, cold and monotonous. The faces of all who figure in the processions should have been of a beautiful character. And, besides, how many of them do we remember?

This plethora of portraits—most of them second-rate—ends by becoming wearisome. Rarely has a ruling family caused the cult of its own fame to be celebrated with so little discretion. Even the palace at Versailles does not offer a general effect comparable to the one in the Palazzo Vecchio, transformed by Vasari into a temple to the glory of the Medici.

Cosimo I's predilections were expressed as much in his art collections as in his commissions to Vasari. We have seen that the inventory of paintings collected by Lorenzo contained very few portraits. On the other hand, in the middle of the sixteenth century there was an imposing number of them in the ducal Palace. The idea came even to Cosimo I to follow the example given by Bishop Paolo Giovio and to form a gallery exclusively composed of portraits. This project was not peculiar to Giovio and others had made such collections before him. Already in the fifteenth century Federigo da Montefeltro had tried to create something of the sort in Urbino. In his library he had surrounded a painting of himself with his son Guidobaldo with twenty-eight portraits of philosophers and famous poets. It is still possible to realise today what this curious collection must have looked like, since the pictures have been preserved partly in the Louvre and partly in the Barberini Gallery in Rome. This cult of illustrious men was very similar to the Florentine practice where the glory of heroes and scholars of antiquity was celebrated, under the guise of Triumphs. The Duke of Urbino presented himself more especially as a humanist paying tribute to the culture of the past, whereas Giovio seemed rather to be a patron of the arts who thought it original to collect in this manner so many different and expressive portraits painted by some of the great artists of his time.

The Bishop of Nocera, that daring intriguer, who has so much in common with his contemporary Aretino, did not recoil from any steps, however difficult, to get possession of what he wanted. His descendant G. B. Giovio said of him that he bought portraits wherever he found any good ones, and every time he met a sufficiently skilful artist; moreover, "he sought them with a boldness which was quite pardonable in a collector"[1]. Like Vasari when he was drawing up a commentary on the frescoes in the Palazzo Vecchio, Giovio wanted to give the idea of the completeness of his museum by declaring in his "Elogia virorum"[2] the considerable number of works which composed it.

This collection, the idea of which came to him in 1521[3], was distributed between Florence and Rome[4] before it was collected together on the shores of Lake Como. According to a manuscript where Paolo Giovio recounts ten years of his life, Gian Battista Giovio was able to fix 1537 as the date of the transfer of the museum to Como. It was about this time that the Marchese del Guasto became Governor of Milan in the name of Charles V; and Giovio who was his intimate friend, decided to go and settle close

---

[1] Letter from G. B. Giovio to Tiraboschi (8 Sept. 1780), (Campori, *Lettere artistische medite*, 1866, p. 235).

[2] It was Doni who had given him the first idea of this publication. Cf. Giovio's letter to Antonio Francesco Doni (14 Sept. 1548): "Ebbe la vostra lettera con la mostra del libro delle Medaglie le quali mi sono piaciute sommamente.... Volesse Dio che di questa maniera si potessero intagliare tutte le immagini ch'io tengo al Museo...." (Bottari, *Raccolta di lettere....*, 1822, V, p. 148). This idea was realised in the Basle edition of 1575.

[3] Cf. Gaye, *Carteggio...*, II, p 151.   G.B. Giovio said that his ancestor began the collection "fin nell'eta piu fresca".

[4] In a letter written by Giovio to the Marquis Federigo Gonzaga (Luzio, *Lettere inedite di Paolo Giovio*, 1885, p. 22), he says (13 Sept. 1522), "Quanto ad exornare el loco di V. Ex. con le imagine de excellenti capitani de la natione italica, io ho in Firenze el Sforza e a Roma el conte Carmagnola, quali madoro in schizo di pictura e cercharo qualce altro".

to him [1]. He continued untiringly to enrich his collection which finished by being of great iconographical value. He never missed an opportunity of enriching it. When Raphael was commissioned to decorate the Stanza in the Vatican, he had at first to get rid of the frescoes by Piero della Francesca, Bramantino, Pietro della Gatta and Luca Signorelli; but he wished at least to keep a record of them, and so he made his best pupils copy several heads of celebrated men which were included in these pictures. These copies after having been the property of Giulio Romano passed into Giovio's collection. As well as this, Vasari, who depicted the features of the Bishop of Nocera in a fresco in the Palazza della Cancellaria, painted for him in a similar picture heads of poets of antiquity. Cardinal du Bellay had sent him portraits of Francis I and of Budé from Paris. And even from Mexico, Ferdinand Cortes had sent his portrait with a precious jewel with a heart of emerald [2].

Thus Giovio was preoccupied right up to the end of his life with the enrichment of his beautiful museum which had become so celebrated. He wanted every form of human activity to be represented in it; he had four sections; deceased learned men and poets, living intellectuals and writers, artists, and finally the supreme Pontiffs, kings and generals; he thought of this classification himself.

Now it is interesting for us to know that a part of this important collection was to begin with assembled in Florence, where it inevitably contributed to the development of taste for historic portraiture.   Gian Battista Giovio says with reason of his ancestor, "not only did he collect for himself these venerable remains of antiquity, but he gave several princes and in particular Cosimo de Medici, the idea of doing the same" [3]. The Duke of Florence was one of the powerful men of the day whom Giovio liked to flatter. The

---

[1] Mr. Carl Frey (*Codice Magliabechiano*, p. LXVII) gives the conjecture that he had the idea of building his museum at Como in 1521 and that it was completed in 1536, a supposition based on no known data. The desire to be neighbour of the Marchese del Guasto was sufficient reason for him to come to Como.

[2] *Elogio di Monsignor Paolo Giovio il seniore vescovo di Nocera, scritto dal conte*, Giovanni Battista Giovio (*Elogi italiani*, 1763, VIII, 38).

[3] G. B. Giovio, op. cit.,   p. 34.

sombre and severe humour of the young sovereign was enlivened by the caustic and dangerous wit of Aretino's rival; relations between these two people were every cordial, and at the end of his life in 1552, Giovio was even lodged by the Duke in a "good house" near the Palace, and he hoped to be able to spend part of the summer there [1].

One of the results of this intimacy was that the Duke became more and more interested in the idea of a collection of portraits. It was, unfortunately, the conception of a sovereign and not of an artist. When we think of the painter he chose to form a collection like the one at Como, we are tempted to attribute an extraordinary talent to the man who was chosen to decorate the halls of the Palazzo Vecchio. Cristofano dell'Altissimo would probably have been entirely ignored—and deserved to be—if the Duke of Florence had not commissioned him to go and copy the paintings which Giovio had collected. In his study of the members of the Academy of Drawing, Vasari dedicates a few brief lines to him: "he was", says he, "a pupil of Pontormo and later of Bronzino; and after having painted in his youth many oil pictures and some portraits, he was sent to Como by the Duke" [2].

One of his letters gives us precise information concerning the time when he arrived at the Museum; the last day of May 1553. He had already been working for eleven months at copying the twenty-four pictures which the Duke of Tuscany had selected. He had already finished them some time past, and he could have painted a larger number if the commission had been more important; this was why he waited impatiently to add other names to those he had already been given [3]. These twenty-four copies sent by Altissimo to Florence in the month of August pleased Cosimo very much and he thanked him for them: "We have received the portraits which you sent by Milan; they have arrived in good condition and we are very satisfied with them. You will continue thus to make others, choosing, as we have written to you, the most famous".

---

[1] *Lettere volgari di mons, Paolo de Como*, 1560, p. 63.
[2] Vasari, p. 608-9.
[3] Gaye, *Carteggio....*, II, p. 389 and following.

Vasari.
53. *Clement VII and Hyppolitus de Medici*. (Hall of Clement VII)
54. *Leo X and Cardinals*. (Hall of Leo X, Palazzo Vecchio, Florence)

55. Bronzino. *Portrait of Guidobaldo II della Rovere, Duke of Urbino.* (Pitti Palace)

Giulio Giovio, the heir of Paolo Giovio, kept the Duke informed of his painter's progress, and spoke of it in terms of excessive appreciation: "he has copied the examples so conscientiously that it is difficult to distinguish them from the originals". The artist himself was no less conscious of his genius; he asked Pagni's impression of a consignment he had just finished on the 26 September 1554: "Tell me if among these portraits there are any which are not perfect, if the answer is yes it is because I could not do otherwise, the original having been badly painted"[1]. Two years later, Altissimo was still at Como complaining that he had nothing to do and no means of living. Giulio Giovio then wrote to the Duke that he was astonished at the collection thus made[2]. It was a long and exacting labour. In his second edition of the *Lives*, Vasari speaks of the portraits which had been painted up till then (1568), which shows that at that date the important commission was not yet completed[3]; but the number of copies was already considerably more than two hundred and eighty. They had been placed in the "guardaroba" of the Duke who was very proud of them.

The habit spread. While Altissimo was working in the Giovio Museum, another painter came there; it was Bernadino Campi, on whom Princess Hyppolita de Gonza had conferred a similar task. Later on Cosimo I's collection was considered to be so interesting that the Archduke Ferdinand of Tyrol sent an artist to Florence charged with the task of copying Altissimo's copies. If we realise that Cardinal Federigo Borromeo, founder of the Ambrosiana at Milan, also had some of the canvases in the Giovio Museum copied, we can understand the prestige of this latter and similarly of the collection made by Cosimo I[4].

This iconographical gallery, which must have given birth to the idea of a collection of portraits of artists which another Medici made later on, is today housed in the corridor leading from the Uffizi to the Pitti Palace.

---

[1] Gaye, II, p. 402.

[2] Gaye, II, p. 413; Gualandi, *Nuova raccolta di lettere sulla pittura, scultura ed architettura*, 1844, I, p. 371.

[3] Vasari, *Le Vite....*, ed. 1568 (*secondo e ultimo volume della terze parte*).

[4] G. B. Giovio, *Elogio*, p. 100-101.

It is a long series of portraits without either character or life; and when one compares the originals which are still existing with these pallid reproductions, we are astonished at the lack of skill of the man who painted them. There may be here a fairly correct record of features, but there is never any record of facial expression. Basically it was then not a collection of works of art that Cosimo wanted, but a series of faces of famous people. He could not himself carry further the taste for portraiture.

It was soon to become an unprecedented craze in Florence; the Duke was imitated, who had himself imitated Giovio: "Truly", says Vasari, "we owe a great deal to the diligence and efforts of each of them as not only the sovereigns' palaces, but even the dwellings of many ordinary citizens were adorned with portraits of one or other of these famous men according to the country, the family and the sympathy of each"[1]. We have then arrived at a period when the form of painting which was an exception in the fifteenth century became the favourite artistic expression of the Florentines.

---

[1] Vasari, VII, p. 609.- Cf. as well G. P. Lomazzo, *Trattato del'arte della pittura*, 1584. book VI, chap. L, p. 436.

CHAPTER X

STATE PORTRAITS, BRONZINO

Influence of Pontormo on Bronzino. Portrait of Guidobaldo della Rovere. *Ugolino Martelli* in Berlin. Bronzino, portraitist to the Florence aristocracy. Portraits of Panciatichi. *The Young Man* in the Louvre. The influence of Rome on Bronzino. *Stefano Colonna. Giannetto Doria. The Young Nobleman* in the National Gallery. Bronzino, official portrait painter to Cosimo I and Eleanor of Toledo. Portraits of the Duke, the Duchess and their children. The series of twenty-four Medici. The characteristics of state portraiture. Bronzino's last portraits: the magnificence of costume.

Among the painters living at the time of the stiff and authoritative Medici, Pontormo was too strong a personality to submit entirely to the rigours of court life. This was, on the other hand, the task of a Vasari or a Bronzino. Vasari's work was a kind of epic, through which passed ceaselessly the faces of the masters of Florence or of those living in their circle. Bronzino was less imaginative; he paid homage to his models in the precise framework of an easel portrait. Wishing above all to please them, he very quickly became a state portraitist.

He could not have received a very deep inpression from the teaching of his first master—Raffaellino del Garbo—a second-rate follower of Ghirlandaio and Botticelli. It was by his intimacy with Pontormo that a personal art full of grandeur was made known to him. Pontormo was between 1515 and 1522 under the influence of Bartolommeo and Andrea del Sarto; he had finished the great *Visitation* in the Santissima Annunziata and the *Holy Family* in San Michele Visdomini. In a painting of this period, today in the National Gallery, and which decorated in the sixteenth century Piero Francesco Borgherini's bedchamber, there is, Vasari tells us, a portrait of Bronzino, hardly adolescent. It is an episode from the Bible, Joseph in Egypt, where the young boy is represented seated on a staircase, with a "lively and marvellously beautiful face"[1]. The master, often hard on his pupils, was full of sympathy for this young follower, to whom this vocation seemed irresistible. Soon a great friendship grew up between the two artists; Bronzino was scarcely twenty years old when Pontormo made him his assistant. While he was decorating the Certosa d'Ema, from 1522, he took him as a helper and a very important one at that; he did not leave him to finish off certain details, but made him paint in its entirety a *Pietà* and a *Saint Lawrence*. Afterwards we find them working together in Santa Felicita between 1526 and 1528. A little later on, when Bronzino was summoned by the Duke Guidobaldo d'Urbino to decorate the Villa Imperiale at Pesaro, Pontormo invited him to come back to Florence as quickly as possible, to help him finish the frescoes begun by Franciabigio at the Villa Poggio a Caiano [2]. Several years later they again collaborated in the decoration of the Villa Medici at Carregi. Finally, when Pontormo died in 1557, it was his former pupil who was commissioned to finish the important work in the Church of San Lorenzo, where he completed the *Resurrection* and the *Deluge*.

These few facts are sufficient to show the intimacy between the two painters. But the constant, almost continuous, contact with the creator of so many expressive portraits did not check the development of Bronzino's personality. Whereas in his religiously inspired pictures he is an imitator of little originality, he can be seen developing little by little in his portraits a technique of great solidity and often remarkable fullness. Vasari affirms that he very soon became famous and received, when still young, numerous commissions. "In those days", says he [3] (it was before the Siege of Florence), "he painted many portraits which gained him a great reputation. Later when he was in Urbino, he painted the duke himself, and a young girl famous for her beauty, the daughter of Matteo Sofferoni". When he came back to Florence to work at

---

[1] Vasari, VI, p. 261.

[2] Octavian de Medici had had the idea of carrying on with this decoration after the death of Leo X.

[3] Vasari, VII, p. 595.

the Villa Poggio a Caiano he was already celebrated as a portrait painter and his renown was to increase.

Unfortunately Vasari only gives us the most vague information about Bronzino's early years. Before his stay in Urbino there is no portrait which can with certainty be attributed to him. The first to give us any idea of the talent of his youth is the one which he painted towards 1532, representing the Duke of Urbino, Guidobaldo II della Rovere [1] *(Plate XXVIII, fig. 55)*.

This picture has a history; it is only recently that it has been recognised as the work which Vasari mentions; it was thought for some time to be Hyppolitus de Medici by Pontormo. Mr. Justi has shown that the model and the painter are different [2]. The Palazzo Albani at Urbino has in fact a portrait which bears a striking resemblance to this latter; it is the same man, older, already greying, with his right hand on the head of a dog; on an envelope there is the following inscription: "Al, Illmo et Eccmo Sigre II Signore Guidobaldo duca d'Urbino". Among the arguments which go to confirm the identification of the picture [3], note the following: the work came from Urbino; it was sent to Florence after the death of the last duke of that town in 1631; it was part of crate no. 136 "quadro con il ritratto del Duca Guidobaldo che tiene una mano sopra un cane" [4].

Bronzino remained with Guidobaldo from about 1530-1532, and the portrait dates from towards the end of his stay. We know precisely that when the commission was given to the artist he was not able to carry it out, because his sitter had not yet received the armour he was expecting from Lombardy, which was to give him the bearing of a leader. Despite an already abundant beard, Guidobaldo's features have an aspect of great youth [5] in the shape of the eyes; here Pontormo's teaching is revealed, as well as in the general

---

[1] Florence, Pitti Palace.

[2] Justi, *Die Bildnisse des Kardinals Hippolyt von Medici in Florenz* (*Zeitschrift für bildende Kunst*, 1897, p. 34).

[3] *Rivista d'arte*, January, 1912.

[4] This conjecture is accompanied by another (a subject for caution) by which the artist would be Zuccaro; in the painting of the picture in the Pitti nothing recalls this second-rate mannerist.

[5] Born in 1514 he was about eighteen years old at the time.

accent of the face, where a certain anxiety is expressed. The lighting gives value to the expression of the gaze and gives a rather dramatic aspect to the whole face. All these elements recall the spirit and technique of Pontormo. But there are others in it which are foreign to the master's manner and which already show new tendencies in his pupil. Guidobaldo, who is represented full face with his body slightly turned to the right, wears the clothes of a Condottiere. He is strapped into a superb breastplate, with the highlights shown as beautiful white streaks. The hands, with tapering fingers, one resting on the helmet and the other on the head of a dog, both of them very slim, almost effeminate, are by a painter who has really grasped the delicate nature which is one of the essential characteristics of his model [1].

This portrait of the Duke of Urbino belongs thus to a period when Bronzino is still under the influence of the artistic environment in which he lived. He was still persuaded that a portrait ought to express a state of mind. This is his first style and recalls, at the same time as Pontormo, Andrea del Sarto and Franciabigio. But the dark materials which used to make the individuality of a face stand out are replaced by a magnificent costume. From this time onwards we find with him a pronounced taste for sumptuous garments.

By the time he came back from Pesaro, Bronzino was already famous; commissions came flowing in even more rapidly than before his departure for the Adriatic Duchy. Among other portraits he made, says Vasari, one of Ugolino Martelli. Today in the Berlin Museum [2], it is certainly one of the most outstanding pictures in Florentine painting. It shows the entire road that had been travelled since the beginning of the sixteenth century. Bronzino's conceptions already differ considerably from those of Pontormo; after having studied the works of his master he began to study Michelangelo. Does not the attitude of Ugolino Martelli recall that of Julius de Medici in

---

[1] Cf. Albèri, *Relazioni degli ambasciatori veneti*, series II, v. The Venetian ambassador Badoera says that is was "sano della persona ed assai forte.... di conplessione melancolica;.... egli senti piu il dolore nelle cose adverse che l'allegrezza nelle prospere" (p. 387-388).

[2] Cf. H. Posse, *Die Gemäldegalerie des K. F. Museums*, I, p. 150.

San Lorenzo? And does it not reveal a love of the monumental style worthy of the great sculptor? *(Plate XXIX, fig. 56).*

Let us first consider the architectural background: it is the interior of the Martelli Palace as it remains to be seen today. This Florentine courtyard with the grey colour of the "pietra serena" leaves an impression of cold simplicity, tempered by the beauty of the marble of the Donatello David which was one of the jewels of the Martelli Collection [1]. It might seem difficult to make a face stand out so clearly against such a background. But Bronzino had other preoccupations besides those of a painter; he wanted first to stress anything which would create the impression of the prestige of his sitter. It is of little importance that attention should be diverted by a series of attributes; for they are precisely there to explain the model's place in society. Already with Guidobaldo the armour is an essential element; with Ugolino Martelli it is even more important: it shows that the young man belongs to one of the most illustrious Florentine families, who takes pride in possessing a beautiful palace and a rich collection of works of art.

Other accessories prove that the model has at the same time a taste for beautiful books and the works of the ancients. On one side there is a Bembo, on the other a Greek text; a book with the inscription Maro which is without doubt a Virgil is on the table. The young humanist with fine head and slim body is dressed in a dark coat which is both simple and elegant. His features are ivory coloured, hardly relieved by the red of the lips and some pink touches on the cheeks. Bronzino's style is taking shape; we see him later often using these cold tones which he was able to develop under the light in an astonishing way. In *Ugolino Martelli* there is nothing more striking than the perfect distribution of tones; the painter has now overcome the difficulties involved in making a face of neutral colour stand out against a background of the same tone. The light comes from the right and illuminates the face and hands; the latter, whose structure recalls Pontormo, make two fine notes of brilliance; the clear white of the right hand is particularly

---

[1] Cf. De Nicola, *Il San Giovannino Martelli di Donatello, Bollettino d'arte,* August 1913.

striking against the binding of the book. Here are real gifts of the colourist; but this painting is by a painter who, unlike one who only knows how to charm the eyes by a display of warm colours, understands extremely well also how to give life to colours without brilliance and also how to mingle them harmoniously.

It is very easy to date this portrait of the humanist. Ugolino Martelli, born in 1519, is here represented quite young; 1535 or 1536 is the probable date. He has no longer the same expression as Guidobaldo; the features are practically motionless. The already cold gaze seems to be acute, and capable of fixing the onlooker with great penetration. Though probably devoid of any feelings of deep emotion, he is the typical elegant and subtle intellectual, more interested in a beautiful work of literature than in the spectacle of life.

It is doubtless between 1532 and 1536 or 1537 that we must date certain of Bronzino's paintings, which are among the most typical of those he has left us of the Florentine aristocracy. *Ugolino Martelli* prepares us for conceptions of a maturity which was rarely to betray any keen sensibilities. But before giving any solemnity to these portraits, Bronzino had allowed them to seduce us like a Pontormo or a Franciabigio, by the distinguished bearing and features of the Tuscan nobility. The Louvre shows us one of these patricians of high descent with a fairly regular profile and a face full of life *(Plate XXIX, fig. 57)*. It was formerly attributed to Sebastiano del Piombo and passed as being Baccio Bandinelli; now nothing recalls the Roman painter's style; as for the face, it is not very like the one we know to be of Bandinelli. In truth it is in no way the portrait of an artist; the pose of the model is becoming more and more of a preoccupation and that of the so-called sculptor is quite usual; a statue becomes a convenient accessory which adorns the picture and which has its interest, although the pose of the sitter at times becomes formalised by it. When it is not a statue it is a musical instrument or a book, which are not necessarily indications of the tastes of the sitter but a growing fashion which was quickly adopted.

In this way landscape backgrounds were definitely disappearing, and we have here one of the most notable effects of Michelangelism. The artist concentrates on depicting man and neglects nature. This tendency became generalised. Beautiful horizons had no longer any justification as a background to a portrait which had become a complete analysis of the sitter and his social rank. The Roman School almost entirely ignored them, and Titian, who is, however, one of the most beautiful landscape painters of Italy, usually painted portraits against a plain background and made magnificent colours stand out against it.

Before becoming official portrait painter to the Court of the Medici, Bronzino had filled a similar role with the Florentine aristocracy, and little by little his gifts of spontaneity were swamped by more haughty and cold conceptions. When these earlier qualities reappear in his work it is only a passing mood. He was destined to express the ideal courtier of his time whose qualities Castiglione had defined several years earlier [1].

"In order that the faces of these elect should be agreeable to look at it was not desirable that their features should be particularly delicate [2]; they must have at the same time power and grace. The body must be harmonious, neither too big nor too small; when it is of exaggerated proportions it is awkward in expressing lightness; the courtier must show vigour and suppleness; and to litheness of body must be added litheness of mind [3]."

And moreover the body must be dressed with elegance and discretion. In the history of costume, the sixteenth century is almost a period of anarchy. Cesare Vecellio says that during this period feminine dress varied even more than the shape of the moon [4]. There was a time when fashion itself disappeared and gave way to the caprices of individual imagination. Castiglione states that the shape of clothes was full of variety; "some dressed in the French style, some in the Spanish, some in the German; certain people even imitated

---

[1] It must be noted the *Cortegiano* did not appear until 1528.

[2] *Il Cortegiano*, ed. Cian, p. 41-42 and p. 50-51.

[3] *Il Cortegiano*, p. 53-58 and p. 109-112. Cf. also *Dialog di M. Lodovico Dolce nel quale si ragiona della qualita, diversita e proprieta dei colori*, 1565, p. 36-37.

[4] Cesare Vecellio, *Habita antichi e moderni di tutto il mondo*, ed. Didot, 1859, p. 115.

the Turks[1]". It was also very difficult for a man of the court to make a choice amidst such confusion. None the less the author of the *Cortegiano* (The Courtier) advises seriousness and gravity; it is thus that in dress, black has the most grace; or if it is not black it should be dark in tone, a remark which applies not only to ordinary dress but also to those for special occasions which are "pomposi e superbi".

These ideas of Castiglione help us to understand Bronzino's aristocratic types; they are charmingly proportioned, dressed elegantly and soberly, not in bright colours. The patricians he painted are nearly always following intellectual occupations. The *Young Noble* in the Sagan Collection[2] has his right hand placed on a book which he half opens with his fingers; the one in the Taylor Collection holds a cameo in his hand; in the Edward Simon Collection in Berlin, it is an antique statue of Venus which decorates the background of the picture[3]. These works, which are perhaps a little earlier than the portraits in Berlin and the Louvre, study with delicacy the essential qualities of representatives of the great Florentine families. The hands are delicate; the material of the costume is rich, but without ostentation: of these three heads the one in the Taylor Collection is the most striking by its distinction; the older countenance of the Edward Simon Collection has a certain seriousness. The drawing of the right hand, the lighting and general bearing make us think of *Ugolino Martelli*. Against a background of grey, Bronzino here plays with cold tones in a very skilful manner; the impression of colour which comes from the grey blue of the statue, the very dark tone of the magnificent dress is full of allure, without the violent red of the doublet for which we must not hold the painter responsible, but an unintelligent restorer, to whom we owe this abuse of loud and unpleasant colours. Unfortunately this passage destroys the harmony of the picture; such as it is, it still keeps a beautiful line and a severe style. On the ivory of the cheeks pale rose appears, which enlivens the character of the face. It is by these small details and a certain

---

[1] *Il Cortegiano*, p. 177.

[2] This work was formerly part of the Portales Collection.

[3] Cf. D. Haldeln, *Die Porträtausstellung des Kaiser Frederick Museumvereins* (*Zeitschrift für bildende Kunst*, 1909).

naturalness in the pose that we recognise works in Bronzino's first manner; they show us an artist different from the one whom Eleanor of Toledo made her official painter.

He understood also how to render the aristocratic bearing of a noble lady. At the beginning of the fifteenth century the feminine ideal was elegance based on simplicity, but soon foreign fashions brought a great deal of variety into costume; *decolletage* disappeared gradually, and luxury, very rich materials and jewels became popular. A curious dialogue entitled "de la bella creanza de le donne" which dates from 1538[1] shows us the general character of the new costumes. One of the speakers, Raffaella, could not conceive of a woman dressing in any way other than with studied elegance. "Young men and women ought to dress in an opulent style with grace and taste; especially women, because they are delicate and were created to help us to support the evils of the world; pure beauty of costume suits their exquisite delicate nature more than that of men, which is harsh and rough." The elegant person of this period was fond of diversity and originality in his apparel. How do we recognise a beautiful dress? By its richness and its lines. Richness does not come only from ornaments such as embroidery, but rather from the splendour of the material. A princess or a great lady should dress in very fine brocades with added pearls, diamonds, rubies and similar things. Raffaella insisted on the choice of materials, which is one of the most difficult things in the art of dressing; the colour in particular must harmonise with the colouring and the "portatura", that is to say the bearing of the person who wears it.

The middle of the sixteenth century was a period when women were incited to display their beauty. Numerous treatises taught them to cultivate it. Firenzuola gave in 1540 at Prato several lectures where he analysed at length the ideal feminine figure[2]; fair hair was always an indispensable adornment: "without lovely hair no woman is beautiful". The ideal brow should be wide, high and of a pretty white colour, the hands should have

---

[1] Alessandro Piccolomini, *Dialogo dove si ragiona della bella creanza delle donne*, 1539 (reproduced in the *Trattati del Cinquecento sulla donna*, ed. Zonta, 1913, p. 1-67).

[2] Firenzuola, *Dialogo delle belleze delle donne*, 1548.

long delicate fingers which taper slightly towards the end. The bearing of the "gentildonna should be full of a majestic gravity, a woman's grace coming from her chaste, virtuous and noble aspect". Some years after Firenzuola, the poet Christofano Fiorentino, surnamed d'Altissimo, resumed in a like manner the canons of feminine beauty: a broad and open forehead, brows clear as if they had been painted, like two arches of a bridge, blacker than ebony or the crow, a straight nose, well set into the eyebrows, teeth of ivory pearl, a neck of marble, circled with a single golden chain, slim and supple arms, skin like alabaster [1]. Is not this the ideal type of feminine beauty that Bronzino set himself to paint?

We have already been struck by these characteristics in some of Pontormo's pictures; they became the essentials of Bronzino's work, such as the one which has gone from the Collection of the Princess of Sagan into Mr. Widener's Collection a *Young Woman with her Child* [2]. The costume and jewellery are magnificent, says Mr. Berenson: "a turban of brocade, earrings, and a chain on the breast, a girdle made of precious stones, rings on the fingers and a dress of red brocade with puffed sleeves." This Florentine patrician, scarcely twenty years old, looks straight in front of her and with a heedless gesture puts her right hand on the shoulder of a young child who takes hold of her thumb. If these delicate slim hands have already an even tone, the face in contrast lives and breathes in a lifelike manner. It is one of the best commentaries to be found on the dissertations of Piccolomini and Firenzuola.

In the portrait of Lucrezia Panciatichi, in the Uffizi, this feminine type has a more pronounced severity, but keeps striking youth and freshness. It dates from the fruitful period between 1535 and 1540 when Bronzino became more and more the fashionable portrait painter. Bartolommeo Panciatichi was one of his admirers; he had commissioned him to paint two Madonnas, his own portrait and his wife's; these were so natural, says Vasari, that they

---

[1] *Opere dell'Altissimo poeta fiorentino*, 1572, p. 3.
[2] *Pictures in the collection of P. A. B. Widener, with biographical and descriptive notes on the Italian painters*, by B. Berenson, Philadelphia, 1916.

appeared to be really alive and only lacked breath[1]; an exaggerated eulogy which this verbose historian wrongly repeated concerning many paintings to which it in no way applied. But this time we understand his enthusiasm. These two portraits of the Panciatichi are superb, and the couple perfectly symbolise the haughty reserve and cold distinction of the Florentine aristocracy of the time.

Pontormo's influence is still apparent: Lucrezia's head recalls in its attitude the preparatory drawing for the pictures in Frankfurt and Oldenburg; Bartolommeo's eyes have the shape which Bronzino's master favoured, but the gaze has not the same fire; it is just as impassive as Lucrezia's. The two sitters are posing in front of the painter: they have arranged their clothes before arranging their pose. Lucrezia's dress is of splendid red velvet, falling in rather stiff folds, broken by a girdle of chased gold and precious stones. On her chest a golden chain has the inscription "Love lasts eternally", around her neck is a collar of pearls with a superb ruby set in a pendant. Against an architectural background which recalls the portrait of Ugolino Martelli, Bartolommeo appears just as richly clad, in black satin with red satin sleeves. He has a less arranged attitude than Lucrezia; leaning on a balustrade, his dog by his side, he holds a book casually in his right hand. His complexion is pink whereas Lucrezia's is dull. In the presence of these faces Bronzino maintains the attitude of an indifferent spectator; but his technique is impeccable and amazingly skilful; the hands are especially well painted: Lucrezia's are sleek and delicate, Bartolommeo's vigorous and expressive.

It is in similar portraits that we see the different tendencies felt by Bronzino between the ages of thirty-five and forty, because it is in that period of his life, about 1538 or 1540, that the Panciatichis were painted[2]. The style is Pontormesque in certain ways, but he has already found the principal elements of his conception of the state portrait. From this point of view the Roman influence would complete the influence of Michelangelo's Florentine School.

---

[1] Vasari, VII, p. 595.
[2] The husband, born in 1507, seems to be thirty-five years old.

His stay in Rome between 1546 and 1548 was like a kind of second stage in his life; without entirely breaking away from his early conceptions of the portrait, he gave his later works an imposing quality, which Tuscan painting had seldom known. These Roman portraits have not the same character as those he painted of the Florentine aristocracy. We may prefer the latter as being more typical, but nevertheless it is undeniable that the others are the work of a gifted painter.

In studying them Sebastiano del Piombo comes immediately to mind. As the latter only died in 1547, perhaps Bronzino had known him and had assuredly admired his last paintings, which were famous in Rome, although they had not the same power and brilliance as during the time when Sebastiano was under the influence of Raphael. In his portraits the influence of Michelangelo was more balanced than in his religious scenes; he brightened them with colours which he had derived from his Venetian origins and which, in a way, tempered the restraint which Raphael had taught him. The dramatic, almost theatrical bearing of a portrait such as Pope Clement VII must have struck the Florentine painter; the impression was very deep, like that which Pontormo's works had left on him in Florence.

The *Stefano Colonna* is the most remarkable example of this powerful and new style by which a portrait became almost a monumental work. Since 1896 it has passed into the Sciarra Gallery in the National Museum in Rome. If it was formerly attributed to Sermoneta, it was because the inscription on each side of the helmet, beneath the name of the sitter, had not been examined. There we find, as well as an indication of the painter, the date 1546[1] *(Plate XXXI, fig. 59)*.

It is one of the works of the beginning of his stay in Rome in which it is easy to recognise the skilful Florentine draughtsman. The extraordinary care

---

[1] The inscription is as follows:

BROSI	MD
FLO	XL
FAC	VI

In the Sciarra Gallery this portrait is opposite that of Francesco, son of Stefano Colonna, actually signed by Sermoneta; thus the confusion (Cf. *La Galleria Nazionale*, III, p. 254).

with which he has rendered the breastplate of Colonna is worthy of admiration; the encrustations of gold which make up its beauty, and those which ornament the helmet and sword, are treated with a precision worthy of a goldsmith. Bronzino was always very detailed in his technique, of a cold and implacable minuteness which does not betray a tremor of sensibility.

Under the influence of Sebastiano del Piombo the model's pose is less stiff than formerly; but more striking even than this naturalism is the powerful bearing and remarkable dignity of the portrait. Besides, we see that the Florentine artist was not impervious to the brilliance of the Roman master's portraits. The pinkish-yellow tones of the face have a certain warmth as well as the hands; the colouring of the background testifies to a good science of colour; the moiré silk shot with violet has a magnificent effect, which would be even more magnificent if the rather stiff lines of the folds did not show that, generally speaking, Bronzino had never attained the facility of a Salviati. There is no doubt that such a solidly painted work reveals Bronzino to be a very gifted colourist. In his dialogue, *della Pittura*, which appeared about this time, Paolo Pini gives him credit for this[1]; while always preferring Titian, he writes that if the Florentine artist continued to make a similar progress he would become the greatest colourist of his times.

The *Giannetto Doria*[2] is in the same vein as the *Stefano Colonna*, with more dash and vivacity in the pose, which is perhaps the most natural this painter ever conceived. We feel that everything has been chosen to enhance the brilliance of the sitter's name and the youthfulness of his face; his hand on his sword, he is ready to make bold decisions and is full of confidence in the greatness of his destiny; a destiny which was tragically interrupted in 1547. It was very likely some time after this that he painted the portrait of the illustrious uncle who found means to avenge the death of Giannetto by mercilessly punishing the conspirators.

This last portrait was commissioned by Paolo Giovio for his Museum at

---

[1] Paolo Pini, *Dialogo della Pittura*, 1548, p. 24.
[2] Rome, Galleria Doria.

Como [1] *(Plate XXXI, fig. 60)*. Bronzino pictured the Genoese admiral as God of the Sea bearing a trident. A myth of this nature is seldom synonymous with life. Andrea Doria draped his body in a sail, and in the foreground, in the shadow, is the great mast on which his name is written. It is a beautiful study of the nude and of muscles, as might be realised by a conscientious pupil of Michelangelo, but it is nothing more. Before a skilful restoration had given back some of its earlier appearance to the picture these sculpturesque qualities were very striking; the monochrome of the general effect even suggested that it might be the work of a sculptor of Michelangelo's school, so obvious is the resemblance to the *Moses* in San Pietro in Vincoli. Now the ivory colour of the skin is entirely in the style of Bronzino, the cheekbones and lips are slightly tinted with pink. As for the face, it is certainly Andrea Doria's; the resemblance to Leone Leoni's medal is striking; it is perhaps less evident in the portrait by Sebastiano del Piombo in the Galleria Doria; it is nevertheless easy to find many similarities between the two portraits [2]. Finally, isn't the copy by Altissimo in the Cosimo I collection a sufficient witness to the authenticity of the picture in the Brera?

It is also undoubtedly from the Roman period that the *Young Nobleman* in the National Gallery dates. The pose is so natural that Bronzino does not come to mind at once. The Gallery catalogue gives the name of Francesco Salviati; and in fact this latter's art is gifted with much ease, but with a very different ease from that which not only the body, but the mind of this model shows. *The Young Man,* in the English gallery, is beautifully drawn, nothing else. The pose is on a small scale exactly the same as in the portrait of Giannetto Doria. This likeness seems to indicate that the two works are almost contemporary. There is an obvious resemblance between the two faces; the same wish to be imposing is manifested in a most ingenious manner by the *Young Nobleman*. The dress is of very rich silk, the garnet-red tone stands out against

---

[1] Vasari, VII, p. 595.

[2] Mr. Lionello Venturi (*Nota sulla Galleria Borghese, L'Arte*, 1909) believes that Bronzino's portrait of Andrea Doria is only a copy of Sebastiano del Piombo's picture. Now in comparing the two works we realise that it is nothing of the sort (Cf. d'Archiardi, *Sebastiano del Piombo*, p. 234).

Bronzino.

56. *Portrait of Ugolino Martelli.* (Kaiser Friedrich Museum)

57. *Portrait of a Young Nobleman.* (Louvre)

58. Bronzino. *Eleanor of Toledo with her son Giovanni.* (Uffizi)

a green background. And it is this same colour, almost identical with that of Giannetto's garment, that Bronzino was to use later on to paint the costume of Don Garzia, one of Cosimo I's sons. One is forced to attribute this picture to Bronzino, since it seems to assemble all the influences of his stay in Rome. The aspirations of his youth towards Pontormo's style are diminished; he is on the way now to his great state portraits.

Some of his portraits have, nevertheless, still at this time a more individual significance. The *Woman in Mourning*, in the Uffizi, that severe portrait where the eyes have not the same tranquil life as in other works of Bronzino's, is surrounded by reminders of Michelangelo. On the table is the *Rachel* which Michelangelo carved for the tomb of Julius II; a marquetry design is practically a copy of the *Day* in the Medici Chapel; the armchair in which she is seated is decorated with athletic nudes. Admiration for the great sculptor is here expressed in a multiple way; another result of Bronzino's journey to Rome is the exultation of his Michelangelism. Is not this latter at least as obvious in his *Young Man with the Lute*, in the Uffizi? The table against which he leans has an inkwell whose essential motif is a woman bathing, who in its style recals the "ignudi" in the Sistine Chapel. Even in the general effect of the picture we feel the influence of Michelangelo's art; there is a visible seeking after a dramatic pose; the severity of the gaze is emphasised by the joining of the eyebrows and by the contrast of the side in shadow with that in the light. The model's complexion is pale, hardly pink at all; it stands out in the effect of contrasted light, as well as the charming drawing of the right hand.

Here are two portraits which show the painter impressed by the sentiments which Michelangelo uttered, at the same time as by the power of his creations in stone. We understand that his technique is influenced by them; he is seen inspired by the most characteristic forms of Roman art, while seeking for an original formula. The gravity of the expression of *The Young Man with the Lute* is not basically the thing which interests him the most. Let us realise that his religious pictures and his nudes became very monotonous, and that the remains of Michelangelism are less expressive there than with

Pontormo or Salviati. The life of the line disappears, only the anatomy remains.

In their turn the colours become less vibrant, like those of a painter deeply influenced by sculpture. This tendency is revealed less in *Andrea Doria* than in the two portraits of women in the Borghese Gallery [1] which have some relationship to the *Woman in Mourning* in the Uffizi [2]. As they were both painted on "lavagna" we might say that this is the reason for a great deal of their metallic lights; but it seems that now the painter sought after effects of this kind in order to give an increasingly impassive aspect to the faces of his sitters.

In the two feminine portraits in the Borghese Gallery, the pose is almost the same as in certain portraits by Sebastiano del Piombo, for instance those in the Huldschinsky and Steinmayer Collections [3]; the head is three-quarters view and there is a coldness in the expression of the face. This is what differentiates them from the painting in the Barberini Gallery, which M. Lionello Venturi also attributes to Bronzino, but which has too much life and brilliance to be his work [4]. While creating portraits of an imposing aspect, in imitation of Sebastiano, the Florentine painter gives them now a rather uniform character. At the same time as the colours diminish in intensity the gaze becomes impenetrable; it is almost steely. The *Young Woman with the Fur* in the Borghese Gallery has such fixed eyes that she seems to be drawn by a painter who does not understand how to give the finer shades of an animated and expressive gaze.

A letter sent by Bronzino to Duke Cosimo tells us that he came back from

---

[1] Cf. Venturi, *Il Museo e la Galleria Borghese*, p. 74 and 82.

[2] There are numerous resemblances between the *Woman with the Fur*, in the Borghese Gallery, and the *Woman in Mourning*, in the Uffizi; the attitude of the right arm is identical; also the drawing of the fingers, especially the forefinger doubled up; the curve of the face, the shape of the nose and lips are other elements of similarity.

[3] P. d'Archiardi, *Sebastiano del Piombo*, p. 204 and 266.

[4] *Note sulla Galleria Borghese*, *l'Arte*, 1909; Cf. Bernardini, *Bollettino d'Arte*, 1911, p. 229.

Rome in April 1548 [1]; it was this time to become permanently official Court Painter to the Medici, and the exact historian of a society usually full of seriousness.

He had helped to decorate Florence for the solemn entry of Eleanor of Toledo; according to Vasari, his paintings, which depicted some glorious episodes in the life of Giovanni delle Bande Nere, were considered the most beautiful among all those which ornamented the processional route, "and that is why the Duke, having thus known and appreciated the qualities of this artist" [2], commissioned him to decorate the Eleanor of Toledo Chapel in the Palazzo Vecchio: a commission which Bronzino spent a long time in carrying out, because it was not yet finished in 1564. Nevertheless he had quickly completed the *Deposition from the Cross* which should have been placed above the altar: and this work pleased the duke so much that he thought it worthy to be sent as a present of great price to Granvelle "the most important living personage then in Charles V circle".

Cosimo I also appreciated Bronzino for his talent in making portraits "with such skill that it is difficult to imagine"; also, he had himself painted by Bronzino while he was still young in full armour with his hand on his helmet. Now in a general way the portraits of the sovereign painted in Bronzino's style are very numerous, so much so that it is often difficult to distinguish the originals from replicas or contemporary copies. It is certain that Bronzino made many portraits of his protector, and Vasari points out several famous ones; but he must have had so many commissions of this kind on behalf of great Florentine families that, to satisfy them, pupils were tempted to reproduce the works of the master. This explains the number of portraits of Cosimo I to be found in the galleries of Europe and America.

In many of them he is dressed as a warrior, especially in the Lucca Gallery, the Cassel Gallery and the Uffizi [3] and even in the Metropolitan Museum

---

[1] Gaye, *Carteggio inedito degli artisti*, II, p. 368.

[2] Vasari, VII, p. 596.

[3] In comparing the portrait in the Uffizi with those in the Lucca and Cassel we have a very definite impression that it is only a second-rate copy; this seems to be true also of the example in the Metropolitan.

of New York. At Cassel and at Lucca the painter has added a laurel as an accessory. The picture at Lucca is the better preserved of the two and by this I mean the least restored; Cosimo's face stands out against a background of black tapestry: he is still young and has a pale complexion; the gaze is hard, almost fierce: it is the tyrant who has just overcome his adversaries' last re-sistance at Montemurlo; the victory has not intoxicated him but has made him understand the necessity for implacable repression and relentless policy. The drawing of this face is in beautiful relief; beneath the skin the muscles are taut with decision. The hand, which is resting on the helmet and which has a rather distorted forefinger, in the Pontormo manner, is like carved ivory. In the general effect the colours are pale and purposely without bril-liance. The armour is iron grey and its basic contours are emphasised by a pale pink highlight. There is none of the splendour which characterises the portrait of Guidobaldo della Rovere.

This likeness of Cosimo I, which dates from about 1540, is much more alive than those which the artist painted after his stay in Rome. Among these last there is one of which Vasari speaks, where the Duke is represented at about forty years old. It is obviously the one mentioned in an inventory of the *Guardaroba Medicea:* "un ritratto dello Illmo Sre Duca Cosimo fatto l'anno 1560 di man' del Bronzino". Unfortunately the original seems to have been lost. In Turin and in the Borghese Gallery there is a Cosimo I represented half-length with rather blurred handling; a similar one in Vienna; a little bust, less dull than the one in the Pitti, shows us the same features. It is likely that these bearded dukes of Florence, with the more or less vacant stare, are fairly good copies of the work where the official painter has depicted the sovereign in full maturity. If we can judge from these portraits there must have been some solemnity in the original, but a technique perhaps drier and less expressive than that used in the *Warrior*, in the Lucca Gallery.

After his return from Rome, it seems that Bronzino had become more especially a conscientious artist who faithfully translated what was before his eyes; the interest of the portraits depends on the interest of the models themselves; as the people he was commissioned to paint had on occasions characteristic faces, their likenesses were not lacking in a certain variety.

Bronzino was still more the painter of Eleanor of Toledo than of Cosimo I. The haughty Spanish woman found in him an interpreter who knew best how to render her physical and moral nature. Besides he did not always give that impassive appearance which we expect to find. It is probable that the first portrait he painted of her was the one in Berlin, where she appears head and shoulders, the neck adorned with a magnificent collar of pearls. We can see revealed here already the taste she was to develop for sumptuous jewellery and unusual materials. With an extraordinary care for finish, the artist details all the parts of the costume, which was for the sitter an essential element and which he had to give in all its brilliance. Nevertheless, there is here more than a talent for painting costume; psychology is not completely lacking in this painting; here we have few traces of Pontormo's psychology. Bronzino prefers to express the personality of his sitters, rather than his own. And it is thus that we are able to judge the evolution of a character or its immutability. The expression of Cosimo I's face has rarely varied; Eleanor of Toledo's is less uniform; it is a little modified with the passing of time.

In the Berlin bust there is an inquisitor's gaze which gives her face a disagreeable expression of hardness; there is plenty of treachery behind the eyelids, which seem to blink. Being only a faithful historian, Bronzino has revealed the depth of a soul which never felt tenderness for anyone. As she became older the duchess's features thickened and the profile lost its angular character. In the later pictures which Bronzino painted we see, in fact, the face changing in shape and expression. A picture in the Uffizi represents her with less severe eyes and an almost round face: it is a second-rate work, doubtless a copy of the lost original; this time the features incline to stillness. It is this calm, this placidity, this implacable coldness, this great mastery of herself, that Bronzino has studied in his portrait of her with her son Giovanni. He studied then, by force of circumstances, this evolution of a temperament which had found no means at first of hiding her deepest inclinations, and who managed by dint of effort to veil them with an impenetrable mask *(Plate XXX, fig. 58)*.

It was then that the cold tones acquired their value and meaning. No emotion seems to disturb this icy gaze. The Duchess of Toledo appears as historians have described her, even those, who, like Galuzzi, were very favourably disposed to the Medici Dynasty: her air is solemn, her bearing full of stiffness; she is laced into her clothes of brocade with velvet relief, which is of unusual sumptuousness. The precious stones which she loved so much sparkle on the magnificent material, on her girdle, in the necklace and in the net which binds her hair. The sitter has, nevertheless, the vanity to leave her beautiful hands bare, white hands very clear in tone, with delicate, long fingers almost motionless, just as insensitive as the features of the face.

In rendering so accurately the beauty of the cloth and jewels, Bronzino gives a new form to the portrait. The impassiveness of the model forces him to take greater interest in everything outside her thoughts and feelings. Nevertheless, when a face is vital and expressive, he does not remain impervious to its charm. Now the faces of children have inevitably less constraint, and more spontaneity, even at a Court where every impulse of the heart is checked. Bronzino was often commissioned to paint the Duke's children. He had already begun, before his departure for Rome with Giovanni and Francesco [1]. The work had given satisfaction, "although Giovanni was depicted with a rather melancholy air". He continued this work after 1548. Cosimo ordered him to Pisa, and commissioned him to paint Giovanni, to begin with, and later Garzia [2]. More than seven months later, Luca Martini, "provveditore" of the ducal galleys, who was living in Pisa, sent to the major domo, Francesco Riccio, seven portraits of Cosimo's children: two of Francesco,

---

[1] *Archivio di Stato di Firenze, Miscellanea Medicea*, folios, p. 27 and 151.
[2] *Archivio di Stato di Firenze, Miscellanea Medicea*, 25 (Bronzino's letter of Dec. 16, 1550 to P. F. Riccio).

one of Giovanni, two of Garzia and two of Maria. The artist worked intensively, because he carried out at the same time, at the request of his patron, two heads of Homer and Euripides[1].

It was doubtless at this period that he painted Luca Martini himself[2] in a picture which recalls the powerful technique of *Stefano Colonna*. But unlike those which inspired him in Rome, here there is exhibited no longer the same fullness of technique; the drawing of the hands, very Michelangelesque, is without emphasis; if in the face there are tones which recall Sebastiano del Piombo, the stiffness of the folds of the dress and the lack of ease of the pose show that, thrown back on himself and in front of such an ordinary face, Bronzino did not know how to express great depth in a sitter; he restricted himself to reproducing conscientiously the features of the model, without adding anything to their insignificance.

Now Eleanor's children were possessed of a certain quality which was bound to impress even an artist devoid of sensibility. We know how their mother brought them up; she gave them an extremely austere education. Having the strictest ideas of woman's honour, she shut up her daughters in the Palazzo Vecchio as though in a prison. One of them, Lucrezia, having been forced to marry Alphonse d'Este, had seen her husband depart for France immediately after the marriage ceremony[3]; she was cloistered as a married woman, just as she had been as a young girl: "I see the Princess every morning at Mass and sometimes at meals", says Susena (whom Alphonse d'Este had left with her); "the rest of the time she hardly sees the sun or a living creature". Prison seemed very long and hard to her[4], and the face of this poor recluse kept, like her sisters', the mark of the dreary life imposed on her.

Bronzino painted her[5] quite young, wearing a dress of Spanish style, made of rich brocade and of austere design; thin and sickly, without grace

---

[1] *Archivio...*, 25. Luca Martini's letter to Riccio of the last day of July, 1551.
[2] Pitti Palace.
[3] G. E. Saltini, *Tragedie medicee domestische (1557-87)*, 1898, p. 77.
[4] Ibid., p. 86.
[5] Uffizi.

or elegance, she had the sadness of a woman who submits to a superior will, and is resigned to her unfortunate fate. The face has nothing haughty about it, her gaze is not without softness. We feel that the painter has understood the significance of this contracted face with its unexpressed sorrow; but it was difficult for him to analyse it; if he had understood in some of his earlier pictures how to veil certain faces with melancholy, he was henceforth incapable of stressing a fleeting impression of a poignant drama.

And now let us look at the painting of Maria [1], Lucrezia's sister: she is hardly thirteen or fourteen years old, and in spite of her childish features, her cold gaze and her gravity belong to a person with neither age nor youth nor spirit (*Plate XXXII, fig. 63*). She is covered in jewellery, and her severe dress recalls by its elegance Eleanor of Toledo's. The artist has taken great care in painting the two sisters, to give the highest idea of their social importance by the sumptuousness of their adornment. Their faces are alike in expression, softer with Lucrezia, graver with Maria. Brought up in the same manner, shut up in the part of the Palace reserved for them, they understood nothing of life and gazed on the outside world with great astonished eyes.

The sitters' ages make it easy to establish the date of these pictures [2]: they were both later than Bronzino's journey to Rome. It was then from the period 1550—1551 that the great qualities of a costume painter were expressed by Bronzino, and that his materials shine with beauty and precision of rendering: he became a kind of Florentine Holbein, but a less powerful one. His drawing has no vigour or subtlety, it is simply accurate; all the details are studied with the care of a miniature painter. Such a conception of portraiture takes us a long way from the ideals of the first thirty years of the sixteenth century, and brings us near to certain manners of thought and painting of the fifteenth century.

Cosimo's sons led a less austere life than his daughters. This difference is shown in Bronzino's portraits. The pictures of Giovanni, Fernando and

---

[1] Uffizi.
[2] Maria was born 1540 and Lucrezia in 1545.

Garzia still remain today among the most interesting examples we have of child psychology. It is Giovanni, and not Fernando, as stated in the Uffizi catalogue, whom we see, with his great questioning eyes, in the portrait of Eleanor of Toledo in the Tribuna. One of the portraits of the Duchess, which Vasari describes to us, is the one which depicts her with her son Giovanni [1]; the inventory of the Cosimo I Collection speaks of two pictures of this kind [2]. In one she is with Giovanni, and in the other with the "principe" (which could only have been Francesco, Cosimo's future heir [3]); there is no question of a work where Fernando is beside her. In the picture of the Tribuna we do not find the features of the latter; the likenesses which Bronzino has left of him give him a long, delicate face with a serious expression, and a certain gravity of gaze; the one in which the Duchess puts her arm on the child's shoulder has on the contrary a robust and square shaped face. Besides, was not Giovanni, with Garzia, the favourite son of the Duchess? Is it not natural then that he should be painted with her? They have the most lively faces of all Cosimo's children: the one with his ingenuous and astonished air, the other with his laughing exuberance; they gave a little gaiety to the formal court of Florence; they were both full of enthusiasm, even a warlike ardour; they often quarrelled; and it is to one of these violent disputes that Giovanni's death was for some time attributed; a legend to which Saltini has given the lie. Bronzino has charmingly analysed, although with a certain stiffness, this note of heedlessness and vivacity. The beauty of the portrait in the Tribuna consists in the contrast of the two faces, of the mother and son, as well as the contrast of the two costumes, one fastidiously severe, the other flowing and of changing colour, seductive in its delicate silk and the delicious refinement of the violet tones. Giovanni is depicted as still a child "quando

---

[1] Vasari, VII, p. 598.

[2] *Archivio di Stato di Firenze, Guardaroba Medicea*, folio 45.

[3] Another portrait of the Duchess and one of her sons used to be in the Guidi da Faenza Collection (*Catalogue de la vente du Musée Guidi de Faenza,* 1902, p. 54). The son is perhaps Francesco, but as far as it is possible to judge from a photograph it is a very second-rate work of a pupil where the mother's face is similar to Eleanor of Toledo with the thickened features in the Uffizi - there is nothing of Bronzino in it except in the intention.

era piccolo", as says the inventory of 1560. We see the painter abandoning the pose of Giannetto Doria, and becoming the scrupulous chronicler of this Florentine court where Garzia, playing with a bird, is the only one to brighten his face with an open smile [1] *(Plate XXXII, fig. 62)*.

His brothers, Francesco and Fernando, are of a more peaceful nature. Fernando's features are full of distinction; Francesco has the wide sensual eyes of an Alexander de Medici [2], the same Alexander that Bronzino painted, with a certain coldness, without trying to render, as Pontormo did, the strange heart of this odd and dissolute sovereign. Thus the face of each of Cosimo's children appears with its individual character *(Plate XXXII, fig. 61)*.

All these portraits are by a very gifted artist, with acute powers of observation, but lacking in imagination, who does not attain the great evocative power of certain other portrait painters. When he had to paint the portrait of Peter the Gouty [3], all he had to inspire him was the rather cold bust by Mino da Fiesole. Now it is striking to see with what faithfulness Bronzino set about depicting the features of the father of Lorenzo the Magnificent as the Florentine sculptor had left them. With its ivory complexion, the head stands out in a half sculptural fashion, and the expression of the face has not been modified. The painter has hardly added anything to the work of Mino. Pontormo's way of animating the chill profile of a medal revealed, as you may remember, far more energy and personality.

Neither is there more originality in the series of the twenty four Medici. Vasari regards it, nevertheless, as one of the best works of Bronzino: "In the little pictures", says he, "made of piastra di stagna, all of the same size, he painted all the great ones of the Medici family, going on one side from Giovanni di Bicci and Cosimo the Elder to the Queen of France, and on the

---

[1] There is in the provincial Pinacoteca of Lucca another portrait of Don Garzia, charming with life and simplicity, where Bronzino has depicted him exactly as in the series of twenty-four Medicis. The painter has here taken particular care with the tones of the costume of a lovely raspberry velvet with a white collar, checked with blue, a very delicate blue, and edged with gold. A portrait of Fernando de Medici makes a pendant to the one of Garzia and seems also to be an enlargement of one Bronzino made for the Medici series.

[2] This portrait is today in Bergamo.

[3] National Gallery.

other from Lorenzo, father of Cosimo to the Duke and his children. These portraits are all natural, lifelike and very good likenesses". We must consider them, according to Vasari, as almost contemporary with the *Nativity* meant for the church of the Cavalieri in Pisa, dated about 1565: since many artists are in the habit of succeeding less well in the last years of their lives, is it not astonishing to see Bronzino doing better than when he was in full maturity? [1]

A first series of similar portraits dates from a much earlier period; they are mentioned, nine in number, in the inventory made in 1553 of Cosimo I Collection [2]: Cosimo the Elder, Lorenzo the Magnificent, Julius de Medici, Leo X, Clement VII, Lorenzo Duke of Urbino and the three children of Cosimo, Francesco, Maria and Garzia [3]. They appear again in the 1560 inventory. It must then have been between 1560 and 1568, date of the second edition of the *Lives*, that Bronzino painted the second series, which included twenty-four little portraits [4]: and these latter show how little the painter varied in his means of expression. A certain warmth in the tones tends to show that he had not been impervious to the influence of the Venetians, especially the *Hyppolitus de Medici* of Titian, whose bust he contended himself with copying. There are in this collection faces which have vague and inexpressive modelling, and they are almost always those which were executed from documentary evidence of the past; others keep life in their pronounced features, and these are the ones which Bronzino was able to study from nature: the Duke Cosimo and his children: Maria, Lucrezia, Francesco, Giovanni, Garzia, and especially Fernando, which recalls, as we have already said, the *Adolescent* of Salviati, in the Poldi-Pezzoli Museum.

---

[1] Vasari, VII, 603. They are today in the pastel and miniature room of the Uffizi.

[2] *Archivio di Stato di Firenze, Guardaroba Medicea*, folio 36.

[3] *Archivio...*, folio 46.

[4] The twenty-four members of the Medici family were: Giovanni di Bicci, Cosimo the Elder, Giovanni di Cosimo, Lorenzo, brother of Cosimo, Pier Francesco, Lorenzo the Magnificent, his brother Julian, Giovanni di Pierfrancesco, Clement VII, Piero di Lorenzo, Leon X, Julius, Duke of Nemours, Lorenzo Duke d'Urbino, Alexander, Hippolytus, Cosimo I, his father Giovanni delle Bande Nere and his children: Maria, Francesco, Lucrezia, Giovanni, Garzia, Ferdinando and Pietro.

Bronzino's talent scarcely altered; it remained stationary like the gaze in almost all his portraits. His solid painting testifies, above everything, to his visual gifts; without getting lost in deep psychological considerations, he describes what he sees; and if, by chance, there is burlesque in the spectacle he offers us, he was in passing a painter of burlesque. This is what happened the day that Cosimo asked him to paint his little court dwarf, Morgante; the two sides of the canvas represent the latter nude, life size, seen front and back view; it was a "beautiful and marvellous work"[1].

This picture, which seems to have been a commissioned portrait, and was found in the cellars of the Uffizi, is certainly one of the most curious of Bronzino's. Morgante is easy to recognise; he has the same features as in the medallion, where Vasari has depicted him with Cosimo I, the engineer Luca Martini and Lorenzo Pagni[2]. Seen front view he has the bearing of a Silenus; his head crowned with vineleaves, a cup in his hand, he drinks deeply; with his malignant and sensual eyes, the squat, almost square, face made hideous by a hooked nose, is more full of life than is usually the case with Bronzino; the body, deformed and fat, seems almost too heavy for the short, fat legs. On the other side of the canvas the dwarf, an owl on his shoulder, is busy driving away birds. Folds of heavy fat can be seen right down his square back.

These two studies, quickly painted, are not lacking in vigour in their realism. This official artist, who created some of the most important state portraits in existence, was not all insensitive to a touch of freedom and fantasy. It is the obvious proof, also, that Bronzino needed a model to free him from the preoccupations imposed on him by the court life. He could not understand how to give interest to a face, except when the face itself was interesting. He seldom goes as far as to sound the life of the soul and mind. Also, he remains above everything the painter of the monotonous and luxurious life led in the court of Cosimo I, and he found the colour, cold and brilliant—but of solid brilliance—which admirably gave its character.

---

[1] Vasari, VII, p. 601.
[2] Hall of Cosimo I in the Palazzo Vecchio, Cf. Masari, VIII, p. 191.

CONCLUSION

THE PLACE OF FLORENTINE PORTRAITURE IN THE EVOLUTION OF ITALIAN PAINTING. ITS ORIGINALITY AND ITS INFLUENCE

If we compare the portraits of Florence with those of Venice, Lombardy, Rome or Flanders, the first impression made by Florence is the very flexible line of its evolution. We find there the gropings of the early years, and the difficulties the artists experienced in individualising faces; then we follow, step by step, all the attempts which finally led to the great state portraits. We do not ignore any hesitations of the painter until he finds a solution to the problem of rendering the physical and moral likeness.

In Venice, the history of this form of art is from many points of view the same as that of Florence; but perhaps we do not find there so much variety. They found successful formuli more quickly, from which they broke away with difficulty. There was, to begin with, Antonello da Messina, then the Bellini, and finally Titian; it is possible that Giorgione also had a great influence in this domain; he, who painted the Saint Liberale at Castelfranco with that face of soft and melancholy charm, must have understood the human face like a poet, and known how to move his contemporaries by the beauty of his analysis.

Now from Antonello to Titian there are certainly not so many gradations as from Pollaiuolo to Bronzino. As in Florence, the portrait was only, to begin with, a bust where a powerful anatomical study was expressed; so in his last years, Giovanni Bellini drew the likeness of the Doge as though he were a sculptured bust. Then the reflection of a soul was shown in a face. From the "historical portrait" we pass on to the "romantic portrait"; after Antonello and Bellini the sitter was caught in a moment of his ordinary existence; represented full length, his clothes, his gestures, and his pose serving to characterise him the better.

Among the Lombards, there was a fairly large uniformity of conception during the fifteenth century; Antonello's influence finished by being equally predominant, and manifested itself right up to the *Portrait of the Musician* in the Ambrosiana in Milan. Leonardo's influence then held sway; it imposed itself on Ambrogio dei Predis and on Boltraffio, even more than on Andrea del Sarto and Franciabigio.

These are the facts which recall what was happening in Florence in the fifteenth and sixteenth centuries. But in Milan and Venice they remained more faithful to certain processes, as long as they satisfied the mind and taste. There was not the same continuous work of elaboration that we find in Florence. Is it not remarkable that the *Doge Loredano,* in the National Gallery, and the *Mona Lisa* are two contemporary works? All the tentative attempts of Florentine painting stand out, in all their originality, when one compares them to the portrait of Bellini. In Venice portraiture besides attained very quickly, and without deviations, a perfectly natural expression which the Florentines found difficult. Portraits of beautiful breadth and magnificent fullness replaced, from then onwards, busts with powerful contours.

Between these different ways of interpreting the human face, it is difficult to say what made up the originality of Florentine paintings. The starting point is very simple: it is the faces of the Gaddi; the conclusion: the state portraits of Bronzino. But by how many different formuli the artists between these two extremes were inspired! Leonardo da Vinci's influence succeeded that of Botticelli; the teaching of Leonardo influenced the young Raphael, Andrea del Sarto and others as well; before losing its grandeur in the monotonies of Puligo, or the strangeness of a Bacchiacca, it successfully inspired the most diverse talents. As for Michelangelism, it fostered around it an enthusiastic pre-occupation with life and movement; from about 1520 onwards, it was the followers of the school of the Master of the Sistine

Chapel who played the most important role in the evolution of the portrait, which seems paradoxical, at first sight, when we think that their master was always averse from this form of art.

It is perhaps the sensibility of Pontormo which is the most related to that of Michelangelo. On occasions, inspiration marks the faces of his sitters. Salviati's and Bronzino's works have quite a different aspect: Salviati looks towards Venice, and Bronzino submitted to the rigours of the court, where he was official portrait painter. Both of them originating from pure Michelangelism, they expressed, in the exact study of human nature, temperaments of astonishing diversity, although there is in their religious paintings a boring monotony.

Thus, whereas the development was majestic and serene with the Venetians, it was, with the Florentines, full of unexpected and original surprises and endeavours. The Florentines were less exclusively painters and quite willingly theorists; they reasoned in their art; they were psychologists and it is that which explains, to a great extent, the subtlety of their interpretation. It was from about 1470 that tendencies appeared which were to lead to so much variety in posing and expression. Until that time the fifteenth century is noted for its impassiveness. It is seldom that a painted portrait reveals any refined sensibilities; the charm of a Baldovinetti is almost an exception; it was, to begin with, the physical resemblance which pre-occupied the portrait painter, wishing to recall, in his picture, the beauty of the lines of a medal, or the impeccable accuracy of a carved bust. He was carried away by the construction of the lines of a face, and he wanted to give them all their relief; it was usually a synthetic and powerful realism.

The fixity of the gaze and the immobility of the features often give the impression of power and gravity in masculine portraits, whereas portraits of women seem haughty and disdainful. But as soon as Botticelli appeared it was, in contrast, the animation of the eyes and features which became the essential element in a portrait. And then follows an admirable series of psychological studies until one returns to the first impassivity, with less grandeur of line and of modelling. These likenesses are among the most curious and the most attractive presented by Italian painting. The different forms of melancholy have been analysed in them, at times with great depth, at others with real subtlety. It appears "mysterious" in the faces depicted by Botticelli. To these impressions of a rather tormented spirit, the technical methods of Leonardo da Vinci were to give an appropriate setting. It was a very attractive theme to present, man and nature united, so to speak, in one same feeling. Lonely landscapes, twilight, harmonised with the thoughts of the people in the foreground; from the *Young Woman* of the Lichtenstein Gallery to the pictures of Franciabigio, the interest of the background completes the expression of the model.

Let us now look at the heroes of the Sistine Chapel; they have no other spectacle but that of their sadness and of their suffering; their anguish weighed on the followers of Michelangelo, and their portraits conserve the memory of this tragic isolation. Through the impulses and emotions of a wakeful sensibility, Pontormo readily clouds the gaze of his characters with sombre thoughts: the overwhelming burden of old age in his *Cosimo the Elder*, the restless anxiety of youth in the *Adolescent* of the Trivulzio Collection, and the melancholy of middle age in the *Cardinal* of the Borghese Gallery. It is a gamut of sentiment which is developed on a plain background, but with a fine richness of psychological interpretation. In the case of Salviati, the melancholy is more refined; the aristocratic faces of his sitters reveal restrained emotion, and he has a far greater sense of measure than Pontormo; but both of them have, moreover, created varied and attractive types of Florentine youth: the *Young Man*, of the Lucca Museum, awaking to the consciousness of life, the *Lute Player*, in the Jacquemart-André museum, wrapped in his dreams but without great joyousness.

To these portraits, Bronzino has added his picture of *The Young Humanist*, Ugolino Martelli, sure of himself and of his knowledge. Even this artist (who has not, however, the enquiring mind of Pontormo) displays the desire to vary the poses, the attitudes, and at times, the expressions, of his sitters, at least in the early part of his career. He is one of the portrait painters whose selection of models is the most varied: next to the Duchess of Florence,

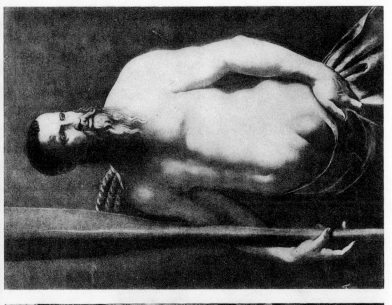

Bronzino.

59. *Portrait of Stefano Colonna.* (National Museum, Rome)
60. *Portrait of Andrea Doria.* (Brera)

Bronzino.
61. *Portrait of Fernando de Medici, son of Cosimo I.* (Uffizi)
62. *Portrait of Garzia, son of Cosimo I.* (Uffizi)
63. *Portrait of Maria de Medici, daughter of Cosimo I.* (Uffizi)

with her inscrutable gaze, there is Giannetto Doria, full of youth, life and frankness: there is also the child playing with the bird, and finally the monstrous anatomy of the court dwarf. Moreover, certain of these faces are full of a melancholy, unknown either to Pontormo or Salviati, derived from the constraint of a life restricted by etiquette, and its accompanying boredom. This court painter had, therefore, a technique not at times devoid of suppleness; but in his work he expressed very little of himself; it is this attribute which explains his power to excel in the presentation of impersonal and frigid faces.

The variety in the expression of feelings, the study of various forms of melancholy, an intelligent psychology, are most certainly some of the most remarkable characteristics of Florentine portraiture at the end of the fifteenth century, and during almost the whole of the sixteenth. Beside the admirable Venetian portraits, with their magnificently coloured costumes, which live by the senses as much as by the spirit, those of Florence may seem rather chill, and at times somewhat mannered. But if we require from a portrait something more than the brilliance of a general effect, we find that these Tuscan painters are endowed with a joy of great quality. The fundamental precepts of Leonardo's art can be applied as much to the pupils of Michelangelo, as to his own pupils: "Il buon pittore ha da dipingere due cose principali, cioe l'uomo e il concetto della mente sua". Florentine portraits are indeed enriched with a presentation of an often profound inner life, which is analysed with skill and subtlety. It is reflected in the features, which are almost always drawn in an impeccable manner, so that the line of the faces and of the bodies becomes yet another element of interest and of beauty.

Through Leonardo da Vinci and Michelangelo, Florentine painting spread its influence over Italian art, in Milan and in Rome. It does not appear, however, that the varied psychology of the Florentine pupils exercised much influence outside Tuscany. In fact the reverse process took place; outside influences modified the evolution of this type of painting; the Roman contribution to Pontormo and the Venetian contribution to Salviati are important factors in its history.

In compensation, Florence contributed in spreading the taste for portraiture; it had been prevalent in the fifteenth century, but in the sixteenth century it became a real passion. From the time of Cosimo I, the Medici had an absolute mania for portraits. The long corridor which leads from the Pitti Gallery to the Uffizi is there to show us to what pitch their enthusiasm could go. This enthusiasm spread everywhere during this period; the history of Spanish painting and of French painting are proof of this; the influence of Flemish art is clearly manifested here, but we must not forget that in France this love of portraiture had a fresh stimulus; the personal taste of a Florentine woman who had become Queen of France [1].

The apartments of Catherine de Medici were crammed with portraits. It appears that she wished to follow the example of Paolo Giovio and of Cosimo I; she even commissioned pictures in Florence itself. According to the registers of the *Guardaroba Medicea*, in 1567 twenty-two portraits of the Casa Medici [2] were painted for her, all of them of the same size, and they were hung in her study, which looked on to the Rue du Four. Just as in Italy, under the influence of Cosimo I and of the Bishop of Nocera, so in France, under the influence of Catherine de Medici, this fashion became a wearisome abuse, for people finished by liking portraiture for its own sake, and no longer as an aspect of art.

Moreover, in Florence, in a court which was growing accustomed to an etiquette full of display and solemnity, it was difficult to find a place for artists full of fantasy and spontaneity. The Official Portrait Painter can only be a painter of state portraits. Little by little, Bronzino gave way to the exigencies of his sitters, and he finished by learning admirably those of the cult of the sovereign. But if his art always preserves a certain grandeur, his followers were only skilful craftsmen. The portraits that are to be found

---

[1] Henri Bouchot, *Catherine de Medicis*, 1899, p. 169 and following.

[2] *Archivio di Stato di Firenze, Guardaroba Medicea,* folio 65, 174: "ventidue ritratti di huomini Casa Medici mandati alla regina di Francia".

in museums under the classification "School of Bronzino" have a fixed gaze and dull colouring. In the case of Christofano Allori, who is the perfect example of the pupil dominated by formulae, all expression disappears from the faces, there is no longer any modelling or delicacy of drawing. The academic spirit pervades even the realm of portraiture; Michelangelo's debilitating influence is added to that of Bronzino, whose chill and impersonal likenesses are imitated, rather than those which have any character. The decadence had by now become irreparable. People no longer knew how to undertake the patient elaboration of a work of art, for technical means were considered essential, and inspiration had practically ceased to count. Vasari boasted that he was much more skilful than his predecessors, because some of them took six years to complete a picture, while he could produce six a year. Later on Santi di Tito took half an hour to make a portrait, and he produced them in countless quantities.

After having been extremely varied, portrait painting in Florence became eventually extremely monotonous in style. The day when the penetrating analysis of features and sentiment was banished because the public ceased to be interested in it brought an end to this type of painting. For many years in the fifteenth and sixteenth century, this originality had been profound. The mobility of a face and the diversity of its expressions filled the painters of the sixteenth century with enthusiasm, for they found in this detailed study a refuge against Michelangelo's crushing mastery of art. Through the portrait, Florentine painting continued to observe living nature; it stripped itself of the intellectuality, void of thought, to which it had been led by the unrestrained imitation of powerful and majestic drawing, whose true beauty it did not grasp. It returned for a certain time to the tradition of some of its best masters, and thus preserved a brilliant reflection of its past glory.

BIBLIOGRAPHY

I. – SOURCES

Archivio di Stato di Firenze: The registers of the Guardaroba Medicea (1-75).

Il libro di ANTONIO BILLI (ed. Carl Frey , Berlin, 1892).

Il Codice Magliabechiano contenente notizie sopra l'arte degli antichi e quella de' Fiorentini da Cimabue a Michelangelo Buonarotti scritte da Anonimo Fiorentino (ed. Frey , Berlin, 1892).

Memoriale di molte statue e pitture della città di Firenze fatto da FRANCESCO ALBERTINI *prete a Baccio da Montelupo scultore*, 1510, republished 1863 in Florence (cf. ed. Horne, 1909).

LEONARDO DA VINCI. *Trattato di pittura* (ed. Ludwig, Vienna, 1882, in *Quellenschriften für Kunstgeschichte*, vol. XV-XVIII).

The literary works of LEONARDO DA VINCI (ed. J.-P. Richter, London, 1883).

Le lettere di MICHELANGELO BUONAROTTI (ed. Milanesi, Florence, 1875).

BALDESAR CASTIGLIONE. *Il libro del Cortegiano*, 1st edition, Venice, 1528 (cf. ed. Gian, Florence, 1894).

FRANCISCO DA HOLLANDA. *Vier Gespräche über die Malerei* geführt zu Rom, 1538 (ed. Vasconcellos, Vienna, 1899).

Apparato e feste delle nozze dello Illustrissimo Signor Duca di Firenze e della Duchessa sua Consorte, Florence, 1539.

La Vita di BENVENUTO CELLINI *scritta da lui medesimo* (ed. Guasti, Florence, 1890).

A. FIRENZUOLA. *Dialogo delle bellezze delle donne*, Florence, 1548.

ANTONIO FRANCESCO DONI. *Disegno partito in più ragionamenti ne' quali si tratta della scoltura et pittura, de' colori*, Venice, 1549.

Due lezioni di M. BENEDETTO VARCHI *nella prima delle quali si dichiara un sonetto di M. Michelangelo Buonarotti. Nella seconda si disputa, qual sia più nobile arte la scultura, o la pittura*, Florence, 1549.

ASCANIO CONDIVI. *Vita di Michelangelo Buonarotti*, Rome, 1553.

GIORGIO VASARI. *Le vite dei più eccellenti architettori, pittori e scultori italiani da Cimabue sino a' tempi nostri*, 3 vol., Florence, 1550 (1st edition).

GIORGIO VASARI. *Delle vite de' più eccellenti pittori, scultori e architetti*, 3 vol., Florence, 1568 (second edition).

BIBLIOGRAPHY

It is in the edition of 1568 that engravings of portraits of artists have been inserted. The most important editions of *The Lives* by Vasari are those of GIOVANNI BOTTARI, Rome, 1759-60, and the one which appeared by LEMONNIER in Florence, 1845 and following years (per cura di una Societa di amatori delle arti belle). The classic edition is today the one by GAETANO MILANESI, volume 9, Florence, 1878 and following years.

Il primo e secondo libro de' ragionamenti delle regole del disegno d'Alessandro Allori con M. Agnolo Bronzino (Manuscript of the Biblioteca Nazionale of Florence, Palat. E.B. 16, 4).

LODOVICO DOLCE. *Dialogo della pittura intitolato l'Aretino*, Venice, 1557 (ed. Battelli, Florence, 1910).

LODOVICO DOLCE. *Dialogo nel quale si ragiona delle qualità diversità e proprietà dei colori*, Venice, 1565.

DOMENICO MELLINI. *Descrizione dell' entrata della Sereniss. Reina Giovanna d'Austria et dell' apparato fatto in Firenze nella venuta e per le felicissime nozze di S. Altezza e dell' Illustrissimo et Eccellentiss. S. Don Francesco dei Medici, Principe di Fiorenza e di Siena*, Florence, 1566.

MELLINI. *Ricordi intorno ai costumi del Granduca Cosimo I* (ed. Moreni, Florence, 1820).

GIO. PAOLO LOMAZZO. *Trattato dell' arte della pittura, scultura ed architettura*, Milan, 1584.

GIO. PAOLO LOMAZZO. *Idea del tempio della pittura*, Milan, 1590.

RAFAELLO BORGHINI. *Il Riposo, in cui della pittura e della scultura si favella*, Florence, 1584, republished in 1730 in Florence with Bottari's notes.

FILIPPO BALDINUCCI. *Notizie de' professori del disegno da Cimabue in qua*, Florence, 1681-1728 (ed. Guiseppe Piacenza, Turin 1768-1817; ed. Ranalli, Florence, 1845-1847).

BOCCHI-CINELLA. *Le bellezze della cita di Firenze*, Florence, 1677.

GIOVANNI BOTTARI. *Lettere pittoriche o sia raccolta di lettere sulla pittura, scultura ed architettura*, Rome, 1757-1773 (cf. ed. Milan, 1822-1825).

GIOVANNI GAYE. *Carteggio inedito degli artisti dei secoli XIV, XV e XVI*, Florence, I (1326-1500), 1839; II (1500-1557) 1840; III (1558-1672), 1840.

GUALANDI. *Nuova raccolta di lettere sulla pittura, scultura ed architettura*, Bologna, 1844-1856.

II. – GENERAL WORKS

Among these, with the exception of the *Storia pittorica della Italia* by Luigi Lanzi (Bassano, 1809), which has nevertheless some value, the most important are the works of CROWE and CAVALCASELLE and of GIOVANNI MORELLI.

J. A. CROWE and J. B. CAVALCASELLE. *A New History of Painting in Italy from the Second to the Sixteenth Century*, London, 1864-1866 (Italian edition, Florence, 1875 and following years), Hutton, London, 1908-1909; LANGTON DOUGLAS BORENIUS, London, 1903 and following years.

IVAN LERMOLIEFF (GIOVANNI MORELLI). *Die Werke italienischer Meister in den Galerien von München, Dresden und Berlin, ein kritischer Versuch*, Leipzig, 1880 (Italian edition, *Le opere dei maestri italiani nelle Gallerie di Monaco, Dresda e Berlino*, Bologne, 1886).

IVAN LERMOLIEFF. *Studien über italienische Malerei. Die Galerien Borghese und Doria-Pamphili in Rom*, Leipzig, 1890 (Italian edition, *Della pittura italiana; le Gallerie Borghese e Doria-Pamphili di Roma*, Milan, 1897).

To these essential works must be added: —

E. MUNTZ. *Histoire de l'art pendant la Renaissance*, Paris, 1889-1895.

GUSTAVO FRIZZONI. *Arte italiana del Rinascimento, saggi critici,* Milan, 1892.

H. WÖLFFLIN. *Die klassische Kunst, eine Einführung in die italienische Renaissance*, Munich, 1899.

ADOLFO VENTURI. *Storia dell' arte italiana,* Milan (the first part of Vol. VII, *La pittura del Quattrocento*, 1911, is devoted to Florentine painting).

BERNARD BERENSON. *The Florentine Painters*, London, 1896 (third edition, 1908).

B. BERENSON. *The Drawings of the Florentine Painters*, London, 1903.

B. BERENSON. *The Study and Criticism of Italian Art*, London, 1901-1916.

III. — SPECIAL WORKS

The Spirit of Italian Painting in the XVI. century:

R. ROLLAND. *La décadence de la peinture italienne* (*Revue de Paris*, 1st January, 1896).

HERMANN VOSS. *Die Malerei der Spätrenaissance in Rom und in Florenz*, Berlin, 1920.

Portrait Painting:

WILHELM WAEZOLDT. *Die Kunst des Porträts*, Leipzig, 1908.

J. BURCKHARDT. *Beiträge zur Kunstgeschichte von Italien*, Basle, 1890 (*Das Porträt in der italienischen Malerei*, p. 163-338).

KARL WOERMANN. *Die italienische Bildnismalerei der Renaissance*, in the volume: *Von Apelles zu Böcklin und weiter*, Esslingen, 1912, I, p. 48-87.

EMIL SCHAEFFER. *Das Florentiner Bildnis*, Munich, 1904.

EMIL SCHAEFFER. *Von Menschen und Bildern der Renaissance*, Berlin, 1914.

Evolution of Portraiture in XV. century:

GIUSEPPE RICHA. *Notizie storiche delle chiese fiorentine*, Florence, 1754-1762.

A. ARMAND. *Les médailleurs italiens des XVe et XVIe siècles* (2nd edition, Paris, 1883-1887). In the body of the work the quotations are taken from the Italian edition.

A. HEISS. *Les médailleurs de la Renaissance*, Paris, 1881-1892.

CH. LOESER. *Paolo Uccello* (*Repertorium für Kunstwissenschaft*, 1898, p. 83 and following).

I.-B. SUPINO. *Il medagliere Mediceo nel R. Museo Nazionale di Firenze* (*secoli XV-XVI*), Florence, 1899.

A. VENTURI. *La Galleria Crespi in Milano*, Milan, 1900.

A. WARBURG. *Bildniskunst und florentinisches Bürgertum; Domenico Ghirlandajo in Santa Trinità*, Leipzig, 1913.

A. WARBURG. *Flandrische Kunst und florentinische Frührenrenaissance (Jahrbuch der königlich preussischen Kunstsammlungen*, 1902).

The monographs which have been published on the Florentine artists of the 15th century often contain information on the art of portraiture. We point out, among others, the work of M. A. VENTURI (*Le Vite scrite da G. Vasari*, I. *Gentile da Fabriano e il Pisanello, edizione critica con note, documenti*, Florence, 1896) and the studies of M.M. E. STEINMANN (Bielelfeld) and H. HAUVETTE (Paris, 1908) on Ghirlandaio, of M. I.-B. SUPINO on *Fra Filippo Lippi* (Florence, 1902), of M. MENGIN on *Benozzo Gozzoli* (Paris, 1908).

Among the Florentine painters Botticelli has perhaps been the most studied. The principal works dealing with this painter are those of HERMANN ULLMANN (Munich, 1893) STEINMANN (Bielelfeld, 1897), SUPINO (Florence, 1900), CH. DIEHL (Paris, 1906), RENE SCHNEIDER (Paris, 1911), BODE (Berlin, 1912). The work of Mr. HERBERT HORNE gives detailed information: *Alessandro Filipepi, commonly called Sandro Botticelli painter of Florence*, London, 1908.

Leonardo da Vinci and his influence:

La Raccolta Vinciana (Installments appeared 1905 to 1922) holds quite closely to the text of that which appeared under Leonardo. It is a useful work to consult.

Much has been written of Leonardo as a portrait painter. We can only indicate here the essential works or articles:

G. SEAILLES. *Leonardo da Vinci, l'artiste et le savant*, Paris, 1892.

EUG. MUNTZ. *Leonardo da Vinci*, Paris, 1899.

W. VON SEIDLITZ. *L.d. V. der Wendepunkt der Renaissance*, Berlin, 1909.

OSVALD SIREN. *Leonardo da Vinci*, Stockholm, 1911 (English translation: London, 1916).

MALAGUZZI-VALERI. *La Corte di Lodovico il Moro, v. II: Bramante e Leonardo da Vinci*, Milan, 1915.

GIOVANNI POGGI. *Leonardo da Vinci, la Vita di Giorgio Vasari nuovamente commentata*, Florence, 1919.

LIONELLO VENTURI. *La critica e l'arte di Leonardo da Vinci*, Bologne, s. d.

ADOLFO VENTURI. *Leonardo da Vinci pittore*, Bologne, s. d.

A. SCHIAPARELLI. *Leonardo ritrattista*, Milan, 1921.

C. CARNESECCHI. *I ritratto leonardesco di Ginevra dei Benci (Rivista d'arte*, 1909).

SALOMON REINACH. *La tristesse de Mona Lisa (Bulletin des Musées et monuments*, 1909).

CH. COPPIER, *Les Vierges aux Rochers et la légende de la Joconde (Revue des Deux Mondes*, 1st March, 1923).

RENE SCHNEIDER. *Le naturalisme de Leonardo da Vinci (Gazette des Beaux-Arts*, November, 1923).

RENE SCHNEIDER. *L'insoluble problème de la Joconde* (*Etudes italiennes*, October-December, 1923).

J.-D. PASSAVANT. *Raphael d'Urbin et son père Giovanni Santi*, Paris, 1860.

EUG. MUNTZ, *Raphael*, Paris, 1881 (2nd edition, 1900).

J. A. CROWE and J. B. CAVALCASELLE. *Raphael, his life and works*, London, 1882, (Italian edition, Florence, 1884 and following years).

A. VENTURI. *Raffaello*, Rome, 1920.

F.-A. GRUYER. *Raphael peintre de portraits*, Paris, 1881.

ENRICO RIDOLFI. *Di alcuni ritratti delle Gallerie fiorentine* (*Archivio storico dell' arte*, 1891, p. 425 and following).

FRITZ KNAPP. *Piero di Cosimo, sein Leben und seine Werke*, Halle, 1899.

ULIMANN. *Piero di Cosimo* (*Jahrbuch der k. preussischen Kunstsammlungen*, 1896).

CH. LOESER. *L'autoritratto di Lorenzo di Credi* (*L'Arte*, 1901).

FRITZ KNAPP. *Fra Bartolommeo della Porta und die Schule von San Marco*, Halle, 1903.

G. POGGI. *Di un ritratto inedito di Cosimo dei Medici dipinto da Ridolfo Ghirlandaio* (*Rivista d'arte*, August-December, 1916).

Michelangelo and his influence:

H. THODE. *Michelangelo und das Ende der Renaissance*, Berlin, 1902 and following years.

C. GUASTI. *Il ritratto migliore ed autentico di M. Buonarotti*, Florence, 1893.

ERNST STEINMANN. *Die Porträtdarstellungen des Michelangelo*, Leipzig, 1913.

P. GARNAULT. *Les portraits de Michel Ange*, Paris, 1913.

Evolution of landscape:

W. KALLAB. *Die toskanische Landschaftsmalerei im XIV. und XV. Jahrhundert, ihre Entstehung und Entwickelung* (*Jahrbuch der Kunsthistorischen Sammlungen des allerhöchsten Kaiserhauses*, ERDD).

J. GUTHMANN. *Die Landschaftsmalerei der toskanischen und umbrischen Kunst von Giotto bis Raffael*, Leipzig, 1902.

Andrea del Sarto and his disciples:

ALFRED REUMONT. *Andrea del Sarto*, Leipzig, 1835.

P. MANTZ. *André del Sarto* (*Gazette des Beaux-Arts*, 1876, vol. II, 1877, vol. I).

JANITSCHEK. *A. del Sarto*, in *Kunst und Künstler des Mittelalters und der Neuzeit*, Leipzig, vol. III.

H. GUINESS. *Andrea del Sarto*, London, 1899.

C.-J. CAVALLUCCI. *Andrea del Sarto* (*Rassegna bibliografica dell' arte italiana*, 1904).

FRITZ KNAPP. *Andrea del Sarto und die Zeichnung des Cinquecento*, Halle, 1905.

F. KNAPP. *Andrea del Sarto*, Bielelfeld, 1907.

CARLO GAMBA. *Di alcuni ritratti del Puligo* (*Rivista d'arte*, 1909).

EMIL SCHAEFFER. *Die Bildnisse des Pietro Carnesecchi* (*Monatshefte für Kunstwissenschaft*, 1909).

CL. PHILLIPS. *Il Rosso by himself* (*Burlington Magazine*, vol. XX).

Pontormo:

A. COLASANTI. *Il diario di Jacopo Carrucci da Pontormo* (*Bollettino della Societa filologica romana*, 1902).

FRITZ GOLDSCHMIDT. *Pontormo, Rosso und Bronzino*, Leipzig, 1911.

FREDERIC MORTIMER CLAPP. *Les dessins de Pontormo, Catalogue raisonné*, Paris, 1914.

F. M. CLAPP. *Jacopo Carrucci da Pontormo, his life and work*, Oxford, 1916.

CARLO GAMBA. *Pontormo* (Piccola collezione d'arte, no. 15), Florence, 1921.

CARLO CARNESECCHI. *Sul ritratto d'Alessandro dei Medici dipinto da Pontormo* (*Rivista d'arte*, 1909).

CARLO GAMBA. *Un ritratto di Cosimo I del Pontormo* (*Rivista d'arte*, 1910).

PIETRO D'ACHIARDI. *Sebastiano del Piombo*, Rome, 1908.

Salviati:

CARLO GAMBA. *Alcuna ritratti di Cecchino Salviati* (*Rassegna d'arte*, 1909).

H. VOSS. *Italienische Gemälde des 16. und 17. Jahrhunderts in der Galerie des kunsthistorischen Hofmuseums zu Wien* (*Zeitschrift für bildende Kunst*, 1912).

F. DE NAVENNE. *Rome, le Palais Farnèse et les Farnèse*, Paris, n.d.

LILI FROHLICH-BUM. *Parmigianino und der Manierismus*, Vienna, 1921.

Taste for portraits in the time of Cosimo I:

GIANBATTISTA CINI. *Vita del Serenissimo Signor Cosimo de Medici, primo Gran Duca di Toscana*, Florence, 1611.

RIGUCCIO GALIUZZI. *Istoria del Granducato di Toscana soto il governo della Casa Medici.* Florence, 1781.

LITTA. *Famiglie celebri italiane*, Milan, 1819 and following years.

L.-A. FERRAI. *Cosimo dei Medici duca di Firenze.* Bologne, 1882.

L.-A. FERRAI. *Lorenzino de' Medici e la societa cortigiana del Cinquecento*, Milan, 1891.

G.-E. SALTINI. *Tragedie medicee domestische* (1557-1587), Florence, 1898.

ANNA BAIA. *Leonara di Toledo, duchessa di Firenze e di Siena*, Todi, 1907.

UGO SCOTI-BERTINELLI. *Giorgio Vasari scrittore* (*Annali della R. Scuola Normale di Pisa*, vol. XIX).

KALLAB. *Vasaristudien*, Vienna, 1908.

BIBLIOGRAPHY

R. V. CARDEN. *The life of Giorgio Vasari, a study of the later Renaissance in Italy*, London, 1910.

G. B. GIOVIO. *Elogio di Paolo Giovio (Elogi italiani*, V-VIII), Venice, 1783.

A. GOTTI. *Storia del Palazzo Vecchio in Firenze*, Florence, 1899.

COSIMO CONTI. *La prima reggia di Cosimo dei Medici*, Florence, 1893.

EUG. MUNTZ. *Les collections de Cosme I de Medicis (Revue archéologique*, January-June, 1895).

FR. KENNER. *Die Porträtsammlung des Erzherzogs Ferdinand von Tirol (Jahrbuch der kunsthistorischen Sammlungen des allerhöchsten Kaiserhauses*, 1896-1897).

EUG. MUNTZ. *Le Musée de portraits de Paul Jove*, Paris, 1900 (Extract from *Mémoires de l'academie des Inscriptions et Belles-Lettres*, XXXVI, 2nd part).

ALLEGRINI. *Cronologica series simulacrorum regiae familiae medicae*, Florence, 1761.

ALLEGRINI. *Serie di ritratti d'uomini illustri toscani con gli elogi storici dei medesimi*, Florence, 1766 and following years.

TRASPESNIKOFF. *Die Porträtdarstellungen der Mediceer des XV. Jahrhunderts*, Strasbourg, 1909.

G. F. YOUNG. *The Medici*, London, 1909.

ROBERT DE LA SIZERANNE. *Les masques et les visages à Florence et au Louvre, Portraits célèbres de la Renaissance italienne*, Paris, 1913.

Evolution of costume:

RODOCANACHI. *La femme italienne à l'époque de la Renaissance, sa vie privée et mondaine, son influence sociale*, Paris, 1907.

CESARE VECELLIO. *Degli habiti antichi e moderni di diverse parti del monde*, Venice, 1590 (2nd edition, 1598). Cf. l'edition, Didot, Paris, 1860-63.

A. LUZIO and RENIER. *Di certo usanze delle gentildonne fiorentine nella seconda metà del sec. XVI*, Florence, 1890.

Bronzino:

A. FURNO. *La vita e le rime di Angelo Bronzino*, Pistoia, 1902.

HANS SCHULZE. *Die Werke Angelo Bronzinos*, Strasbourg, 1911.

JUSTI. *Die Bildnisse des Kardinals Hippolyt von Medici in Florenz (Zeitschrift für bildende Kunst*, 1897).

G. CAROTTI. *Il ritratto di Andrea Doria (L'Arte*, 1898, p. 182).

S. REINACH. *De quelques prétendus portraits de sculpteur (Revue archéologique*, January-June, 1916).